Religious Postures

Religious Postures
Essays on Modern Christian Apologists and Religious Problems

G. A. Wells

Open 🌣 Court
La Salle, Illinois

First printing 1988.

Library of Congress Cataloging-in-Publication Data

Wells, George Albert, 1926-
    Religious postures: essays on modern Christian apologists and religious problems /
G.A. Wells.
    p. cm.
    Bibliography: p.
    Includes index.
    ISBN 0-8126-9070-2: $28.95. ISBN 0-8126-9071-0 (pbk.): $14.95
    1. Christianity—Controversial literature. I. Title.
BL2775.2.W45 1988
230'.09'03—dc 19
                                     88-1526
                                        CIP

CONTENTS

Preface

In two recent books I have given detailed reasons for regarding the New Testament as unreliable. I refer to my *The Historical Evidence for Jesus* (Buffalo: Prometheus, 1982) and *Did Jesus Exist?* (second edition, London: Pemberton, 1986). In the present work I am concerned with the methods of apologists, both fundamentalist and liberal, and with general issues often raised in connection with religion, including the question of miracles and the foundation of moral behaviour. I have included in my title the provocative phrase "Religious Postures" rather than the neutral 'Religious Attitudes', as a good many of the attitudes I discuss may fairly be designated as posturing.

After an account and criticism of Fundamentalist Christianity (today no insignificant phenomenon) I outline (in chapter 2) the rise of radical biblical criticism in the nineteenth century. De Wette and Strauss are my examples of theologians whose work destroyed the credibility of much in the Old and New Testaments respectively, and thus made the Fundamentalist position untenable, although this is not appreciated even by many educated persons today. (Fourteen professors of science recently signed a letter to *The Times*, London, affirming their belief in the virgin birth, the resurrection, and the gospel miracles generally; cf. below, p. 221). The legend of Wilhelm Tell is adduced as what I call a "parallel" case, in that it illustrates how what has been proved a fiction can, even in a historical period, find general acceptance, and also the enormous efforts required to discredit a popular fiction even when the plainest evidence is against it.

My third chapter is a criticism of liberal theologians of yesterday and today who know about this radical work, and who do not for the most part dispute its cogency, but nevertheless try to rescue something from the ruins. One very common line of defence (discussed apropos of Collingwood in chapter 5) is to claim that religious truth is a special species, which need not be compatible with scientific truth. What repeatedly appears in chapters 3 to 7 is that the flimsiest of ideas can be linked with the strongest of emotions. I do not wish to deny the importance of emotion as supplying the underlying impetus to inquiry and to behaviour. As Hume long ago pointed out, the rational element in behaviour is merely that part of the mechanism which guides an animal to its goal; and the goal must exert some kind of attraction before this mechanism can be brought into play. My chapter on Bonhoeffer shows how important the strong sustaining power of moral emotion can be in difficult circumstances. Yet it is surely indisputable that sound reasoning depends on (among other things) adequate knowledge, for which strong feelings are no substitute.

If the inadequacy of a predominantly emotional basis to ideas and the frequency with which it nevertheless occurs in religious apologetics is one major thesis of this book, another is the futility of the quest for absolute truth, truth which is final and not subject to any revision. The chapter on miracles culminates in denial of all such absolutist claims; and the three final chapters (9–11) are specifically directed against hankerings after 'necessary truth' and absolute moral principles, and answer the charge that no religion means (or should logically mean) no morals. The argument of this book is that, although there is no thought except under the impulse of some emotion, all thought depends on experience, which differs for each individual; and further that, as all the fundamentals of the thinking process can be seen in the higher mammals—the dog obviously recognizes the same house, the same people, and the same cat as does his master, for his whole behaviour is manifestly related to them—it is ridiculous to suppose that the only marginally better human brain can attain to absolute truth.

In the 'Conclusion' to this book I to some extent indicate the relatedness of its various chapters, but am mainly concerned to account for the success of Christianity in surviving destructive criticism.

For many people today, religion is old hat and the real problems of society lie elsewhere. Some such people are prepared to conform outwardly so far as it happens to be convenient, and so long as they are not expected to modify their way of life in accordance with alleged religious principles. Their view is that we should not be expected to take religion very seriously, but must not be seriously opposed to it. Live and let live, particularly as religious writers and teachers are ready to make all kinds of concessions. I am writing primarily not for such people, but for those who have not yet finally made up their minds about religion, particularly about Christianity, who are exposed to the influence of liberal and not-so-liberal apologists and need factual information and rational arguments to protect them from such blandishments. I have tried to argue a case on a maximum basis of fact, not to encourage readers to replace one set of unthinking prejudices with another.

In English (unlike Greek or German) the word 'man' can designate both the adult male of the species and the species as a whole, and I have not undertaken circumlocutions to avoid using it in the latter sense.

Biblical quotations are from the Revised Version of 1881–1885 (unless otherwise stated), and I understand from Oxford University Press that this version is now in the public domain.

Much of the material in this book has been adapted from articles which I have published in journals, and my thanks are due to their editors for permission to re-use it here. The details are:

> *The Publications of the English Goethe Society*, 45 (1975) and 50 (1980): articles on Strauss and on 'Kant Contra Hume'.
>
> *German Life and Letters*, 22 (1968) and 39 (1985): articles on 'Criteria of Historicity' (covering de Wette's work on the Pentateuch and the legend of Wilhelm Tell) and on Bonhoeffer.
>
> *Scottish Journal of Religious Studies*, 7 (1986): article on Julian Huxley.
>
> *Trivium*, 21 (1986): article on Collingwood.
>
> *New Humanist*, 101 nos. 2 and 4 (1986) articles on Tillich and on Fundamentalism.

The substance of chapter 8 (miracles) and of part of chapter 10 (ethics) appeared in my articles in *Question* 10 (1977) and 13 (1980) when I was myself editor of that journal. There is also some overlap in chapter 10 with what I have written in my account of J. M. Robertson's views in *J. M. Robertson, Liberal Rationalist and Scholar* (London: Pemberton, 1987), a volume of essays by several hands, to which I was both contributor and editor.

I have tried to make the notes (collected at the end) easy to correlate with the text of this book by giving the name of an author in the relevant note as well as in the text.

I wish to express my very sincere thanks to my secretary, Mrs. Bärbel Selvarajan, for her constant help with the typing and finalizing of my manuscript.

Chapter One
The Fundamentalist Mentality

(i) Jehovah's Witnesses

From time to time one finds oneself answering the door to well-demeanoured callers offering the latest number of *Awake!* and *The Watchtower*, both published by the Watch Tower Bible and Tract Society and embodying the policy and doctrines of Jehovah's Witnesses. If the Witnesses were merely a fringe minority, they could safely be ignored. In fact they are in many respects typical of powerful Fundamentalist groups which thrive, particularly in North America, on ignorance of the origin and nature of the various books composing the Bible. In 'Christian' countries this ignorance has for centuries been fostered rather than dispelled by traditional teaching, from Sunday Schools upwards.

The Witnesses rely on God to come in the near future, destroy all those who have not been living in accordance with 'Bible principles'—of course, as interpreted by the Watch Tower Society—and leave the survivors in possession of an earthly paradise (1, p. 12).[1] "Only Jehovah's Witnesses" are urging people to heed the commandment of Revelation 18:4: "Come forth, my people, out of her", namely "Babylon the Great", interpreted by the Witnesses to mean "false religion". Hence they "will not be in line for destruction" (3, p. 7). It is clear from this that they share with the worst of more orthodox Christians that *odium theologicum* which has contributed so much to the misery of the European peoples and which for many centuries made the history of Christianity a perpetual crusade against 'heretics'. Once the truth has come to be regarded as a goal to be striven for, and the possession of truth as a mark of superiority, there arises jealousy between rival claimants. The scientific seeker after truth seeks to establish his claim by demonstration, but it is an arduous process, and honest claims of this kind must always be modest. Others, more impatient and less well-equipped for investigation and reflection, are apt to claim some special inspiration or revelation. But this claim is still more difficult to establish against the miscellaneous rivals of the same type; and so the demonstration of reason is bolstered by the emphasis of assertion, and defence of one's own position by denigration of rivals, particularly of those who seem most formidable.

As they are expecting God to come quickly, the Witnesses are not concerned to improve the condition of mankind. They are not the only religious movement (Christian or otherwise) whose belief in a future life has led them to despise this one. If we are to spend eternity in paradise, why worry ourselves about a few short years on this corrupt earth (especially as St. Paul has told us (Romans 8:18) that "the sufferings of the present time are not worthy to be compared with the glory which shall be revealed to us")? Is it not more important to convert as many as possible to the faith so that they shall be acceptable when the time comes, and to discipline the faithful so that they are not contaminated by their missionary or other contacts with unbelievers? The additional misery that has been caused over the centuries by acting on these principles is surely beyond calculation. But because the Witnesses accept them, they disapprove of those Christians who try to influence political and social policies. This general alienation from the world is one factor in the Witnesses' success; for, thrown back on each other as they are, their *esprit de corps* is very strong, and has been further strengthened by the persecution they have suffered in both totalitarian and democratic countries (in the latter because of their wartime refusal of military service). In isolated societies creeds can be preserved. It is where people of different traditions, outlook and creeds mingle freely and exchange ideas that religious beliefs begin to be eroded (cf. below, p.66). No one changes his beliefs without some instigation, some novel experience, some modification of the customary course of things, and in a closed society people believe what all their fellows obviously believe. Only when they are brought into contact with persons whom they respect holding different views do they begin to look at their inherited beliefs critically.

Regarding efforts to reform this world as misdirected contributes to the Witnesses' present success also because, as Professor Medawar has noted in a quite different connection, "the Predicament of Man is all the rage now that people have sufficient leisure and are sufficiently well-fed to contemplate it, and many a tidy literary reputation has been built upon exploiting it; anybody nowadays who dared to suggest that the plight of man might not be wholly desperate would get a sharp rap over the knuckles in any literary weekly". He added that, "instead of wringing our hands over the Human Predicament, we should attend to those parts of it which are wholly remediable, and above all to the gullibility that makes it possible for people to be taken in".[2] Medawar had in mind the appeal of hollow but apparently profound philosophizing in the manner of Teilhard de Chardin's The Phenomenon of Man. But his remarks allow of wider application.

What the Witnesses chiefly protest about in rival Churches is, apart from social involvement, the condoning of what they regard as sexual licence. They attempt to show that any other Church accepts a lower standard of morality than the Bible demands, and that they alone uphold the old and true standard (4, p. 12).

A rational system of ethics does not condemn an act unless it has, or may be expected to have undesirable consequences. If it is true that homosexuality, fornication, or smoking have such consequences—and Awake! argues repeatedly that this is so—then it is quite unnecessary to collect, as Awake! also does, isolated verses from the various books of the Bible and in this way to show that such behaviour conflicts with Biblical teaching. In any case it is somewhat anachronistic to regard the Bible as an authority on smoking. And as for sexual conventions, these are not uniform throughout the Old Testament, as they changed considerably during the history of the Jewish people. The patriarchs had each more than one wife, and many concubines, and nobody suggested that there was anything wrong in this. 2 Samuel 5:13 tells that, after David moved to Jerusalem, "he took more concubines and wives" from the city. Such an ethic was probably inspired by tribal interests: a large number of children needed to be produced to enable the tribe or nation to stand up to its enemies. James Fenton (writing in The Times, 10 October 1985) thinks that the Old

Testament's prohibition of sodomy was "similarly functional. Seed was extremely precious and was not to be wasted in such a way".

It is well-known that much or even all of the Jewish law is repudiated in some New Testament passages. Paul says that "Christ is the end of the law" (Romans 10:4); Matthew makes Jesus repudiate the Old Testament doctrine of "an eye for an eye and a tooth for a tooth" and replace it with "resist not him that is evil" (5:38–9). Mark (at 7:19) understands Jesus to have declared "all meats clean", thus contradicting the prohibition of Leviticus 11:4–7 against eating the flesh of the hare or the pig. At Exodus 31:15–16 the Lord tells Moses that abstention from work on the Sabbath is a perpetual (Hebrew: 'ohlahm') covenant. The Witnesses have their own 'New World' translation of the Bible, where they claim that this Hebrew word does not mean 'perpetual' but only 'time indefinite'.[3] They also appeal to Jeremiah 31:31–2 about the promise of a "new covenant" and to New Testament passages which maintain that it has been brought in to supersede the Lord's agreements with Moses. If, then, the Witnesses believe that many Old Testament rulings are no longer valid, there is little point in quoting the Old Testament as profusely as they do in order to justify their various standpoints. But although they cannot altogether deny that the moral and other ideas endorsed in the Bible are far from uniform, they do not regard it as a miscellaneous collection of books which can be understood only in the light of their various dates and authors, but as true, prophetic, and self-consistent—a collection of oracles derived directly from the deity. They support these claims by selective quotation and arbitrary interpretation. When they say 'the Bible says', what they mean is that they have collected one or more short passages from it, which they then proceed to apply quite arbitrarily to justify the favourite doctrines of their organization.

Let me illustrate their method. They refer to Exodus 22:21–2 and Leviticus 19:32 to establish that "Jehovah wants everybody to be treated with respect, regardless of sex or age" (1, p. 19). But no mention is made of Exodus 21:20–21 which reads (in the New English Bible): "When a man strikes his slave or his slave-girl with a stick and the slave dies on the spot, he must be punished. But he shall not be punished if the slave survives for one day or two, because he is worth money to his master".

One could fill an issue of *Awake!* with such outrageous sayings taken out of their context from the Bible. Thus one might say, in the manner of the Witnesses: 'The Bible says that a man may beat his servant to death and must go unpunished if the victim lingers a couple of days before he expires'. Such arbitrary quotation would no more prove that the Bible was inspired by the Devil than the Witnesses' equally arbitrary method proves their claim (4, p. 4) that it was inspired by God. If one makes an honest attempt to understand the conditions under which this collection of old writings came to be compiled, one reaches a more intelligible view. So bien-pensant a handbook as *The Oxford Dictionary of the Christian Church* informs us (in its article 'Pentateuch') that the first five books of the Old Testament (Genesis, Exodus, Leviticus, Numbers, and Deuteronomy) are considered by "most Biblical critics" to be "made up of various written documents dating from the 9th to the 4th century B.C." I do not need to argue the details, as there are any number of lucid accounts which justify this dating,[4] and some of the evidence for it will occupy us in the next chapter. I need note only that chapters 21 and 22 of Exodus are regarded as forming, in the Pentateuch, or first five books of the canon, one of its earliest strands (the so called Elohistic Document, centuries older than the material in Deuteronomy, which in turn is older than the 'Priestly' regulations in Leviticus and Numbers) and that much in the code of these two chapters is closely parallelled in the Code of Hammurabi, which was recorded many centuries before the earliest books of the Bible. The editor of Exodus in *The Century Bible*, published at the beginning of this century, found the view of the relation between master and servant stated in Exodus 21:20–21 rather barbarous and commented:

> It is fairly certain that these verses and verses 26 and 27 are a mitigation of more primitive custom which gave the master absolute control over his slaves, including power of life and death. Thus the harshness does not belong to the author of these laws; their point is the limitation of the master's rights; the intention of the legislator is humane, and his provisions for the welfare of slaves were not restricted by lack of humanity, but by practical difficulties. If he had made his laws more unfavourable to the master they would have remained a dead letter.[5]

The Witnesses quote Psalm 103:8 and part of Exodus 34:5–7 to show that Jehovah is "abundant in loving kindness" (3, p. 29). But a great deal of the behaviour ascribed to him in the Old Testament implies injustice according to our views. According to Genesis 7:23, by means of the Flood from which the inhabitants of Noah's ark (eight persons and some animals) were saved, God wiped out "every living thing" that existed on earth, "both man and cattle and creeping thing and fowl of the heaven". The Witnesses interpret this to mean that God "flushed out everything that was bad" (4, p. 11). At Genesis 11, God, seeing that all mankind spoke one language, deliberately confused their tongues so that they would not understand what they said to each other—otherwise they would be able to achieve anything they put their mind to (verses 6–7). At Deuteronomy 20:13–14 the Lord gives instructions that, when a resisting city is captured, the males are to be slaughtered, "but you may take the women, the dependants, and the cattle for yourselves, and plunder everything else in the city" (New English Bible. The Revised Version has "take the women . . . for a prey unto thyself"). But this applies only to distant cities. In those near at hand, nothing is to be left alive (verse 16). In 1 Samuel 15:3 the instruction is "slay both man and woman, infant and suckling, ox and sheep, camel and ass". In 2 Samuel 8, "the Lord gave victory to David whithersoever he went", and this involved, among other things, the destruction of 22,000 Aramaeans (RV: Syrians) and 18,000 Edomites (Syrians according to some manuscripts). All this can be understood only as tribal ethic, with Jehovah interested exclusively in the welfare of his chosen tribe. This is why he leaves other peoples to worship entities that are not gods at all (Deuteronomy 4:19), he being the only God (verse 35). There are, of course, other passages, from other authors and periods, which view him quite differently, but it is grotesque to claim that 'the Bible' shows him to be abundant in loving kindness. The Witnesses criticize the Churches for their sanction of wars (3, pp. 5–7), but it would be hard to outdo Jehovah in indulgence in violence. At Isaiah 45;5–7 he is even represented as the creator of evil: "I am the Lord, and . . . beside me there is no God . . . I form the light and create darkness; I make peace and create evil; I am the Lord, that doeth all these things". Determination to uphold monotheism and to admit no independent evil principle has led to the idea that it must be God who inspires even evil acts, as when Exodus 7:3 makes him declare his intention of "hardening Pharaoh's heart". Later strands of the Old Testament attribute evil to a spirit other than God—subordinate to him but allowed independence—at first described merely by the title 'the adversary' or 'the Satan' (see the notes in the New English Bible to Job 1 and Zechariah 3:1–9), but finally bearing the latter ascription as a proper name (1 Chronicles 21).

One of the very passages to which, as I have noted, the Witnesses appeal because it mentions what they call God's "loving kindness", namely Exodus 34:6–7, contains the additional statement that he "visits the iniquity of the fathers upon the children". This doctrine is included even in the Decalogue (Exodus 20:5 and Deuteronomy 5:9) and appears also in the very first chapters of Genesis, which are normally taken to imply that the whole human race is condemned to bring forth children in sorrow and to till the ground in the sweat of their faces because of the ill-advised behaviour of Adam and Eve. This doctrine that children will be punished for their fathers' vices is repudiated by Jeremiah (31: 29–30) and Ezekiel (18:1–10), but accepted by Jesus, if we can believe that he really said what Matthew makes him say to the scribes and Pharisees at 23:29-36: " . . . that upon you may come all the righteous blood shed on the earth, from the blood of Abel the righteous. . . . " As so often with Biblical stories, one can see how the underlying idea could easily and naturally arise, even though one is not inclined to endorse it. The conviction that God is just naturally leads to the expectation that the virtuous will be rewarded and the wicked punished; but as it is very hard to believe, on the basis of our experience, that happiness and unhappiness are distributed in this world on any such principle, some other theory had to be thought of. The idea that God will compensate the individual in an after-life for injustices suffered in this one was not available to the early Hebrews, as they had not come to believe in immortality (a belief represented only in the later strands of the Old Testament, and only sparsely even in them).[6] And so the idea that naturally suggested itself was that the virtuous individual who was unfortunate in life was being punished for the sins of a wicked ancestor. It is always possible to imagine some wicked ancestor.

In this case as in others, amendment of an earlier more naive theory about God solves one problem only to create others, for if we are to be punished for the sins of our ancestors, what can we do? What is done cannot be undone. Must the good in each generation go on being punished for their wicked fathers? The Christian idea of the Atonement aims at coping with this new difficulty: we are cleansed from the sin we have inherited by the blood of Jesus, provided we have faith in him. The Witnesses make the Atonement into a straight one-for-one deal. Adam, created a perfect man, sinned and was sentenced to death. Jesus, the only other man ever to have been born perfect, was alone able to compensate God for Adam's transgression by accepting death.[7]

These premisses—that both Adam and Jesus were alone of mortals originally sinless—have two obvious consequences: they make it impossible for the Witnesses to accept any theory of human evolution from a more primitive creature; and they tie them to literal acceptance of Jesus's virgin birth, by which they suppose he escaped inheriting sin.[8] As is well-known, the virgin birth is documented only in the two nativity stories of Matthew and Luke (each one of which is incompatible with the other, as well as being full of its own difficulties[9]), and is unknown to the other New Testament writers. Paul's statement that Jesus was "born of a woman" (Galatians 4:4) does not suggest acquaintance with the doctrine. Many Christian scholars have therefore come to concede that it is a mere legend,[10] although they often argue that it nevertheless conveys some kind of profound truth. The Witnesses themselves are sometimes willing to allow that a Biblical narrative can be interpreted freely—in fact they insist that it must be if its plain meaning contradicts their moral sense. Jesus tells (in an apocalyptic vision, not, as is so often claimed, in a 'parable') that, at the final judgement, the "goats" will be sent "into the eternal fire which is prepared for the devil and his angels", and will "go away into eternal punishment" (Matthew 25:32–3, 41 and 46). According to the Witnesses, this merely means that they will experience eternal annihilation, not eternal torment. But the Witnesses believe that to allow any other than literal interpretation of Jesus's virgin birth would undermine their whole theological position.

When the Witnesses quote various New Testament passages that condemn violence, they do not in this connection refer to Jesus's behaviour in the temple:

> And Jesus entered into the temple of God and cast out all them that sold and bought in the temple, and overthrew the tables of the money-changers . . . (Matthew 21:12)

Elsewhere, in the same inspired document, Jesus is made, as we saw, to say: "Resist not him that is evil" (Matthew 5:39). The obvious explanation of such discrepancies is that the gospels, like so much in the Old Testament, have been compiled from a multitude of materials of different provenance, representing entirely different standpoints. If, however, one takes them as records of what a historical Jesus actually did, then it is clear from his behaviour that he approved of violence in certain cases; and it does not appear that he anywhere defined more precisely when resistance is justifiable. According to the Witnesses, he "set a perfect example of long-suffering" and "never dealt harshly with his disciples" (3, p. 29). But he did call Peter "Satan" (Mark 8:33), and in Matthew 23 he fiercely denounces his sectarian opponents, intimating that they will not escape being sentenced to hell (verse 33).

(ii) Biblical Prophecies About the End of the World

If all this illustrates the Witnesses' policy of selective quotation, their treatment of the final book of the New Testament, entitled (in literal translation from the Greek) 'A Revelation of John', shows how arbitrary their exegesis can be. They agree with the majority of Biblical scholars that this apocalypse was written about A.D. 96 (4, p. 4), when Christians were being persecuted by the Roman authorities. Apocalypses are characteristically products of times of affliction. They seek to keep alive the hope of believers by promising early deliverance (a technique the value of which the Witnesses of today obviously appreciate!); and the author of this one describes his visions of forthcoming untold destruction and suffering, to be followed by the general resurrection and judgement of souls. The opening verse claims that all this must take place soon, and the transfigured Jesus reiterates this at the end of the book. At 17:3 the writer in his vision "saw a woman sitting upon a scarlet-coloured beast full of names of blasphemy, having seven heads and ten horns". That this is a reference to the hated Rome is obvious when verse 9 explains that "the seven heads are seven mountains on which the woman sitteth". Rome had long been known as *urbs septicollis* and a festival was celebrated every December to commemorate the enclosure of the seven hills within her walls. The next verse says that these seven heads are also "seven kings", five of whom have fallen, "the one is, the other is not yet come". The "kings" are Roman emperors. The number seven may not be meant literally, and if it is, it is not clear from which emperor one starts counting—possibly from Nero, as the first who persecuted Christians. But the suggestion seems in any case to be that there will be only one more reign before the grand consummation. The writer had no interest in what was to happen in two thousand years' time. His work is the agonized cry of a community under persecution, looking for an immediate intervention of God. Nevertheless, the Witnesses interpret the beast with seven heads as meaning the United Nations! (3, p. 7).

There is today a strong appetite for this kind of nonsense, and the Witnesses are not the only ones who cater for it. In his valuable book on *Fundamentalism* (second edition, 1981), James Barr (Regius Professor of Hebrew in the University of Oxford) has drawn attention to Hal Lindsey's *The Late Great Planet Earth*, first published in America in 1970, which claims to have had 26 printings in the first year and a half, and to have more than 1,700,000 copies in print in December 1972. It teaches that the ten horns of Daniel 7:24—which form the model for the ten horns in the passage from Revelation discussed above—refer to a *revived* Roman Empire, namely the then ten-nation European Economic Community.

It is particularly at times of political upheaval, or in international situations fraught with danger when people are very frightened and suggestible, that attention is called to apocalyptic programmes, and attempts are made to relate them to those situations. At such times, the desire to read the future becomes acute. The liberal theologian Jackson Case deplored how the world war which began in 1914 had given new opportunity for the advocacy of millennial views, whose adherents had "not been slow to avail themselves of this advantage".[11] Marley Cole, in his sympathetic account of the Witnesses, claims that during that war, a joint manifesto was published by a group of England's most noted clergymen, representing Baptists, Congregationalists, Presbyterians, Episcopalians, and Methodists, saying that "the present crisis points to the close of the times of the Gentiles"—an allusion to Jesus' 'prophecy' at Luke 21:24 that "Jerusalem shall be trodden down of the Gentiles until the times of the Gentiles be fulfilled"— and that "the revelation of the Lord may be expected at any moment".[12] More recently Paul Tillich declared that atomic physics has at last confirmed the prophecy of Isaiah 24:18–20 ("The foundations of the earth do shake" etc.), and that only those who have faith in the God of the Bible will survive the imminent catastrophe (cf. below, p. 87).

For the Witnesses, the date of Jesus's second coming is stated in Revelation, and elsewhere in the Bible, but in enigmatic language that requires interpretation. If the reader finds it puzzling that a divine revelation should be enigmatic rather than a perfectly clear guide, then he will doubtless be told that such obscurity has the approval of Jesus himself, who at Mark 4:11–12 is represented as being deliberately unintelligible to outsiders so that they shall not have any chance of repenting and being saved: "Unto them that are without all things are done in parables, that seeing they may see and not perceive, and hearing they may hear and not understand; lest haply they should turn again and it should be forgiven them." Jesus himself is here doing no more than following in the long tradition of Jewish apocalyptic writings which were intended to transmit secret knowledge to special circles of initiates.

Fundamentalists do not realize that there is no uniform teaching about the end of the world in the Bible, that for instance the discourse on this subject put into Jesus's mouth in the gospel of Mark was rewritten by Luke so as to give a different timetable.[13] Their method is to join together portions of Scripture which were never intended to go together, and, as an eminent textual critic has noted,[14] by thus "decontextualising" passages, it is possible to prove anything from the Bible. "The method", he adds, "is seen to be reduced to an absurdity if one should quote in succession the following":

> Judas went out and hanged himself (Matthew 27:5)
> Go and do thou likewise (Luke 10:37)
> What thou doest, do quickly (John 13:27).

As one might expect, such an arbitrary 'method' has led to a multiplicity of interpretations. The Old Testament scholar H.P. Smith referred in 1921 to 27 different dates which were fixed as the time of the end of the world and of the second coming between the years 557 and 1734, and added that further disparate calculations—all drawn from the same scriptures—had continued up to his own day.[15] The Witnesses themselves have repeatedly made false predictions. Professor Penton, himself a former Witness, has noted in his recent full-length study of the movement that "during the early years of their history, they consistently looked to specific dates—1874, 1878, 1881, 1910, 1914, 1918, 1920, 1925, and others— as having definite eschatological significance".[16] When the end did not come in 1914, they reinterpreted their doctrine that it would to mean that "the coronation of Jesus Christ in heaven" had taken place in that year (4, p. 6), and that—as stated on the opening page of many numbers of *Awake!*—"a peaceful and secure New Order" will begin "before the generation that saw the events of 1914 passes away". Their latest failure in prediction is that the end would come in 1975.

The scientist regards a theory as discredited if evidence falsifies it. The belief that 'the Bible' forecasts events of hundreds, even thousands, of years ahead has repeatedly been falsified. Apart from the failure of apocalyptic timetables, it is today widely admitted by New Testament scholars that, for instance, the passages in Isaiah, Micah, Hosea, Jeremiah, and so forth, to which the author of the gospel of Matthew alludes as prophecies of Jesus's birth at Bethlehem from a virgin mother, of his parents' flight into Egypt, and of other episodes from this evangelist's nativity story, have no real relevance to the episodes in question.[17] Who, ignorant of Matthew 2:16–19, could suppose that Jeremiah 31:15 (Rachel weeping for her children) referred to Herod's slaughter of the Innocents? The word 'prophet', as applied to these Old Testament writers, is itself misleading, as it suggests a foreteller, whereas the Hebrew word denotes rather "one who speaks for another, specifically one who brings the message of God, whether the message concerns the past, the present or the future".[18] The prophecies of Isaiah—I mean those which may fairly be regarded as genuine, and not the apocalyptic material beginning at chapter 24, from which I have quoted above and which, in the words of an eminent Old Testament scholar, is "quite certainly not Isaianic" and "totally different in outlook and in spirit from anything else in the book of Isaiah"[19]—these genuine prophecies refer to the political situation of Isaiah's own times: to the Syro-Ephraimite war of 735 B.C. and to the threatened invasion of Judah by Sennacherib of Assyria (701 B.C.). It is to the first of these two situations that the famous 'Immanuel' prophecy—taken in Matthew 1:22–3 as a reference to Jesus—really refers.[20] Once the prophetic canon was closed (about 200 B.C.), further disclosures had to be put into the mouth of an ancient personage if they were to find acceptance. And so the author of the book of Daniel, thinking that the persecution his contemporaries were suffering circa 165 B.C. from the Seleucid ruler Antiochus Epiphanes must surely provoke God to intervention, pretended that Daniel had lived during the Exile (in the sixth century B.C.), had prophesied with extraordinary precision the details of Antiochus's reign, and had outlined the consummation that, so he believed, would immediately follow it. As was early this century noted in the very valuable *Encyclopaedia Biblica*, on the assumption that the book was really written during the Exile, "it is very hard indeed to understand how, out of the ten pieces of which it is composed, so many as five, in which the coming of the Messianic kingdom is predicted, should stop short at the reign of a Seleucid sovereign whose kingdom—not to speak of the Greek kingdom out of which it and the other Seleucid kingdoms had arisen—had no existence in the days of the exilic Daniel".[21] Early Christian authors, however, took what they read in Daniel as genuine prophecy and looked for its fulfilment not in the author's times but in theirs. To this day each generation continues to produce enthusiasts who interpret the data both of Daniel and of the New Testament apocalypse modelled on it so as to make these data applicable to their own age. The technique is at all costs to salvage an underlying theory (in this case that the Bible foretells events in the remote future)—a technique not confined to religious apologists. Some psychologists who insist that a certain man has an Oedipus complex will not be deterred if he gives evidence that he has never got on at all well with his mother. They will simply allege that he has the complex in an inverted form. Sir Karl Popper has recorded in his autobiography how impressed he was in the Vienna of his youth by the difference between the method of Einstein—who gave a "clear statement that he would regard his theory as untenable if it should fail in certain tests"—and "the dogmatic attitude of Marx, Freud, Adler, and even more so that of their followers".[22]

The Witnesses are among the many groups who have been able to endure present ills patiently in the expectation of a future recompense. The Stoics and Epicureans were religious in this sense: they too aimed at an interpretation of things which counterbalanced the evils and accidents of existence. But their views, unlike those of the Witnesses, were adequate only for few individuals, since they are based on conceptions too general for average intelligence. Involved in all these attitudes is a vivid imagination, a strong conviction of the reliability of one's expectation and of its adequacy as compensation for the present. Ideally, the realization of the hopes must also be remote enough not to be shown up as false in the devotee's life-time, yet believed to be near enough for him to have the satisfaction that he is slowly but surely approaching it. Few things are more satisfying than the consciousness that one is drawing ever nearer to a major goal—whether this be the completion of a book, the winning of a war, or any other enterprise. The belief in a relatively prompt end to the present dispensation is necessary to keep the Witnesses working at the level of commitment shown by their canvassers. It is to some extent a source of weakness that such a timetable is liable to be falsified by history. But the movement, like many others within and outside Christianity, has shown that it can survive destructive criticism of any kind by reinterpreting the primary data.

(iii) Biblical Inerrancy and Authoritarian Sects

Awake! urges us not merely to read the Bible, but also to notice how its different parts connect (1, p. 20). I would recommend those who believe the Bible to be inerrant to implement this excellent advice by comparing the books of Samuel and Kings on the one hand with those of Chronicles on the other. They cover the same period of history (from David to the Babylonian Exile), but Chronicles was written centuries later than the others, and suppresses or contradicts unpalatable statements in the earlier works. It omits the chequered picture of David's family troubles: his adultery with Bathsheba, his callous arrangements for the murder of her husband Uriah (2 Samuel 11–12), and his terrible treatment of seven of Saul's sons—hung "before the Lord" to appease the deity who had punished the sins of his chosen people with a famine (2 Samuel 21:6 and 9). In its biography of Solomon, Chronicles makes no mention of his idolatry and polygamy; and whereas 2 Kings 15:1–4 tells that King Uzziah (also called Azariah) "did that which was right in the eyes of the Lord", except that "the high places were not taken away", 2 Chronicles 26:4 omits this proviso. The high places were the old sanctuaries of Yahweh, regarded as legitimate before the building of the Jerusalem temple. They came in time to be regarded as confusing the minds of the people as to the one national god, who was therefore to be regarded as being present only in one unique shrine in the holy city. The Chronicler and his generation could not imagine a good king tolerating them, and in one passage he actually contradicts what Kings had said on the subject:

1 Kings 15:11–14	2 Chronicles 14:2
And Asa did that which was right in the eyes of the Lord . . . But the high places were not taken away.	And Asa did that which was good and right in the eyes of the Lord his God: for he took away the strange altars, and the high places . . .

These are no isolated instances, for the Chronicler systematically revises the narrative of his predecessors. A well-known example is the crowning of the young king Joash. In 2 Kings 11:4–12 he is placed on the throne by the royal bodyguard acting under the direction of the priest of the temple. In 2 Chronicles 23:1–11 this bodyguard does not appear; it is the Levites who do what is necessary, and care is taken that none but consecrated persons enter the sacred building. This Chronicler clearly could not conceive that a bodyguard of laymen, including probably foreigners, could be admitted to it, or that the chief priest could make use of them when he had Levites at his command, and so he amended the account he found in his predecessor—in perfectly good faith. This is something that I wish to stress very heavily. We are so often told that either we must allow that a Biblical narrative is true, or we must admit that we are calling it a sham, a lie, a fraud, or worse. But there is no reason to believe that the Chronicler regarded the earlier account as inspired; and he will have found it much more plausible to suppose that his predecessor had got things a bit wrong than to believe that they could have happened in the way described.

The reader may think that contradictions about what Jewish kings did centuries ago are a trivial matter. In fact they show how a Biblical writer can be inspired by the conceptions of his own times rather than by God; and they also form part of the case argued by de Wette in 1806 that the standpoint of the Chronicler was unknown to Biblical writers of earlier date and certainly does not go back to the time of Moses; and therefore that the actual history of the Jewish people is quite different from what large sections of the five opening books of the Old Testament (the Pentateuch) allege that history to have been (cf. below, pp. 25 ff). Subsequent research, culminating in the case argued by Julius Wellhausen in 1878, has shown that, of the variegated matter of different age and provenance welded together in the Pentateuch, it is only the so-called 'Priestly' material (dominating the books of Leviticus and Numbers, but represented also in sections of Genesis and Exodus) that shares the standpoint of the Chronicler; that this material, with its elaborate ritual prescriptions (allegedly promulgated by Moses), its genealogies and its statistics, is much later than the folklore represented in the patriarchal stories of Genesis, and somewhat later even than the legislation (also allegedly Mosaic) recorded in Deuteronomy; and that the really early material shows Israelite religion to have been much less elaborate and less regulated in the early days of the nation's history than the Priestly Code would allow, so that this Code's ascription of complicated ritual and other legislation to Moses in these early days is mythical. It was, however, an ascription which will have been made in perfectly good faith. The compilers of the Priestly Code no doubt believed that the traditions they collected were very ancient, and so what could be more appropriate than to ascribe them to the founder of Israel's religion?

The initial page of many issues of *Awake!* states that the journal "probes beneath the surface and points to the real meaning of current events". The Watch Tower Society insists that "personal reading" of the Bible is "not sufficient", that the "help" of the Society is indispensable.[23] It is of course the very latest teaching of the Society to which we must all be beholden. Only in the publications of its critics (for example in the books by Rogerson or Penton already cited) does one discover how often it has changed its views. In a recently published guide book of nearly 450 pages, designed to help the Society's field activists to answer questions likely to be put to them, less than half a page is devoted to the topic of changes in doctrine, which remain unspecified. Assurance is simply given that "increased knowledge often requires adjustments in one's thinking", and that "Jehovah's Witnesses are willing humbly to make such adjustments."[24] Changes in teaching would indeed be no discredit to the Witnesses if, like scientists, they regarded all their theories as provisional. But the rest of this guide book is sheer dogmatism, totally lacking in the tentativeness suggested in the passage quoted.

This dogmatism goes hand in hand with intolerance toward any deviation in opinion among the membership. The Society insists that, if we recognize God as a "Grand Instructor", then "we will not doubt or criticize the methods of instruction Jehovah's 'faithful and discreet slave' class is using today. Rather, we will support disciplinary actions that are sometimes necessary in instructing" (4, p. 30). This last sentence may fairly be linked with the statement on p. 13 of the same issue that, during 1985, "36,638 individuals had to be disfellowshipped from the Christian congregation"—"the greater number", it is claimed, "for practising immorality". But it is apparent from the increasing number of critical publications by former Witnesses that some have been expelled for questioning the received teaching. Such authoritarian demeanour has always been typical of sectarian leadership. F. C. Watson has recently shown how, in the first and second centuries of our era, the Jewish Qumran community, the Pauline Christians, and the Christian Johannine community all re-interpreted the Jewish sacred books—all in different ways, in the interests of their sect—and denounced all who did not accept the sect's interpretation.[25] Paul, for instance, begins his letter to the Galatians by twice cursing Christians who viewed things differently.[26] He also betrays the importance to a sect of the mutual reassurance generated by communal worship, saying: when we cry "Abba, Father!", it is "the Spirit himself bearing witness with our spirit that we are children of God" (Romans 8:15–16). Meeks has recently stressed (apropos of early Christianity but with an awareness of more general implications) how much a group's cohesiveness is promoted by meeting together with ritual speech, music, reading of scripture, and preaching.[27]

Sectarian dogmatism is one of the implications of holding by any sacred book, be it the Bible, the Koran or *Das Kapital*. The book requires interpretation, the interpreters cannot agree on what constitutes the correct interpretation, and so any person or group that cares to pose as an authority declares that theirs is the exposition that must be unquestioningly accepted. And authoritative ruling is what many people want. Society could not cohere if all were rebels, and although some educationalists are apt to stress the value of independence and originality, the great majority of people are far better equipped to do things in a traditional manner, to follow a clear lead rather than to take the initiative. In the presence of a forceful leader, an individual who would feel weak when left to his own devices is more confident, braver, and stronger. What the Christian craves, says the psychologist William James, "is to be consoled in his very powerlessness, to feel that the spirit of the universe recognizes and secures him, all decaying and failing as he is".[28] The strong human protector, the father or leader of the group, and not 'the spirit of the universe' (or, as it is usually called, God), is the first and most natural object of this craving. But a complex community has many strong men and leaders at loggerheads, and none of them, in their human capacity, able to supply adequate protection. And so men contrive to find in God a power greater than any human power, and to put their trust in this unchallengeable champion. "The Lord is my light and my salvation; whom shall I fear?" (Psalm 27:1).

(iv) Conservative Christianity Generally

For Western Europeans and Americans, brought up to regard the Bible with respect if not reverence, this turning to God means turning to the Bible. They are largely ignorant of what non-conservative Old and New Testament scholars have established about it in the past 150 years. Today these scholars themselves (with a few honourable exceptions) make little attempt to come to terms with ultra-conservative Christians—partly because they regard the battle with them as fought and won long ago, and partly because they find Fundamentalism at any rate preferable to 'materialistic' atheism. In this sense the liberal theologian Professor John Hick has stated that "fundamentalism, or extreme conservative evangelicalism, can be an important phase through which to pass, though not a good one in which to get stuck."[29] And the conservative camp is still able to produce its own scholars, arguing for at any rate an approximation to the older doctrines, holding for instance that Daniel was written in the Exile and merely 'reissued' in the time of Antiochus Epiphanes, and that the Pentateuch 'in some sense' goes back to Moses. Conservative spokesmen are anxious to give the impression that, minority among scholars as they are, they nevertheless give as good as they get, and that—as one of them has recently put it—"the counter-arguments . . . are pressed home with as impressive a display of scholarship as is used on the other side".[30]

Some of the conservatives deal with 'the other side' by largely ignoring it. An example is James Dunn's *The Evidence for Jesus* (London, 1985). Dunn is Professor of Divinity in the University of

Durham, and his book is an expansion of four public lectures delivered in a Methodist Church to an audience of presumptive piety. The book aims at rectifying the distress experienced by many Christians who watched the London Weekend Television series entitled 'Jesus: the Evidence' (April 1984), and proposes to "set the record straight as to what scholarship can and does say on a number of key issues relating to Jesus and the beginnings of Christianity" (p. xii). Scholarship here means conservative scholarship, as Dunn's bibliography reveals. To take a minor example from his own text: when pleading for the historical reliability of the gospels, he refers to the evidence of Papias (a bishop in Asia Minor, circa 150 A.D.) without indicating that many of his theological colleagues regard it as valueless. (Hans Conzelmann, for instance, noted in a history of the earliest Christianity published at Göttingen in 1971, that Papias's "jottings about the origin of the gospels are, to this day, endlessly discussed". They are, he added, "one and all historically worthless"). At the ends of his first, second, and third chapters Dunn appends notes criticizing statements made in the television series by myself, by the historian Professor Morton Smith, and by the theologian Professor Helmut Köster respectively. He makes no attempt to direct the reader to the relevant books published by these three persons. The only reference to publications in these three notes is to a work which, in contrast to the scholar criticized (Köster), takes a traditional view of the issue in question. Dunn must know that a substantial fraction of what is filmed for a television programme is liable to be edited out; in my own case, what was left was a caricature of my views which he can easily dispose of.

The triumphant conclusion of Dunn's book is that "Christianity has nothing to fear from scholarship" (p. 103). The old-time faith, however, has something to fear from scholarship even as conducted by Professor Dunn—as when his only reference to the virgin birth is an allusion to the opening chapters of Matthew and Luke as testifying to the "fact" that "there *was* something odd about Jesus' birth" (p. 19).

Since Strauss, whose work we shall study in the next chapter, it has been obvious that biblical writers often alleged as historical fact what they deemed necessary on theological grounds. Conservative apologists still do the same. The attitude is less blatant. There is more parade of erudition and open-mindedness. But the conclusions always turn out to be in accordance with desire, in harmony with what is regarded as essential doctrine.

The non-specialist reader is ill-equipped to make an informed choice between warring voices, and the individual is always more open to suggestion in matters where he has not the means of judging for himself. In this situation he is tempted to resign his own will and submit to an authority—particularly as he is told that it is a virtue thus to 'humble himself'. His suggestibility is today further increased by fear, for he is living in an unstable international situation with terrifying developments in armaments, and so wants a faith that gives him more than mere tentative reassurance. Dr. David Jenkins has told (in The Guardian, 17 December, 1984) how disconcerted he was to find, on relinquishing his theological chair for appointment as Bishop of Durham, that what his flock requires from him is not the "exploration, critical re-assessment and discovery" which, as liberal theologian, he would be happy to provide, but rather "assurance", and "reinforcement in opinions and positions already held". Liberal theology, recognizing as it does difficulties in what has for centuries been taught as Christian doctrine, cannot provide such assurance; its qualifications and hesitations testify only to doubt, and "he that doubteth is like the surge of the sea, driven by the wind and tossed" (James 1:6). The author of this epistle knew—as many have known (they include Nietzsche and Hitler)—that emphatic assertion is often more effective than careful statement of pros and cons; that arguments suggest the possibility of dissenting views, and that to defend one's opinions is to admit that they are open to attack.[31] What is called the old-time Bible faith, promulgated by well-organized groups with massive propaganda, gives certain and unhesitating answers, and is welcomed for that.

The dogmatic moral guidance given by the Witnesses, by Fundamentalists generally, and by conservative Christian spokesmen has a particularly strong appeal today. Now that the disadvantages of permissiveness—in the form, for instance of sexually transmitted diseases and of contempt for all kinds of authority—have become a little obvious, we find a widespread reaction in the form of a reindorsement of moral absolutism which goes well beyond Fundamentalist circles. Paul Johnson claims (in *The Times*, 22 August, 1985) that Western civilization has inherited "a core of moral absolutism" from its Judaeo-Christian tradition, and that "by accepting moral absolutes we concede the limitations of human wisdom." It would be juster to say that, by accepting such absolutes, we can act without having to justify our actions; and that on this view we must implement what we take to be God's laws even though they do not seem wise to us. (If they do, then we are not, in accepting them, going beyond 'the limitations of human wisdom'.) Reaction of this kind is just as irrational as the excess of permissiveness that occasioned it. But it is a reaction from which Fundamentalism is nevertheless profiting.

The return to the Bible is much more marked in America than in Britain. Caspar Weinberger, U.S. Secretary of Defence, stated in an interview to the *New York Times* (23 August, 1982), apropos of the present international situation: "I have read the Book of Revelation and, yes, I believe the world is going to end—by an act of God, I hope—but every day I think that time is running out." Perhaps such statements need not be taken very seriously, as politicians are apt to talk in the kind of terms that they think will be acceptable to whatever audience they happen to be addressing. Nevertheless it is somewhat frightening to find even statesmen looking to the Bible for elucidation of our present perils.

Adequate religious education would make a big difference here. I do not believe that what is called 'Religious Education' in schools tells the pupils how the Bible came into existence, how limited is its historical value, and how confused and contradictory are the ethical principles that are proclaimed in its various books. How many schoolchildren learn that the gospels are relatively late documents and therefore more questionable as sources for Christian origins than many of the epistles which view Jesus so differently? How many are aware that the fourth of the canonical gospels is in significant respects incompatible with the other three, and that a given story even in them can often be shown to be not straightforward reporting but manipulation of an earlier and contrary tradition? How all real problems are avoided in books designed for use in schools is well illustrated in Michael Keene's *Steps in Religious Education*, published in three booklets by Hutchinson in 1986. Misstatements of fact are also not wanting,[32] and the booklets are lavishly illustrated with pictures romanticizing religion and appealing to readers who would find a continuous text burdensome. One of the pictures shows "Paul writing his Epistle to the Ephesians from prison." No indication is given that many Christian scholars regard this epistle, among others ascribed to Paul in the New Testament, as not his work at all, but as an adaptation of some of his ideas to the needs of certain Christian communities a generation or more after his time.[33] It is in the interests of all the Churches that pupils are not encouraged to be critical about the Bible and are seldom told about the criticisms which have been made in the past and which continue to be made by scholars in the present. And on the resulting ignorance Fundamentalism thrives.

Postscript: Since I completed this chapter, Macmillan Press has published *Studies in Religious Fundamentalism*, edited by Lionel Caplan, 1987. All its nine chapters, by various scholars, repay careful study, but particularly relevant to the present work is Steve Bruce's account of the "Moral Majority" in the U.S.A. Bruce has first hand experience of conservative Protestantism (he lectures on sociology at the Queen's University, Belfast) and stresses the fierce pace of change in American lifestyles to which fundamentalism is, in part, a reaction: "Although it is fashionable for liberals to characterize the New Christian Right as 'extremists', it is worth remembering that the world they wish to recreate was the world of most Americans as little as thirty years ago. Where once two-thirds of the states' legislatures were willing to vote for prohibition, there is now talk of legalising marijuana. Where once divorce brought considerable social stigma, there are now single parent, lesbian and male homosexual 'families'. In what was once 'one nation under God', public prayer is no longer permitted in public schools" (pp. 180–1). The considerable amount of 'God talk' at federal level must be such as to offend nobody, and so has "so little content as to have few behavioural consequences" (p. 179). This gives the fundamentalists, with their specifics, their chance.

Chapter Two
The Rise of Radical Biblical Scholarship

(i) Old Testament: W. M. L. de Wette (1780–1849)

In the first five books of the Old Testament, the so-called Pentateuch, we read of God's dealings with mankind from the Creation to the Flood, the call of Abraham (Genesis 12), the oppression of the Israelites in Egypt, their exodus from that country under Moses (who is supposed to have lived circa 1300 B.C.)[1], and their subsequent forty years' wandering in the wilderness before they established themselves in Canaan. The final four of these five books (Exodus, Leviticus, Numbers, and Deuteronomy) record the laws which God gave the Jews via Moses during these forty years. Their conquest of Canaan is the subject of the next two books (Joshua and Judges), and the books of Samuel and Kings deal with the establishment and history of the Hebrew monarchy up to the collapse of the Jewish state and the deportation of Jews to exile in Babylon in 586 B.C.

Until the end of the eighteenth century it was supposed that the bulk of the Pentateuch was written by Moses, and it is still convenient to refer to these five books as 'the Mosaic books', as they include the divine legislation revealed through Moses. De Wette was the first to press considerations which have brought most scholars to conclude that the Pentateuch is in fact a blend of documents dating from pre-Mosaic times down to about 400 B.C.[2] John Rogerson, the most recent historian of the Old Testament criticism of the nineteenth century, has justly noted that de Wette "inaugurated a new era in critical Old Testament scholarship", and that his *Beiträge zur Einleitung in das Alte Testament* (Contributions to an Introduction to the Old Testament), published in two volumes at Halle, 1806–7, was his most significant contribution to this end. It is "the first work of Old Testament scholarship to use the critical method in order to present a view of the history of Israelite religion that is radically at variance with the view implied in the Old Testament itself".[3] In the following account of de Wette's case, page references will be to the first volume of the *Beiträge* (unless introduced by a II, indicating the second volume).

De Wette observed that the laws which, according to the Pentateuch, God promulgated through Moses, and which allegedly laid the basis of Israelite life at such an early date in the nation's history, appear to be unknown to the later history of the nation as recorded in Judges, Samuel and most of Kings; that the life and worship of the nation in the period covered by these books seems to proceed in complete ignorance of the Mosaic stipulations. In particular, there is no suggestion that Yahweh is to be worshipped only at one fixed central sanctuary; there are no precise regulations about the manner in which sacrifices are to be offered; and there is no established priesthood to regulate worship. 1 and 2 Samuel and 1 and 2 Kings cover the period from Saul and his successor David (who reigned about 1000 B.C.) until the exile in Babylon (586 B.C.). Samuel, de Wette says (p. 152), makes no reference to the Mosaic books, nor to the matter contained in them, and Kings only very occasional reference to Mosaic laws until it tells of the discovery of the "book of the law" in the temple in the reign of Josiah in 621 B.C., 400 years after David (2 Kings 22). De Wette says that this book is unlikely to have been the whole Pentateuch, but probably only Deuteronomy (pp. 175–6), since the narrative represents Josiah, once he has become acquainted with the book, as carrying out reforms in accordance with the deuteronomic stipulations that the passover is to be a national festival, attached to the feast of unleavened bread, and to be celebrated at the unique sanctuary. Josiah's knowledge of the book is certainly represented as the basis of an entirely new departure in the religious life of the nation, for we are told (23:21 ff.) that he "commanded all the people, saying, keep the passover unto the Lord your God, as it is written in this book of the covenant". And the narrator adds that "surely there was not kept such a passover from the days of the judges that judged Israel, nor in all the days of the kings of Israel, nor of the kings of Judah". Now de Wette argues that if the Pentateuch had been written in the time of Moses (or,

Chronicles: revises & contradicts kings & Samuel

though written later, accurately records what had then happened), it really is extraordinary that none of the kings or judges earlier than Josiah (many of whom are said in the books of Judges, Samuel, and Kings to have been extremely religious) should have kept the passover according to the rules of Deuteronomy (pp. 178–9). On the other hand, if these rules were not in existence until the period of Jewish history we reach with 2 Kings 22, then the total absence of their stipulations from Judges and Samuel is quite intelligible.[4]

One passage in Kings, if taken at its face value, implies that Mosaic laws existed at the time of David. For the dying David is represented as urging his successor Solomon to act "according to that which is written in the law of Moses" (1 Kings 2:3). Now Kings was written (or the material on which it is based collected into the book as we know it) hundreds of years after David, for, as we saw, it records the collapse of the Jewish state in 586 B.C.; and its author, acquainted as he was with Deuteronomy, could well have put this reference to the law of Moses into the dying king's mouth. De Wette notes that even the most honest historian can be tempted to embroider speeches, and that a pious tirade might well have been thought appropriate as the final utterance of this paradigmatically pious king (pp. 159–161).

At 2 Kings 14:6 King Amaziah (king of Judah from about 800 B.C.) is said to have refrained from punishing the children of the murderers of his father, "according to that which is written in the book of the law of Moses". De Wette says that this clear reference to Deuteronomy again gives evidence only of the beliefs of the author of Kings and of his times (p. 167). It is not said in this passage that Amaziah himself had any knowledge of Mosaic laws. The passage is simply the author's comment on his behaviour.

In sum, the history narrated in Judges and Samuel is not in accordance with the Mosaic laws, which therefore were unknown when these books were written and which a fortiori did not exist when the events they describe took place. By the time Kings was written, Deuteronomy, but not necessarily the other books ascribed to Moses in the canon, had come into existence.

De Wette checks this hypothesis by comparing Samuel and Kings with the two books which follow it in the canon, namely the books of Chronicles. They cover the same period of history as do

Samuel-Kings, but were written much later. Kings takes the history up to the beginning of the captivity of the Jews in Babylon, but Chronicles ends with the statement that this exile lasted seventy years. Its language also stamps it as late (p. 44). The overthrow of Babylonian power was due to the rise of Persia from circa 538 B.C.; and de Wette notes that Persian coinage was sufficiently familiar to the author of Chronicles for him to commit the ineptitude of reckoning in darics for Davidic times (1 Chronicles 29:7).[5] De Wette believed, as many have done since, that Chronicles was in fact written in the period of the Greek Empire of Alexander which succeeded the Persian about 300 B.C. (pp. 45-6). But the most recent scholarship favours a date late in the Persian period.[6]

Chronicles has many passages verbally identical with Samuel-Kings and also many that are irreconcilably at variance with what is stated in these earlier books. The question naturally arises whether Chronicles drew directly from them, taking over some of their passages but rejecting or embellishing others, or whether the agreements are due to a common source and the disagreements to independent deviations from it. De Wette believes that the former of these two alternatives is the case, as it is always Samuel-Kings, not Chronicles, that give what is obviously the simpler and more primitive account of a given incident.[7] The Chronicler, for instance, delights in miracles, and at one point manages to introduce one by means of an obvious insertion into a narrative as he found it in Kings. According to 1 Kings 22:32–33, Syrian soldiers at first take Jehoshaphat for King of Israel and make to attack him; but when he cries out—presumably thus making his true identity known to them—they realize their mistake and turn away from him. 2 Chronicles 18:31 implies that Jehoshaphat cried out *to Jehovah*, who heard his call and caused the Syrians to turn away. Comparison of the two passages shows at once that this is an insertion (italicized in my quotation) rupturing the original context:

Kings	Chronicles
And it came to pass, when the captains of the chariots saw Jehoshaphat, that they said, Surely it is the king of Israel; and they turned aside to fight against him: and Jehoshaphat cried out. And it came to pass, when the captains of the chariots saw that it was not the king of Israel, that they turned back from pursuing him.	And it came to pass, when the captains of the chariots saw Jehoshaphat, that they said, It is the king of Israel. Therefore they turned about to fight against him; but Jehoshaphat cried out, *and the Lord helped him; and God moved them to depart from him.* And it came to pass, when the captains of the chariots saw that it was not the king of Israel, that they turned back from pursuing him.

The natural causation of Jehoshaphat's survival that is alleged in Kings is thus not abrogated in Chronicles but merely clumsily supplemented by supernatural causation. De Wette observes that the Chronicler will have thought it entirely appropriate for the pious Jehoshaphat to have been saved by miracle (pp. 79–80).

Chronicles also suppresses or contradicts unpalatable statements made in the earlier works, omitting or even denying their admissions that pious monarchs failed to suppress the 'high places'—local sanctuaries, forbidden by the Deuteronomic legislation, which restricts sacrifice to the one central shrine at Jerusalem (cf. above, p. 15). De Wette summarizes the evolution as follows: The early Hebrew monarchs, and the early historians who wrote of them, knew nothing of the Mosaic laws; the author of Kings, who drew on the work of such earlier historians, knew Deuteronomy, which insists repeatedly that Yahweh is to be worshipped at one place only, that sacrifices must be offered and the annual festivals celebrated only there; and so although the author of Kings recorded the failure of the monarchs to suppress the high places, he was careful to designate it a crime; finally the author of Chronicles redacted previous traditions so drastically that he suppressed the failure to abolish the high places.

De Wette gives many examples which show how Chronicles expands the narrative of Samuel or Kings so as to include references to the law conspicuously absent in them. For instance, 1 Kings 9:25 says that Solomon offered burnt offerings three times a year on the altar he had built. De Wette observes (pp. 52–3) that in 2 Chronicles 8:12 this is expanded to say that he did so

> even as the duty of every day required, offering according to the commandment of Moses, on the sabbaths, and on the new moons, and on the set feasts three times in the year, even in the feast of unleavened bread, and in the feast of weeks, and in the feast of tabernacles. . . .

Similarly 2 Kings 11:18–19 is expanded in 2 Chronicles 23:17–20 in order to include a reference to "the priests, the Levites" and to show that they offered "the burnt offerings of the Lord as it is written in the law of Moses". Again, the bare mention in 2 Kings, 23:21–22 of the feast of the passover under Josiah is turned at 2 Chronicles 35:7–19 into an elaborate description (pp. 55–6).

De Wette puts together (pp. 225ff.) all that Samuel and Kings tell us about the religious life of the nation, and compares this with the requirements of the Pentateuch. The number of omissions and breaches is formidable, and he comments that, if the laws were really written by Moses, they have had a most remarkable fate. Instead of being kept at the time of their institution and forgotten later, the reverse is the case: the period following the lawgiver is marked by flagrant transgressions of his most important laws, and a total silence of the historians about his law-book; while a thousand years later they are followed with a punctilious, almost superstitious, exactitude (pp. 223–4). One can, he argues, make better sense of the data by assuming that the laws were framed after, and as a corrective to, the ungodly behaviour of the early kings. Solomon's conduct seems, in particular, to have been the stimulus for some of the prohibitions of Deuteronomy, where the king is forbidden (17:16–17) to "multiply horses to himself", or to "cause the people to return to Egypt, to the end that he should multiply horses. . . . Neither shall he multiply wives to himself. . . . Neither shall he greatly multiply to himself silver and gold". From 1 Kings we learn that Solomon had 40,000 stalls of horses (4:26), obtained horses from Egypt (10:28); that he "made silver to be in Jerusalem as stones" (verse 27), "loved many strange women" and had "seven hundred wives" (11:1,3); and that "the weight of gold which came to him in one year was six hundred three score and six talents" (10:14). It seems, then, that the law of Deuteronomy for

the Hebrew monarchy was framed after the nation had had

experience of kings, and not in the desert under Moses. De Wette suggests accordingly (II, p. 22) that a written book of the law may not have existed before Josiah, in whose reign it was, according to Kings, discovered. The prophets, he argues, knew nothing of a Mosaic law-book. "They allude continually to laws, but not to a book of law" (p. 184). Even Jeremiah, who was active after the 'discovery' of the law book under Josiah, deemed it of little account, for he repudiated its authority, saying:

> I (the Lord of Hosts) spake not unto your fathers, nor commanded them in the day that I brought them out of the land of Egypt, concerning burnt offerings or sacrifices (7:22).

This passage, says de Wette (p. 185), shows that the prophet did not accept the Sinaitic authority of the legislation recorded in Leviticus and elsewhere. The very orthodox *New Bible Commentary* (edited by F. Davidson, London, 1961) has recorded (p. 615) that subsequent scholarship has in the main endorsed de Wette's view that "what Jeremiah is proclaiming is that the entire ritual scheme of sacrifice had never been instituted by God".

De Wette is a little confused about the relation between Deuteronomy and the other books of the Pentateuch. The view subsequently established is that the so-called 'Priestly Code' contained in Leviticus and Numbers (and in parts of Genesis and Exodus) is even later than Deuteronomy.[8] His confusion, however, does not impair his principal arguments, namely that "up to the time of Josiah there is no trace of the existence of the Pentateuch, whereas afterwards, particularly after the Exile, there are abundant and unambiguous traces of it" (p. 182); that Kings knew at any rate Deuteronomy, while Esra and Nehemiah, which continue the history of the Jews from the point at which Chronicles ends, show knowledge of all the Mosaic books (p. 180); and that Chronicles itself corrects earlier narratives, as if its author had Moses's law-book in his hand (pp. 80–1). As we saw, it is today acknowledged that de Wette was the first who clearly stated the inconsistency between the starting point of Israelitish history, as stated in the opening books of the Bible, and that history itself.

In his second volume, de Wette attacks the method then prevalent in German theology of reinterpreting Old Testament narratives so as to eliminate their allegations of miracle and make them records of incidents which could well have happened. Abraham, it had been urged, did not converse with God, but had some kind of psychological experience; and God did not appear as a 'flaming torch' as he walked between the pieces to seal the covenant, but there occurred some kind of 'volcanic phenomenon' or a streak of lightning (II, p. 82). Such commentators were called in those days 'rationalists' because they tried to turn Bible stories into narratives which reasonable people can believe. De Wette complains that in fact they merely disfigured the Bible with their "tasteless, prosaic views"; that—to revert to the incident concerning Abraham—the documents which alone gives us any information about him state clearly that God spoke to him (II, pp. 59–61); so that when we have rejected what they say there remains no supporting evidence for any assertion about psychological or any other experiences. We are left alleging an event which is possible, or even probable, but this is no proof that it occurred (II, p. 73). George Grote was soon to make the same comment on attempts to discern a kernel of historical truth in Greek legends. Deletion of their miracle stories leaves one with incidents similar to those in a modern novel, and

> to raise plausible fiction up to the superior dignity of truth, some positive testimony or positive ground of inference must be shown.... A man who tells us that on the day of the battle of Plataea, rain fell on the spot of ground where the city of New York now stands, will neither deserve nor obtain credit, because he can have had no means of positive knowledge; though the statement is not in the slightest degree improbable.[9]

De Wette stresses the relevance to the Hebrew stories of methods freely argued in connection with Greek myths. Early man, he says, was acquainted with a tradition about a universal flood which had destroyed all mankind, and yet knew that somehow the race had survived. How could this be? He says that numerous stories arose as an answer to this question, and that the one about Noah is clearly no more historical than the equivalent tale of Deukalion and his wife Pyrrha (II, pp. 70–9).[10] Furthermore, the two discrepant Flood-stories united in Genesis by a redactor show that poetic writers felt free to adapt existing traditions, just as the Greek myths were treated differently by the tragic and the epic poets (II, p. 74).

In Britain radical criticism of the Pentateuch came only later in the nineteenth century, but signally when J. W. Colenso, missionary Bishop of Natal from 1854, published his *The Pentateuch and the Book of Joshua Critically Examined* in seven parts between 1862 and 1879. Intelligent questioning from one of his Zulu converts had made him dissatisfied with orthodox views on the subject; and he began reading critical accounts, including that of de Wette. Colenso's first volume in turn convinced the Dutch scholar Abraham Kuenen that the text contains "difficulties" which he had before "not at all or not sufficiently considered".[11] Kuenen's shift of opinion was to have profound consequences for Old Testament criticism. The most recent account of this whole episode concludes that Colenso "exhausted the credibility of the older defences of orthodoxy, and showed to a younger generation of scholars facts in the Bible that orthodox schemes could no longer explain".[12]

If de Wette caused something of a stir in Germany, Strauss was soon to give even greater offence by extending some of his predecessor's principles from the Old Testament to the New; for it was de Wette's work that taught Strauss to regard so much in the gospels as 'tendency-stories'. De Wette had, for instance, observed that Genesis 9:18–27 makes Canaan receive the curse that (if anybody) his father Ham deserves; that it is the progenitor of the hated Canaanites that must be cursed, even though the narrative is but clumsily adapted to this end (II, p. 76).[13] If in this instance the tendency that inspired the story is patriotic, in others, so de Wette maintained (II, p. 51), it is priestly—the obvious purpose of many of the narratives being to supply a quasi-historical basis for the theocratic laws (the holiness of the Sabbath, circumcision, and the prohibition against eating blood). Sometimes, he holds, the underlying tendency is merely artistic. In his view the story of the promise of a son to Abraham owes its origin to the fact that Jewish mythology requires the birth of outstanding individuals to be miraculously foretold (II, p. 67). This is something that Strauss had very much in mind when he traced Luke's story of the annunciation of the birth of John the Baptist to Old Testament models. (Luke makes the Baptist born of aged parents, as are Isaac, Samuel, and Samson, and in circumstances which are to a large extent parallelled in Old Testament narratives about these three.) Again, de Wette discerns a literary tendency in the similarities of the two genealogies of Genesis 5 (from Adam to Noah) and Genesis 11:10ff. (from Noah's son Shem to Abraham). The writer, he says (II, pp. 48–9, 69), wished to mark out two epochs: from man's origin to his destruction in the Flood, and from the subsequent new beginning to the inauguration of the Hebrew theocracy with Abraham. To effect a neat division the writer has supplied each epoch with the same number of generations—each genealogy contains ten names and in each the facts are stated with the same turns of phrase. De Wette points to similar features of symmetry in Matthew's genealogy of Jesus, thus giving Strauss his cue.[14] Strauss was well aware of the general similarity of his method to that of de Wette, and noted that, while the latter's view of the post-Mosaic origin and mythical character of the Pentateuch was then widely accepted, the application of an equally critical method to the study of the New Testament had not yet become quite respectable.[15]

(ii) New Testament: David Friedrich Strauss (1808–1874)*

Many have been introduced to the problems of the New Testament by Albert Schweitzer's The Quest of the Historical Jesus. This famous account of the debate concerning the historical Jesus from H. S. Reimarus in the late eighteenth century to William Wrede's work of 1901 sends the reader to Strauss with the assurance that his Das Leben Jesu kritisch bearbeitet (The Life of Jesus Critically Examined), 1835—I shall call it his first Life—is "one of the most perfect things in the whole range of learned literature". Schweitzer has particular praise for the author's ability to marshal evidence: "His analysis descends to the minutest details, but he does not lose his way among them".[16] Certainly, to

---

*In what follows I use the names Mark, Matthew, etc. sometimes to mean the authors of the relevant gospels, and sometimes to mean the gospels ascribed to them. Which meaning is intended will be clear from the context.

compare and contrast four gospel accounts of each alleged incident in Jesus's life without blurring the issues is one of the expositor's great difficulties, and Strauss surmounts it with skill. Another fine feature of his book—although it gave offence at the time—is his scientific detachment towards his material. Strauss's teacher F. C. Baur, who even then was no more of a believer than Strauss, complained (in a letter to L. F. Heyd, 10 February 1836) of the book's "often offending coldness, especially towards the person of Jesus". If, then, Strauss had been more enthusiastic for the person of Jesus, he would, in Baur's opinion, have been juster. In the opinion of others, Baur would have been juster had he been less fearful of giving offence to piety.

Strauss's book was—in the words of his recent English biographer, Dr. Horton Harris,

> the most intellectually reasoned attack which has ever been mounted against Christianity . . . the first open and public assault on the bastions of the traditional Christian faith, in an age where atheism was treated with abhorrence and attacked with the weapons of academic and social ostracism.[17]

Theologians are fond of these military metaphors, and sometimes work them rather hard. The 'weapons' of academic and social ostracism were certainly both used against Strauss. His sympathizers, in fear for their own position, dared not protest against his dismissal from his theological lectureship, which promptly followed publication of his book. Strauss's defence was that his views were not unique, but represented one trend in the Protestant scholarship of the day, which could appropriately be represented in a theological seminary by one of its staff, just as other directions were represented by others.[18] But in the Tübingen of 1835 lecturers were not safeguarded by any such ruling. Strauss not only lost his job but was cut off from his friends; for in those days "the Church was so bound up with society that . . . he could not openly visit them for fear of bringing them into disrepute" (Harrris, p. 117). His isolation is well illustrated in the dedication to his merchant brother, thirty years later, of his *Das Leben Jesu für das deutsche Volk bearbeitet*, 1864 (I shall call it his second *Life*), where he explains that he has hitherto avoided dedications so as not to compromise his friends:

> But you, dear brother, are independent . . . by the happy privilege of
> commercial pursuits . . . [of] the favour or displeasure of spiritual or lay
> superiors. The appearance of your name on the foremost pages of a
> book of mine can do you no injury.

Although, then, his book of 1835 cost him dear, he could never
regret having thus made available its critical information. "Many a
. . . . man", he wrote in 1860, "who dates the liberation of his mind
from the study of this book, has been grateful to me for this
throughout his whole life" (quoted by Harris, p. 193). I can endorse
this from my own experience, and to that extent this chapter is a
tribute.

The Reformation was an appeal from the authority of the
Church (regarded by the Reformers as a merely human institution)
to the Bible (the book of God). In time this assumption that the
Bible is a divine revelation was bound to be questioned. "From the
time of the Reformation", wrote Baur, commenting in 1836 on his
pupil's recently published book, "one has set Scripture in too high
a place", and emancipation from it "therefore lies fully in the
natural course of events" (quoted by Harris, p. 88). The method of
Strauss's major predecessors Reimarus and H. E. G. Paulus had
been merely to set aside the gospel miracles as misunderstandings
on the part of Jesus's entourage. The results were often grotesque.
Paulus explained the healing miracles by positing special medi-
cines, known only to Jesus. The feeding of the five thousand occurred when he and his disciples shared their provisions with
each other, thus setting the multitude an example which was
promptly imitated, with the result that there was soon food
enough for all. Again, according to Paulus, Jesus's resurrection was
only apparent, for he did not die on the cross, but when laid in the
cool tomb recovered consciousness. The earthquake rolled the
stone away and enabled him to creep out unnoticed. From time to
time he showed himself to his followers, until finally, on the
Mount of Olives, a passing cloud came between him and them;
they lost sight of him for ever and came in time to describe his
departure as an ascension (after Harris, p. 44).

Strauss was convinced of the nullity of all this. He was
particularly scornful about this explanation of the resurrection.
Can we really believe, he asked, "that a being who had stolen half-

dead out of the sepulchre, who crept about weak and ill, wanting medical treatment . . . could have given his disciples the impression that he was a Conqueror over death and the grave?"[19] The absurdity of Paulus's argument, he insists, follows naturally from his attempt to combine two incompatible premisses: the modern scientific view that miracles do not occur, and the traditional view that the gospels were written by eye-witnesses of the events narrated in them. Combination of these premisses means regarding the gospels as the work of men who had lived with Jesus and yet, with consummate stupidity, completely misunderstood all that he had actually said and done.

Strauss begins by challenging the assumption that the gospels are eye-witness reports. He notes that these works are in themselves anonymous, and that it is only their titles which ascribe them to named authors. But these titles, he adds, became established only in the latter part of the second century. And how little reliance can be placed on the ascription of any Biblical book to a named author! Who now, he asks, believes that the book which records Moses's death and burial was written by him (with prophetic foresight), as its title ("the fifth book of Moses" in Luther's Bible) purports? How many psalms bear the name of David even though they clearly presuppose the Babylonian Captivity, which came only hundreds of years after his time? And Daniel, supposed to have been written at the time of this captivity, in fact shows a detailed acquaintance with the reign of Antiochus Epiphanes of nearly four hundred years later.[20] Strauss also realized that a very powerful argument against the ascription of the gospels to eye-witnesses is the presence in them of so-called literary doublets. Mark, for instance, which today is accepted as the earliest of the four canonical gospels, includes accounts of two miraculous feedings, of the five thousand and of the four thousand. The sequence of events, and even the vocabulary, is in both cases remarkably similar. That two separate incidents are involved is hard to believe, since in the second the disciples—who are represented as having recently witnessed the first—have so completely forgotten it that they think it impossible for food to be supplied to thousands in a desert place (Mark, 8:4). The doublet is best explained by assuming that a tradition of one such feeding

—the doublets show that Matthew was not an eye-witness

existed, before Mark wrote, in two slightly different written forms, and that the evangelist who drew on these written sources incorporated both because he supposed them to refer to different incidents.[21] If he supposed this, he obviously could not have been present as a witness of such a miracle. Different written, and not merely different oral forms, underlie such doublets, of which there are a number in Mark. Two oral traditions that are slightly discrepant can easily be combined into one story. But as soon as a tradition is fixed in writing, discrepancies between it and a kindred tradition can result in both these literary forms of the story being told.

Strauss discusses the doublets as they occur in Matthew rather than in Mark. In his book of 1835 he was not much concerned with the order in which the New Testament books were written, or whether the earlier ones were known to and used by the authors of the later. His purpose was to show that many narratives, no matter in which gospel they occur, cannot be accepted as historical. He has often been criticized for failing to discriminate the documents. But that was the work of his successors, to which his own was a natural preliminary. He regarded Matthew, not Mark, as the earliest of the four, and it was rational for him to consider Matthew as of great importance to this question of eye-witness reports; for Mark is not assigned, even by Christian tradition, to an eye-witness, whereas Matthew, in the gospel which bears his name, is listed as one of Jesus's twelve disciples. Strauss points out that the doublets show that the author was not, in fact, an eye-witness; "for the apostle Matthew [the man who actually was Jesus's companion] could not possibly take one event for two and narrate a new history [e.g. a second miraculous feeding] which never happened".[22]

Today it is almost universally agreed—even now, nothing in theology is quite unanimously settled—that Mark, written of course in Greek, was adapted and expanded by Matthew and Luke (each of whom wrote in ignorance of the other's work). And so if it is now asked whether Matthew is an eye-witness report, the answer is likely to be that its use of Mark, a Greek gospel of a non-disciple, makes such a hypothesis "completely impossible".[23] Matthew, then, not only includes doublets, but took them, with other material, from Mark, where their presence proves that even this, the earliest of the four, was compiled from written sources. As to the titles of our gospels, it is today agreed that gospels and other writings used for reading in church at first existed without titles, and were supplied with them only when Christian communities acquired more than one gospel and needed some means of distinguishing between them. For this purpose they did not designate the documents 'A' and 'B', but hit upon the more homely ascriptions of 'Matthew', 'Mark', etc., which are now admitted to be "second-century guesses".[24]

Strauss, then, impugned one of the two premisses of Reimarus and Paulus, namely that the gospels are based on eye-witness reports. But he accepted their second premiss—that miracle stories cannot be literally true. He has often been criticized on the ground that his denial of the miraculous and the supernatural element in the world is never proved but merely presupposed (so Harris, p. 42); and that it was therefore quite arbitrary of him to treat all the New Testament miracles as myths. I shall try to show that, on the contrary, his standpoint was one from which he could proceed to make sense of the evidence. And no more can be required of any hypothesis. His critics have naturally been anxious to stamp his procedure as arbitrary. Those who cannot defend their own position seek to undermine their opponent's; and when everything has been undermined it becomes merely a matter of taste which we adopt. In this way the supernaturalist standpoint can be defended as no more arbitrary than any other. It is, of course, true that Strauss did not show by philosophical reasoning that belief in miracles is unjustified. To my mind, this is no defect, for, as I shall explain in chapter 8 below, I do not believe that the credibility or otherwise of a belief can be established by *a priori* rules. To say that all that happens must accord with the laws of nature does not settle everything, because these laws are, even today, very imperfectly known. An event may be improbable, but we should need extraordinary confidence in our own conception of the world to be able to determine, without regard to the evidence, that the report of an event, however marvellous, is false. If all this is conceded, Strauss's arguments remain unaffected. For his point was that natural causation was accepted as applicable everywhere except in the case of events portrayed in the Bible, and that it was therefore reasonable to see if these could also be explained on a natural basis. Furthermore, if the New Testament miracle stories are to be accepted as genuine, they must—he argued—be both well attested and internally coherent; and he showed that neither of these conditions is fulfilled: for external evidence of the gospels (that is, mention of them by other writers) is late, and does not suffice to establish that they were written by eye-witnesses—a hypothesis which is in any case excluded by the internal evidence of the doublets. And the gospel narratives also include many contradictions, not just on minor matters, but on essentials, as we shall be seeing.

Strauss, then, asked whether it was possible to explain gospel stories, including the miracle stories, in a non-supernatural way, without, like his predecessors, imputing gross stupidity or even fraud to their authors. His argument was that many of the stories are the outcome of Old Testament expectations. If the evangelists believed, as they did, that Jesus was the Messiah, then they will also have believed that he must have been, done, and suffered all that was expected of the Messiah. He must, for instance, have been a descendant of David, born in David's city of Bethlehem.[25] Hence it was natural for stories to circulate in Christian communities giving him these qualifications. Since they were not based on fact they varied a good deal; and so we find that what one evangelist says on the subject is excluded by the narrative of another. Jesus's healing miracles are likewise constructions from the Old Testament. Isaiah 35:5 tells that "then the eyes of the blind shall be opened, and the ears of the deaf shall be unstopped; then shall the lame man leap as a hart and the tongue of the dumb shall sing". This passage, he says (NL, II, 151), originated when the Babylonian captivity of the Jews was coming to an end, and describes how the exiles, overjoyed at the prospect of return, will forget all their sorrows. But when, after the return, the expected period of bliss did not occur, it was thought by later generations reading Isaiah that his reference was to miraculous healings which would occur in Messianic times. Hence the authors of the gospels, who believed Jesus was the Messiah, recorded incidents where he cures blindness, deafness, dumbness, and paralysis. He also had to raise the dead and supply food miraculously, otherwise he would have been inferior to Elijah and Elisha.

Strauss's great contribution, then, was to demonstrate a plausible mechanism for the origin of many gospel stories (not only those involving miracles)—a mechanism which today is admitted to have been of decisive importance. Put in its most general terms, the principle which guided him is this: written descriptions (in the Old Testament or in any respected document) of some event (historical or imaginary) may be read by persons who know nothing of the real subject represented, and who may freshly interpret the document in accordance with their own knowledge. In this way they may take the writing to refer to people and events entirely unknown to the actual writers. In the Psalms, for instance, the term 'the anointed' or 'the Messiah' is used to designate the reigning king. Later generations, reading the Psalms when the historical kingship had ceased to exist, nevertheless assumed that the meaning of the Psalmist had some relevance to present times; and that since there were no more kings in the old sense, his reference must be to another king or Messiah, perhaps in heaven. In this connection Strauss points to the evangelists' technique (particularly common in Matthew) of stating that certain events in Jesus's life happened in order that certain scriptures might be fulfilled.[26] The evangelists, then, and also the authors of the Christian traditions on which they drew, lived so entirely in the earlier history of the Jewish people, and in the sacred books in which it was laid down, that they found in them everything that subsequently took place, everywhere prophecies and symbols of what was to come. For the Jews of the first century A.D., all truth was contained in the scriptures; "and so science consisted exclusively in an utterly wretched and arbitrary kind of exegesis, of which we have all too many specimens in the New Testament" (Glaube, p. 66).

The difficulties besetting any attempt to interpret the gospels as historical records are well illustrated by the narratives of Jesus's birth and infancy. Today serious defence of them is uncommon, because we now know, as Strauss did not, that Matthew and Luke, in which alone they occur, are both relatively late documents. There is no mention of the circumstances of Jesus's birth in any

— Pauline letters written before the gospels?

New Testament epistle. In the Pauline letters—which are the earliest extant Christian documents, written, as Strauss was already aware (NL, I, 183), well before the gospels—Jesus is said to have been a descendant of David, but born of a woman (Galatians 4:4), not a virgin. Mark, the earliest evangelist, introduces Jesus as an adult, and records nothing of his early life. Matthew and Luke supplement Mark with introductory genealogies, and accounts of his birth and infancy. These introductions were obviously not drawn from reliable material; not only are they, as I have been stressing, late, but each one is full of its own difficulties and implausibilities and the two—as Kümmel says in his standard handbook—"contradict each other in essential features" (op. cit., p. 43). To have given a detailed demonstration of all this is one of Strauss's achievements.[27]

Strauss follows incident after incident of Jesus's life, as given in the gospels, and notes the Old Testament parallels for each one. He stresses, for instance, that some events in his public ministry were invented in order to show that he was a greater prophet than Moses. The forty days' temptation in the wilderness parallels Moses's time on Sinai; and since Moses had been transfigured upon the mountain top, Christ must also have a transfiguration to show that he was in no way inferior. All this, although it may still shock the laity, is barely disputed any more even by relatively conservative theologians. A. E. Harvey, in so bien-pensant a work as the New English Bible Companion to the New Testament (Oxford and Cambridge University Presses, 1970) specifies a number of details peculiar to Matthew in the gospel transfiguration stories, and says that "these details perhaps show Matthew at work, deliberately presenting Jesus as the new Moses, the definitive lawgiver" (p. 70). That early Christians constructed their picture of Jesus from the Old Testament is obvious from the statement of Paul—the earliest extant Christian writer—that the Old Testament consists of prophetic writings, written down for our instruction in order to elucidate facts about Jesus (Romans 15:3–4; 16:25–6). In other words, if study of the Old Testament showed that the Messiah was to behave in a certain way, then, for early Christians, Jesus must have behaved in that way, whatever eye-witnesses or historical records said or failed to say. As

Hoskyns and Davey put it, in their disarming way: "In the Church at the end of the first century the Life and Death of Jesus were recounted in the context of the Old Testament Scriptures".[28] F. C. Grant writes more bluntly of the evangelists' tendency to state the facts of Jesus's life "as they could be inferred from the Old Testament".[29] That ideas among Jews at the beginning of our era originated as a result of such musing on sacred texts is today obvious from the Qumran discoveries. Fr B. Lindars has shown that, like the Qumran scribes, the early Christians developed major aspects of their beliefs in this way, interpreting the texts in the light of their experience and their experience in the light of the texts.[30]

It is, then, no longer in dispute that the historian must treat the gospels as he would treat propaganda material. Hence, says Robert Morgan in a Cambridge symposium on Jesus's trial, "the arguments from prophecy and miracle have lost all force".[31] This is due, ultimately, to Strauss, who further, in 1872, insisted that a purely human Jesus on whom various elements from the Old Testament were subsequently foisted, is hardly compatible with any form of worship of this individual. Morgan also warns against uncritical acceptance of the non-supernatural elements in the gospels: "The sorts of motives which led to miracle stories being told about Jesus were also responsible for the preservation and transmission within the Christian communities of the passion narratives" (op. cit., p. 139). This was also clear to Strauss, who wrote in 1835: "Every narrative, however miraculous, contains some details which might in themselves be historical, but which, in consequence of their connection with the other supernatural incidents, necessarily become equally doubtful".[32]

What, then, is left in the gospels as historically true? Strauss's argument that New Testament stories are myths based on Old Testament expectations does not account for the crucifixion and resurrection. The former he does not need to explain away, for he accepts it as historical, as sufficiently attested by the evidence of Tacitus.[33] The resurrection he of course does not accept, and he shows in detail that no stories could be more discrepant than the relevant gospel narratives. It is often alleged that discrepancies do occur in eye-witness accounts, which are not thereby discredited.

But if those who purported to be witnesses of, say, a street accident, disagreed as to all the details; if one affirmed that it took place in London, while another sited it in Manchester; and if additionally there were no damaged vehicles or injured persons to corroborate this contradictory testimony, then we should certainly doubt whether the event had occurred at all. This is exactly the position with the resurrection testimony. There is no external evidence; and the gospel narratives contradict each other in essentials: as when one evangelist makes Jesus's appearances to his disciples occur exclusively in Galilee, while another sites them exclusively 80 miles away at Jerusalem. Strauss is perfectly justified in saying, of the resurrection: "rarely has an incredible fact been worse attested, and never has a badly attested one been intrinsically less credible" (*Glaube*, p. 72). He finds it greatly to Christianity's discredit that it is based so fundamentally on the resurrection. Jesus, he says, could have done and taught what he liked, it would all, however sublime, have been forgotten but for this "delusion about his resurrection".

How does he explain the origin of this delusion? Since he concedes that there was a historical Jesus who was followed by a group of disciples, and since he cannot explain the resurrection appearances from the Old Testament, he has to suppose that the resurrection belief originated in some actual experiences these disciples had after Jesus's death. In his first *Life* he simply demonstrates the shortcomings of the resurrection narratives. His own theory is given in his second *Life*, and I will outline it later.

In spite of his destructive analysis of the virgin birth, miracles, resurrection and ascension, Strauss insists at the outset of his first *Life* that they "remain eternal truths, whatever doubts may be cast on their reality as historical facts". This kind of double-think is distressingly familiar in more recent apologists. Bultmann, for instance, holds that the resurrection, although it never happened, is an event of the greatest significance (cf. below, p. 73). He thinks that we can know practically nothing of the historical Jesus. Yet, he declares, God (whatever that may mean) challenges us to authentic existence (whatever that may mean) through this—to us unknown—Jesus. The thought is found reassuring in this world of doubt and ignorance and uncertainty. If today existentialism underlies such sleight of speech, Hegelianism performed the same function in Strauss's day, and it is only in this aspect of the book that the Hegelian views he then held make themselves apparent. Strauss, then, insists that "the religious truth" remains unaffected by his criticism, calls the contrary view "frivolous" and refers the reader to the concluding dissertation of his book, which, he claims, demonstrates that "the dogmatic import of the life of Jesus remains uninjured". And so this elaborate treatise of 1,500 pages, written to disprove every supernatural occurrence connected with the life of Jesus, begins and ends with the assurance that it all makes no difference to religion, and that those are frivolous who think otherwise.

This looks like blatant insincerity, but in fact such philosophizing was as completely sincere with the young Strauss as it was the other day with Bultmann and J. A. T. Robinson. It was—and is—nevertheless also very opportune: for its effect is to save the existing religious organization, and this—not the historical tradition—is what matters to the faithful. If this religious organization can be more securely based on 'spiritual' truths than on historical facts, then why worry about the latter? I cannot pretend to understand the spiritual truths of Strauss's concluding dissertation. "It is the essential property of the Spirit", he there says, "in separating itself from itself, to remain identical with itself and possess itself in another than itself". One would need a lexicon of Hegelian jargon; and such a lexicon would, if honest, include a good many words of which it could only be noted that, although of frequent occurrence, they had no particular meaning. Nietzsche justly called the Hegelians "the most unscrupulous of all those who pervert German", and he believed that Strauss's flirtation with Hegel permanently damaged his prose style. He wrote of the last work which Strauss ever published: "One can see that in his youth he stammered out the Hegelian jargon."[34] Nietzsche tickets various sentences in the book in the manner of a Professor marking an essay by a freshman—comments like "lax in the extreme in expression" and "miserable as to style". But this criticism is not without force, and Strauss never succeeded in writing with the clarity of a Schopenhauer.

Soon after the publication of his first *Life* Strauss abandoned Hegel, and declared in a letter of 1839 that giving such philosophical support to Christian dogmas is vain affectation (quoted by

Harris, p. 136). In his second *Life*, and in his final work of 1872, there is no trace of double-think. Nothing that is set aside is brought back through another door. This is one reason why these later works have so frequently met with even more adverse comment than his first *Life*.

The next task for New Testament criticism after Strauss's first *Life* was to ascertain the growth of early Christian tradition about Jesus by arranging the books of the New Testament in a chronological sequence. To assess the value of Strauss's book, it is necessary to say a little about this next task, and how his book facilitated it.

F. C. Baur was struck by the fact that in some gospel passages Jesus tells that only the Jews will be saved, whereas in others he promises salvation to the gentiles and says the Jews are to be damned. Baur also noted that the gospels contain many pro- and anti-Jewish narratives of a more general kind. Now there can be no doubt that Christianity began as a Jewish sect. Early Christian documents accept the God of Israel, the Old Testament, Jewish apocalyptic and angelology, and Jewish ideas about the Messiah. A non-Jewish origin for a sect which embraced all this is out of the question. Therefore, argued Baur, the most Jewish gospel, Matthew's, in which Jesus is made (at 5:18) to endorse every jot and tittle of the Jewish law, must be the earliest of the four, and the least Jewish, John's, the latest. Even Matthew's gospel, however, is, in Baur's view, to some extent a redaction of pro- and anti-Jewish tradition. Incidents which represent the twelve Jewish disciples as jealous, selfish, stupid, unsympathetic or traitorous were, he thought, invented by gentile sectaries who wished to be completely independent of the Jews; while later in the development of Christianity, when the Jewish Church was no longer so formidable a rival, stories were produced glorifying the twelve by making them perform miracles as stupendous as those of Jesus himself, so that the prestige of the old religion should pass on to the new, and the new Church seem founded on the old.[35]

Baur's claim that Matthew is the first of the four has long since been abandoned, and I shall later try to indicate the grounds on which that place is now accorded to Mark. But Baur's attempt to discover the 'tendencies' which inform gospel stories has become the basis of a great deal of twentieth-century theology, and has made him, justifiably, more influential than Strauss. It is no criticism of Strauss to say that, having laid the basis for the work of his successors, he did not go on to do it himself. It is a criticism of Baur to have to say that he did his best to belittle Strauss's achievement, calling it "negative" criticism, because Strauss does not, as he did, discriminate the documents. "Strauss", he said, "takes the gospels all together and always refutes one with the other", holding all alike to be suspect (quoted by Harris, p. 101). Baur agrees that "the majority [sic] of the gospels are obviously tendency-writings", but he adds the corollary that "the historical truth is most probably to be found where a tendency character shows itself the least". He calls his own criticism "positive" also because it thus does not deny the historical credibility of at least one gospel, namely Matthew's—"in a relative way", since even Matthew mixes pro- and anti-Jewish material which cannot all be authentic. Now when those who had not followed the details of the debate gathered that Strauss's theology was to be called 'negative' and Baur's 'positive', they could readily suppose that, while Strauss denied essential Christian doctrines, Baur upheld them. Certainly Baur never used the words positive and negative in this sense, "but it was in no way disagreeable to him if others should receive such an impression" (Harris, p. 104). His termi-nology thus created the impression that he rejected Strauss's work. But in fact he made it the basis from which he himself proceeded; for to seek out the 'tendencies' which inspired the narratives presupposes that they are not to be taken at their face value as straight-forward historical reports. As Strauss wrote to him: "In the criticism of the New Testament, my negation must precede your position" (quoted by Harris, pp. 98–9).

The textual analysis practised by Baur has been continued by form-critics and redaction critics. The former analyze gospels and epistles into short passages ('pericopes') of distinctive literary form (e.g. creeds, short sermons). Each pericope is held to have originated as a result of some liturgical or doctrinal need, and the evangelists have combined all this material, of very different provenance, into a continuous narrative, where, however, suture lines between the originally independent pericopes are still visible. Redaction criticism observes how an evangelist modified the material as he moulded it so as to make it fit the overall thesis which he wanted his gospel to proclaim. The theologians of today can carry out this highly critical work without giving offence because it is possible to leave the question of truth and reason in the background, and simply to ascertain the doctrinal or liturgical 'Sitz im Leben' (life-situation) of each pericope, or the theological ideas which guided an evangelist in his editing of it. The question, how much of the material is based ultimately on solid history, is often simply not raised. Strauss, however, was concerned almost exclusively with this question, and so his work is much more obviously 'negative'.

In his second *Life*, Strauss does discuss the relative ages of the gospels, but simply accepts the findings of Baur. Matthew is the earliest evangelist because the most Jewish, and Mark wrote an abridgement of Matthew's gospel (*NL*, I, 152 and 176). Now it is true that Mark's gospel is much shorter than Matthew's and that Matthew's contains a wealth of material absent from Mark's. But this non-Marcan matter is today regarded as added by Matthew to his edition of Mark's gospel, for when the two evangelists do overlap, when they tell the same story, it is nearly always Matthew who gives it in the shorter form. Matthew, then, abbreviated Mark's work (not vice-versa), and supplemented his abbreviation with material unknown to Mark. This view was argued as early as 1835 by Lachmann, and more decisively by Holtzmann in 1863. In 1865 Strauss called Holtzmann's Marcan hypothesis "a temporary aberration" on a level with Wagner's "new noise" or "music of the future" ("ein Zeitschwindel wie die Zukunftsmusik")[36]—an aspect of his taste which did not endear him to the young Nietzsche.

It is easy to see, with hindsight, that Strauss and Baur were wrong in dating Matthew earlier than Mark. But Strauss's discussion of passages which occur in both their gospels shows how misleading the evidence can be. The New Testament contains statements to the effect that the end of the world is very near indeed, and others which suggest that it is not so very imminent. Critics, even today, hold that the latter represent a later stage in the developing tradition, written when the earlier expectation of a speedy end had failed to come true. From this premiss Strauss compared Mark 9:1 with its parallel in Matthew 16:28, where Jesus says:

> Verily I say unto you, there be some of them that
> stand here which shall in no wise taste of death till they see the Son of
> man coming in his kingdom.

The Marcan version is: *Spread of the Church*

> Verily I say unto you, there be some of them that stand by, which shall in
> no wise taste of death till they see the kingdom of God come with
> power.

He infers that Matthew's version represents the earlier tradition, for here Jesus is made to declare that some of his auditors will still be alive at the time of his second coming. In the Marcan parallel, the prophecy seems to be given in a more guarded form; it says nothing about the return of Jesus; the coming of "the kingdom of God with power" is surely formulated so as to suggest that Jesus was prophesying the spread of the Church, not his own second coming (NL, I, 172). A modern commentator has replied[37] that the phrase "the kingdom of God" shows this Marcan version to be the more primitive. In Matthew's version, the kingdom is no longer God's but belongs to Jesus: the "Son of man" will come in *his* kingdom. It is characteristic of developing Christology that Jesus takes over functions of God until, in second-century Christian writings, he is actually called God.

Matthew, although for Strauss the earliest evangelist, is still "but a writer at second-hand", as is clear from his literary doublets (NL, I, 153). And we are not to assume that the historical Jesus was the narrow-minded Jew that Matthew sometimes makes of him. On the basis of Baur's 'tendency' analysis of the documents Strauss points out in his second *Life*, and in yet later books, that even if the pro-Jewish passages in Matthew derive ultimately from reports of Jesus's disciples, they were probably prevented from understanding him by their own "thick stratum of Jewish prejudices" (NL, I, 185). Furthermore, Matthew includes anti-Jewish material. Matthew 8:5–12 tells of a centurion who asked Jesus to cure his boy (who was lying sick at home), not by going to the house, but simply by ordering, from the distance of Capernaum, the cure to occur. Jesus is astonished at the faith this gentile has in him, says he has not found such faith in Israel, and adds that the Jews will not be saved, but "cast forth into the outer darkness" where there is "weeping and gnashing of teeth". A modern commentator follows Strauss (NL, I, 154) in regarding this comment as put into Jesus's mouth by a gentile Christian community which looked back to the Jews' rejection of him and to their consequent exclusion from the kingdom as to events of quite some time ago.[38] Strauss insists that such utterances, although never made by Jesus, were ascribed to him in perfectly good faith. For on matters of such importance as who is to be saved, or whether one is to keep the Jewish religious law, it was felt that he must have given his opinion (NL, I, 155). Early Christians who reserved salvation for Jews, or who respected the Jewish law, would have felt convinced that he had done so too, and so they assumed that he endorsed these attitudes in his speeches. The faction which did not wish to preserve the law would, arguing from opposite premises, reach the reverse conclusion; and in this way sets of mutually contradictory statements could come to be ascribed to him, and eventually brought together in one gospel, written by a redactor of available traditions. Thus, a few chapters after the anti-Jewish story of the centurion at Capernaum, Jesus refuses, initially, to heal the daughter of the Canaanitish woman on the ground that he has no concern with gentiles, but was "sent unto the lost sheep of the house of Israel" (15:24). When he goes on to call the gentiles "dogs", the woman replies that even dogs may eat of the crumbs which fall from their master's table: whereupon Jesus, after all, complies with her request and "her daughter was healed from that hour". Strauss thinks that this story represents a period when the admission of gentiles to the faith was, albeit grudgingly, conceded; whereas the story of the centurion belongs to a later stratum, or, alternatively, derives from a more liberal Christian community (Glaube, pp. 57–8). In between the two stories, Jesus instructs his disciples to have no truck with Samaritans or gentiles (10:5); whereas after his resurrection he dispatches them "to make disciples of all the nations" (28:19). It is not, Strauss insists, a case of change in his outlook, for the evangelist puts pro-gentile utterances into his mouth early in his ministry. Here, Strauss's view has certainly been endorsed by later scholarship. Form-critics have argued the futility of trying to discern any psychological development in Jesus, since the gospel stories came to our evangelists as isolated, independent units of tradition, with no indication when, or even where, Jesus said or did what was involved. The sequence of events, and the places where they occurred, are today widely regarded as a creation of Mark, whose order is, on the whole, followed by Matthew and Luke.

Strauss's second *Life* is often regarded as inferior to his first. Its final part is an effective abridgement of what he had said in 1835. But this is preceded by an extended discussion of the relation between the first three gospels where, as we have seen, Strauss is demonstrably wrong, and by an attempt to reconstruct the character of the historical Jesus—unsatisfactory, like all other such attempts, since the evidence is not forthcoming. We can never be sure whether what an evangelist says represents the real Jesus or merely what a Christian community believed. In his final work of 1872 Strauss admitted this. The gospels, he said, are "distorted at every turn by conflicting party ideals and interests", and we have no 'control' account from a disinterested source. Furthermore, the supernatural powers they ascribe to Jesus make futile any attempt to describe his character in human terms (*Glaube*, pp. 58, 76).

Perhaps the most notable new feature in this second *Life* is Strauss's attempt to account for the origin of the belief in the resurrection. Critics of his first *Life* had objected that, if the resurrection is a legend, Jesus, to have occasioned it, must have been a more commanding figure than emerges from Strauss's investigation. This criticism clearly assumes that the idea of Jesus's resurrection originated in the minds of persons who had followed him during his lifetime. Strauss never challenged this assumption, and unfortunately it still underlies almost all present-day discussions of the resurrection. He always insisted that Jesus had made a strong impression on his followers, but in his later works he argued that it was precisely the least rational and sober of Jesus's ideas that, after his death, suggested to them that he would rise again. Either our gospels contain no reliable information about him, or—if they are in the least trustworthy—he foretold that he would soon return to earth on the clouds (*Glaube*, p. 79f). After his death the disciples would have pondered on this, and would have searched the scriptures for elucidation. There was, for instance, Psalm 16: "Thou wilt not leave my soul to sheol; neither wilt thou suffer thine holy one to see corruption". Whoever composed this Psalm certainly intended no statement about the Messiah, and expressed only his complete trust in God. But a Christian, who of course believed that David was the author, would argue that David could not be speaking of his own body, which did see corruption, and that the reference must be to Jesus. This is how Peter interprets the Psalm in his Whitsuntide address to the Jews in Acts 2:27–8. And once the disciples were convinced that Jesus was still alive, it was but a short step to the conviction that he had appeared to them (*Glaube*, pp. 77–83).

One criticism to be made of this argument is that Peter's speeches in Acts—although they undoubtedly represent early Christian attempts to justify the resurrection—are not evidence of what was said or thought by the Peter (if there ever was such a person) who had been Jesus's companion. Ernst Haenchen, whose commentary on Acts is one of the outstanding achievements of post-war New Testament scholarship, has shown that Peter and James repeatedly appeal in Acts to the Jews of Jerusalem with arguments which presuppose the Greek translation of the Jewish scriptures, and which are not available in the Hebrew original. From this alone it is clear that Peter's speeches in Acts cannot be taken as a true reflection of the ideas of the Jerusalem Christians he is supposed to have led, but could have been drawn up only in a Hellenistic community.[39]

Strauss supposes that Jesus was buried with other executed criminals in a dishonourable place, with the result that neither friend nor foe could, after an interval of weeks, check on what had become of the body. Matthew's story that the rich Joseph of Arimathea buried him in a tomb originally intended for himself is set aside as inspired in part by Isaiah, 53:9 "they made his grave . . . with the rich in his death". And, of course, nothing but a tomb yet unpolluted by any corpse would, for the early Christians, be good enough for their god-man, just as they had considered it right that no one had ever sat on the ass which he used on his entry into the capital. Strauss goes on to argue that, from fear of the Jewish authorities in Jerusalem, the disciples left for Galilee after the burial, where, with no nearby grave to contradict their phantasies, their faith began to revive. This did not happen quickly, and there is no need to accept the gospel stories that the risen Jesus was seen within three days of his death; for Paul, whose account of appearances is by far the oldest extant, says indeed that he rose on the third day, but not that he appeared to anyone at such an early date. Paul simply lists the appearances, beginning with that to Peter, and ending with that to himself. This latter, even on the orthodox view, took place some time, perhaps even years, after Jesus's death; and Paul gives no indication of the time of occurrence of the appearances which he places earlier in his list. Furthermore, whenever Jesus's appearances are to be dated, the idea that he rose as early as the third day is a natural one. A resurrection to life must occur soon after death, if it was to occur at all. Death must be allowed to have power over him for but a short time, and his victory over hell must be quickly decided (NL, I, 429–39).

In his final work *Der alte und der neue Glaube* (The Old Faith and the New) Strauss declares that he is no longer a Christian, and that Christianity survives among educated peoples only by dint of the corrections which secular reasoning has introduced into it (p. 64). He goes on to say—what a number of theologians have since conceded—that the New Testament is, for modern man, an alien work. The Mainz theologian Herbert Braun, for instance, says: "Its statements are to a great extent legendary in character; it shares the ancient belief in demoniacal possession; it reckons on the world coming to a speedy end".[40] Strauss declines to salvage it by symbolical interpretation: "Why these detours, why embroil ourselves at all with what we can no longer use, in order finally to reach what we need?" (p. 88). For the enemies of critical theology this his last book is a classic illustration of the truth that all criticism leads inevitably to unbelief. Gladstone held it up to school-children as an awful example of what they would come to if they once began exercising their own faculties.[41] And as recently as 1967 an American theologian, H.J. Hillerbrand, said it shows that those who "repudiate the religious status quo", that is who "think themselves wiser than all . . . who have gone before", run the risk of rejecting the faith completely. "All radicals perform a tight-rope act".[42] Clearly, then, *il faut s'abêtir*.

Strauss here does not confine his criticism to the New Testament, but asks with what right we refuse to acknowledge the obvious facts of death by positing the persistence of a part of our being of which there is, in any case, no ascertainable trace (p. 123). He insists on the physical basis of mind—mental capacities develop and decline with the body (pp. 129, 205). He does not find it humiliating to be related to the gorilla (cf. p. 194), and observes that the fossil record gives strong support to Darwin's theory, from which man cannot be arbitrarily exempted (p. 192). Strauss seems to have thought, by this time, that the dogmas of the Church would not survive the discoveries of the nineteenth century. But he was mistaken, and religion was destined to take on a new lease of life in the twentieth.

Strauss called this book "a confession". Who, asked Nietzsche, cares about a man's confession of faith, who would want to know the credo of a Ranke or a Mommsen? (*op. cit.*, p. 19) But it is surely of interest to know whether a theologian accepts Christianity, immortality, and recent biological discoveries. These are not, for a theologian, private beliefs which can be divorced from his scientific work. The really weak points in Strauss's 'confession' are his naive optimism and his exaggerated patriotism, and here Nietzsche's strictures are perfectly justified. Strauss insists that anyone who thinks that the evil-doer is happy and the good man miserable in this life does not know how to distinguish appearance from reality. We can accept this sort of thing from theodicies of the eighteenth century, but in a writer of 1872 it may justly be called what Nietzsche called it, namely "philistine optimism" (*op. cit.*, p. 38), particularly when coupled with talk of "nature's great law of progress" (*Glaube*, p. 239). For Nietzsche these, together with complacent patriotism, were aspects of the satisfaction engendered in German thinking by victory over France in 1871. He did not see that Strauss's patriotism may fairly be regarded as an example of the natural willingness in innovators to be on a friendly footing with the majority at least on some questions, and hence unduly to stress what notions they do happen to have in common with that majority. During the war, Strauss had found in the German cause a ground of union with his countrymen which for the first time put him into sympathetic relation with them after his long exposure to their Christian wrath. The open letter he wrote to Renan about the war aroused jubilation throughout Germany. And when the fighting was over, he said it had been caused by "passion and unreason" on the part of the French—"a restless and vain people"—whereas the German decision to go to war had been purely rational, and if Kant himself had been the king's minister, he could have given him no other advice (*Glaube*, p. 256). This drivel of course no more discredits Strauss's work on the New Testament than Newton's ramblings on the prophecies invalidate his discoveries in the sciences. And even Nietzsche allowed this; for what he missed in the book of 1872 was precisely Strauss as he used to be (*op. cit.*, pp. 68f).

Strauss seems to have expected that a book which included the patriotic views which had recently made him so popular would be acclaimed. But acclamation was not accorded to a theologian who rejected Christianity and immortality, accepted Darwin, and declined to view morals or art as something indefeasible. And so he found himself, in what were to be the final months of his life, relegated to his old status of ostracized heretic.

How can one characterize his achievement? His view of the mythical nature of much of the New Testament was not new, but he was the first to work this view out in detail, as even Baur conceded (quoted by Harris, p. 107)—Baur, who did so much to stress his own contribution to New Testament Studies, and to minimize that of Strauss. Strauss, then, was original only as Colenso or Darwin were original. The Pentateuch had been criticized before Colenso, evolution advocated before Darwin. But it was they who argued their respective theses with such over-whelming evidence that the whole issue could no longer be brushed aside. That was what made all three of them so hated: they had let the cat out of the bag. Strauss was told—as Lessing was when he published fragments from the critical account of the Old and New Testaments that Reimarus had left as an unpublished manuscript—that none of this should have been set before the

public, but published, if at all, in Latin in decent obscurity. Writing
as he did, the impact of his first *Life* was enormous, and in later
years he was able to note, with a touch of justifiable pride, that
during a quarter of a century "not a significant line" had been
written on the questions with which his book had dealt "in which
its influence is not to be perceived" (quoted by Harris, p. 193). This
influence has been permanent—Hillerbrand, who, we saw, points
to Strauss's career to illustrate the principle that radical criticism
leads inevitably to agnosticism, nevertheless concedes that neither biblical scholarship nor theology have been the same since
(*op. cit.*, p. 129). But his influence has been at best grudgingly
acknowledged. The scientists of today speak of their predecessors
with pride and appreciation. Thanks to the great and real progress
that has been made, it is possible for them to look back on pioneers
with sympathy for their difficulties and admiration for their
achievements. But in theology there is no neutral vantage-point
from which the student may survey dispassionately the successes
and failures of the past. The hypotheses of his predecessors are
still in competition with his own, and he must discredit them if he
would establish his claim to have superseded them. Karl Barth, for
instance, invokes derision for this purpose. "Proper theology", he
says, "begins just at the point where the difficulties disclosed by
Strauss and Feuerbach are seen and then laughed at".[43] Counter-
arguments come less easily than laughter.

Perhaps the most endearing feature of Strauss is his uncom-
promising honesty. He was clear that he could not have lived with
himself had he suppressed or disguised his real views instead of
publishing his famous book (quoted by Harris, p. 193). Only once
did he falter. The babble of voices opposing him led him to make
concessions in the third edition of his first *Life*. They delighted the
orthodox, not because they amounted to much, but as evidence
that he had begun to contradict himself. And so, still *persona non
grata*, Strauss realized that he had allowed criticism to lead him
astray, and in the fourth edition of 1840 he reverted to the positions
taken up in the first. George Eliot, whose fine English translation of
this fourth edition appeared in 1846, met him in 1858, and found
that he spoke as "a man strictly truthful in the use of language"
(quoted by Harris, p. 233). One may have a calling, he said in 1865,

even if one has no professional position; and his calling, he added, is directed against make-believe ("Falsch-münzerei") which he found rather prominent in the theology of the day.[44] Have things changed much? Schweitzer wrote, early this century: "The apologists, as we learn from the history of the Lives of Jesus, can get the better of any historical result whatever".[45] And more recently Zahrnt has declared that, if historical study proved that Jesus had never lived, "even then we theologians would succeed in finding a way out—when have we not succeeded in the past?"[46] Strauss is today not gladly remembered because he finally declined all ways out.

(iii) Criteria of Historicity: The Parallel Case of Wilhelm Tell

The Mosaic origin of the institutions described in the Pentateuch long remained a question of some delicacy, and T. H. Huxley (1825–95) has told in his *Science and Christian Tradition* that, although he sought no quarrel with the Bible, every path in his scientific investigations brought him to "a tall and formidable-looking fence" with "a comminatory notice-board—No thoroughfare. By order, Moses". But the questions discussed by de Wette and by Strauss also raise more general issues: namely, how can we ascertain whether a personage of a remote age ever existed, or whether an institution originated in the way alleged in ancient documents? In this connection it is of interest to note the criteria which have led historians to regard the story of the founding of the Swiss Confederation by Wilhelm Tell as a legend. The parallel between Moses, Jesus, and Tell is not a forced one, for most of the following six points are relevant to more than one of them, if not to all three: (1) some of the deeds alleged of them had been told of previous heroes; (2) there are discernible motives for the origin and growth of the stories; (3) the silence of the earliest documents has been remedied by interpolations and forgeries; (4) although there is no testimony contemporary with the time of the hero's supposed existence, references which assume his achievements become legion later, even hundreds of years later; (5) the later documents give more precise details (for instance, exact names and dates) than the earlier; and finally (6) the evidence of scholars has been fiercely resisted by parties committed to the traditional view.

De Wette's concern was with the Mosaic law rather than with Moses himself. Early this century T. K. Cheyne cautiously wrote in the *Encyclopaedia Biblica* (art. Moses, 22) that he greatly sympathized with "those who . . . feel compelled to treat Moses as to some extent a historical personage". But the same writer had no hesitation (art. cit., 3) in rejecting the story of the ark of the bulrushes as "of mythic origin" since it duplicates pagan traditions— he instances the story of Sargon, whose mother placed him in a basket of reeds and abandoned him to the river.

Some of the earliest writers to doubt Tell's existence were influenced by evidence of this kind, i.e. that stories of obviously mythical origin had been transferred to Tell. According to the traditional story, Tell, a native of Uri, failed to bow to the hat (placed on a pole as a symbol of authority) of the cruel Habsburg bailiff Gessler, whereupon Gessler ordered him to shoot an apple with his cross-bow from the head of his own little son. This he successfully did, but when the watching tyrant asked why he had a second arrow in reserve, Tell replied that he would have killed the bailiff with it, had he killed his own son with the first. About the same time, Swiss conspirators against the harsh Austrian rule met at night on a meadow known as the Rütli, and there followed a general uprising, with Gessler being killed on a narrow pathway by Tell. All this is supposed to have occurred at the beginning of the fourteenth century.

In 1760 U. Freudenberger, a Swiss Protestant clergyman, published a pamphlet *Tell: ein dänisches Mährgen* which proved that the apple episode, including Tell's story of the second arrow and its purpose, had been told of a Danish hero, Toki, before Tell's alleged time. Freudenberger's work was condemned by the government of Uri and burned by the common hangman. As early as 1727 the Swiss historian Isaak Iselin had pointed to the priority of the Danish story, and doubts concerning Tell were voiced by Voltaire and, apparently, Gibbon.[47] But a more powerful attack came in 1835 and 1851 when J. E. Kopp was able to show that extant documents of the early fourteenth century mention neither Tell, nor the Rütli meeting, nor the alleged rising of the forest cantons against cruel Austrian bailiffs which was long believed to have inaugurated the Swiss Confederation in 1308. Kopp has been described by the three modern historians referred to in the previous note as a "sceptical historian of the documentary school" (*op. cit.*, p. 79), and he proved that all these incidents are first recorded in documents of the late fifteenth and early sixteenth centuries, which tell what was then believed to have happened in the fourteenth. Kopp's *Urkunden zur Geschichte der eidgenössischen Bünde* has been justly declared to mark the beginning of a new era in Swiss historiography, even though the complaint has been made, with equal justice, that he presented his findings in almost unreadable form.[48] The principal of the later documents to which Kopp referred (and the one containing the first reference to Tell and his exploits that has not been proved a forgery or an interpolation) is the manuscript written about 1470 known as the White Book of Sarnen. Its author supposed that the antagonism which then undoubtedly existed between Swiss and Habsburg had also been a reality 200 years earlier, and had brought the Confederation into being.

The three modern historians of Switzerland already quoted have declared (*op. cit.*, p. 75) that "at what date, under what circumstances and for what precise purposes Uri, Schwyz and Unterwalden first reached the state of permanent alliance are among the most obscure questions of Swiss history". The first documentary evidence is a treaty of 1291 (found in the archives of Canton Schwyz in 1760) in which the three valleys pledge mutual support. The Emperor Rudolf had just died, and it is now thought that the treaty may represent "an attempt on the part of the valleys to minimize in their own area the effects of . . . foreseeable disorders" following his death (*ibid.*, p. 76). It makes no mention of Tell, nor of the cruelty of Austrian bailiffs. And Kopp showed that at the time of the supposed uprising in 1308 there was no grievance against Rudolf's son Albrecht, who was a severe but just ruler, never guilty of any atrocity, and who had no occasion—neither as King nor as Duke of Austria—to send bailiffs into the cantons. Nor,

Kopp added, is there any cogent evidence that any bailiff of his, of whatever name or rank, entered them.[49]

The oldest reference to an uprising in the cantons is in Johannes von Winterthur's chronicle written about 1340. It has nothing to say of either bailiffs or Tell. Traditions about cruel bailiffs first appear in Conrad Justinger's Bernese Chronicle of 1420, and were also alleged by Felix Hemmerlin who wrote about 1450. Neither makes any mention of Tell.[50] Hemmerlin advances on Justinger, who had confined himself to general terms, by giving details of the cruel acts. He tells how the Count of Habsburg's bailiff in Schwyz was killed by two men for having seduced their sister. When the Count determined to punish the murderers, they formed a league with others from their valley against him. This, says the writer, was the basis of the Confederation which was later joined by Unterwalden, Luzern, Bern, Zug, and then Uri.

Tell is mentioned in a ballad composed about 1477 which gives a quite different account of the origin of the Confederation, and which claims for Uri the honour of instigating it. There is no mention of the bailiff's hat, but we are told how he made Tell of Uri shoot an apple from his son's head. Tell was to die unless he succeeded with his first shot. After praying night and day he made his attempt and was successful. But he informed the bailiff (without being asked) that he had intended to kill him with his second arrow had he killed his child with his first. A great commotion followed in which "the bailiffs" persecuted the local people. Finally we are told that "he"—the bailiff is now again referred to in the singular—was driven from the country. Here, then, is a piece of patriotic fiction which aims at glorifying the canton of Uri, and which illustrates the oppressive rule of bailiffs with the story of Tell.

The sense of superiority of the men of the three forest cantons (Schwyz, Uri, and Unterwalden) is expressed in a work of about 1440 (questionably ascribed to Johann Fründ), *Von dem Herkommen der Schwyzer*, wherein the forest men are said to be of different ancestry from their peasant neighbours and to have been free from immemorial times. In the White Book of 1470—the first extant document to combine the Tell story with stories of atrocities committed by bailiffs—we read that the Emperor Rudolf made the three cantons subject only to the Empire, while other parts of what is now Switzerland were ruled by the Counts of Habsburg or Tyrol. This is a new variant of Fründ's belief in the privileged political status of the forest cantons, and the whole tradition was discredited when Kopp's documents showed (I quote Huber's summary, op. cit., p. 10) "that by far the majority of the inhabitants of the forest area were not freemen but bondsmen of ecclesiastical and secular landlords; that Uri in particular was largely in the possession of the Abbey of our Lady at Zürich, and that the Habsburgs did not merely possess a few estates in the three forest areas, but as landgraves of Aargau (which had spread its territory so as to include Unterwalden, Uri and Schwyz) had rights of jurisdiction there".

The White Book also tells of the atrocities in the cantons which led to the nocturnal meeting on the Rütli, and gives the story of Tell's refusal to salute Gessler's hat. It provides no dates for these events. These were supplied by Tschudi, who died in 1572 and whose chronicle was for long the standard history of Switzerland. Kopp was amazed at Tschudi's "insolent self-confidence and the honest manner he assumes"; and the chronicler's confident way of naming the very day on which an event occurred has been described as "breathtaking".[51] J. von Müller added a few further details in his Geschichte der schweizerischen Eidgenossenschaft, 1786, and it is to his imagination that we owe the oppressor's full name, Hermann Gessler von Bruneck. Finally, once Tell's existence became an accepted fact, some of the earlier documents were redacted. For instance, his name was forged in the register of deaths at Schattorf.[52]

The important fact is that Tell is not mentioned for over a hundred years after his supposed exploits even though documents are extant from this period which describe the circumstances in which he was (according to the later traditions) concerned. That so much of the material concerning him is tendentious is not in itself decisive. We know from other instances that, although the needs of writers to prove a thesis dear to them can lead to the compilation of biographies which are largely fictitious, the person in question can sometimes be proved to have existed, e.g. from extant letters of people who, quite independently of each other, witnessed and commented on his behaviour.

What criteria of historicity emerge from all this? The examples discussed show the importance of contemporary evidence.[53] Where the earliest documents specify circumstances in which a personage was (according to later documents) concerned without mentioning him, we can be fairly sure that he did not do what is alleged of him, if he existed at all. In such cases our suspicions will be confirmed if we find that the later stories duplicate traditions told of another hero and if we can discern obvious motives for their concoction. Of course, earlier documents are not invariably more reliable than later ones. De Wette realized (pp. 42, 49) that a later writer might use his sources more critically. And today Aristotle is for this reason regarded as a more reliable source on the Athenian statesman Solon than is Herodotus who wrote a century earlier. Contemporary evidence, then, does not always mean contemporary documents. Quotations from ancient documents by later inquirers are valuable if there is reason for believing that the later writer was able to consult the earlier documents, and that these latter were either contemporary with the events described, or later copies of contemporary documents. This is always a matter of inference. Furthermore, contemporary evidence attains its greatest cogency if independent witnesses agree in affirming it. A century ago, Andrew Lang, outlining the precautions which the anthropologist must observe when collecting his evidence, wrote (in an appendix at the end of his *Myth, Ritual and Religion*) of "corroboration which is derived from the undesigned coincidence of independent testimony" and called this "the touchstone of anthropology".

It is often alleged that argument from silence is not permissible. But in fact my examples show that the silence of a writer may or may not be significant according to the subject he is discussing. The silence of the earliest documents about Tell is important because the conditions they describe are relevant to his supposed circumstances. And the silence of Samuel-Kings about the Mosaic law is significant because (as de Wette showed, pp. 6–7) these books neither lack interest in religious and cultic matters, nor are they aiming at extreme brevity. He demonstrated well enough (e.g. p. 152) that their author had occasion to mention the Mosaic laws if they had been known to him.

J. M. Robertson has justly noted that the fortunes of the Tell myth serve to illustrate both "the fashion in which a fiction can, even in a historical period, find general acceptance", and also "the time and effort required to dispossess such a belief by means even of the plainest evidence". When at last the pressure of criticism could no longer be resisted by the learned, recourse was had to the position that, "while the apple story is plainly myth and Tell a non-historical person, there is some reason to believe that *some* disturbance occurred about the time in question". To this day, Robertson said, "the great majority of the Swiss people . . . probably believe devoutly in the Tell story . . . so little do the studies and conclusions of scholars represent popular opinion in any age." The relevance of all this to the persistence of belief in the principal tenets of Christianity, in spite of what scholars have done to discredit such belief, is obvious enough; and, as Robertson added: "those rationalists among ourselves who go about proclaiming that Christian supernaturalism, being detected, is 'dead', do but proclaim their own immaturity."[54]

Chapter Three
The Liberal Defence

While Strauss and his successors were undermining traditional views of the New Testament, John Henry Newman remarked: "How often has the wish risen in the hearts [of many Catholics] that some one from among themselves should come forward as the champion of revealed truth against its opponents." Newman was urged to do so himself, but there were difficulties and he found that true wisdom counselled silence: "Fear ye not, stand still: the Lord shall fight for you and ye shall hold your peace".[1]

A historian of the Oxford Movement has noted that, if an undertone of uncertainty runs through Newman's book, "it must not be inferred that he entertained any misgivings as to the intrinsic soundness of his position."[2] In other words, he was unwilling to relinquish his conclusions, but had some difficulty in finding plausible premises. This is a common form of thinking; it consists in the search for a set of conceptions or arguments which will appear to justify a belief or an attitude which is found desirable for other reasons.

The dilemma of more recent apologists has become acute. In former times unbelievers formed but a negligible proportion of the population and could be consigned to damnation without serious opposition or inconvenience. Today they have grown in numbers and the more educated among them cannot be frightened so easily. They must be approached in a different spirit, in the spirit of compromise. In 1963, A.R. Vidler, then Dean of King's College Cambridge and lecturer in ecclesiastical history, advised Christians—in a way that would have horrified Newman—not to "try to lay down a hard and fast line between what are the essentials and the non-essentials of belief."[3] Evidently he thought it inadvisable to commit oneself to any particular belief because it might become untenable, and believed that if Christianity was to be preserved, its creed must remain fluid.

Taking this advice makes it impossible for apologists to present a united front. Among educated populations, flexibility in ritual or belief encourages independent ideas, and this variety of opinion advertises the uncertainty of the true doctrine. In this connection the long history of religious ideas generally is instructive. In an organized society or tribe with strong traditions in the hands of an established priesthood, spontaneous departure from orthodoxy will be resisted and ascribed to evil powers. But when mixture of races and interpenetration of communities produces confusion, contrast, and scepticism, the bonds of tradition will be more easily thrown off. This was the situation in the Roman Empire when Christianity originated, and as a result we find that the earliest Christians of whom we have record could agree on practically nothing. Paul complained of "false apostles" and of Christian missionaries who were preaching "another Jesus" than the one he preached (2 Corinthians 11:4 and 13). The epistle to the Hebrews warns the faithful not to be led astray by "divers and strange teachings" about Jesus (13:8–9). The pseudo-Pauline pastoral epistles repeatedly complain of "false teachers"; Jude and 2 Peter also castigate heretics, and 2 John warns against Christians who do not bring the true doctrine. Christianity in time developed into a strictly controlled and fairly uniform set of beliefs laid down in creeds, but when central control was abolished at the Reformation, Protestant Christianity reverted for a time to a medley of warring sects. Our own day sees something similar as to variety of opinion, and in some cases also as to mutual hostility.

Vidler's colleagues and successors have nevertheless had to take his advice, for, as the Claremont theologian John Hick puts it, "the pressure upon Christianity is as strong as ever to go on adapting itself into something which can be believed."[4] J. S. Bezzant, formerly Dean of St. John's College, Cambridge, and lecturer in the New Testament, even argued that we ought to go on trying to make sense of Christianity with the same energy and perseverance with which we persist in trying to find a cure for cancer. Attempts to find the causes of the disease have, he said, so far failed, but "the sponge is not thrown in with anything like the ease with which difficulties in and objections to Christianity are allowed to be negatively effective."[5]

Let us return to Vidler, for although his book is now 25 years old, his successors have made out no better case. He quotes Paul Tillich, to the effect that "the affirmation that Jesus is the Christ is an act of faith and consequently of daring courage" (p. 76). Now we do not know anything about Jesus except what is contained in the 27 books of the New Testament, which are far from reliable documents. We know even less about 'the Christ' except that the Jews had a tradition that there would one day come a Messiah, a Christ, to save his people, and that there were different opinions about how he would come, what he would be like and what he would do. So what does such a vague and uncertain affirmation as 'Jesus is the Christ' amount to, and why is it "an act of daring courage"? We show courage in the face of danger. What is the danger incurred in making such a vague affirmation which in any case is generally regarded as orthodox and respectable? The meaning can surely only be that it is courageous to affirm a belief when the evidence for it is so flimsy.

Vidler suggests that "the hard core of the Christian story" is generally accepted, although he concedes that experts differ widely as to the extent of its "legendary embellishment" (p. 72). As he speaks in purely general terms, it is not clear what he assigns to the hard core. He does however say that we cannot decide whether to accept this core by studying the New Testament alone but must consider also the Old Testament and "the subsequent history of the Christian movement", "the total Christian phenomenon in history". This is dangerous ground. The Christian phenomenon in history might by some be held to justify the belief that the religion had been inspired by the Devil himself; and he concedes that "the Christian movement in history has a brighter and a darker side" (p. 73).

As, then, the experts are admitted to disagree widely, everyone who does not claim to be an expert must, in Vidler's view, be guided by one or both of two things. First, by the emotions he experiences under the impact of Christian ritual. He may feel "convinced that there is something there which, despite all his puzzlements, holds him and speaks to the deepest levels of his being" (p. 76). It is of course true that emotions of awe and wonder can be evoked by the solemn music of a cathedral service, by the voice of the intoning priest, the candlelight, and so on. But this does not authenticate the religious doctrines on which the ritual is based, nor even necessarily go with clear ideas about them. I shall show repeatedly in this volume how readily powerful emotions can be linked with flimsy ideas.

The second factor which Vidler thinks may appropriately guide a non-expert in deciding whether to be a Christian believer is not much different from the first. It is whether the story in the gospels, true or false, appeals to some emotion. He speaks in this connection of "the enduring impression or impact that is made . . . by the person of Jesus as he is portrayed in the gospels". He admits to difficulties in "getting at" this, but nonetheless claims that "the authentic personality of Jesus does still make its impact" (pp. 75–6). But wherein this authentic personality consists is precisely the problem. Are the words and deeds attributed to him by the evangelists authentic? W. D. Davies, author of a standard theological work on the Sermon on the Mount, concedes that many experts have regarded the majority of the sayings ascribed to Jesus throughout the gospels as creations of the primitive Church, and that, on this view, the Sermon "cannot fruitfully be discussed" in relation to his teaching, because we cannot know what he taught, only what the early Church credited to him.[6] F. W. Beare, theologian and author of the first major commentary on the gospel of Matthew to appear for many years—he describes it as "a grim book" and finds the Christ it presents "on the whole a terrifying figure"—says that all the major discourses in this gospel are agglomerations: "The materials which they contain were of many different origins and came into the hands of the evangelist through many different channels and after a long history of transmission".[7] D. Cupitt (Dean of Emmanuel College, Cambridge, and lecturer in the philosophy of religion) and P. Armstrong have noted, in a book based on a series of BBC television programmes, that

> If we put Mark, Matthew and Luke in parallel columns and look at them in detail, it is obvious that Matthew and Luke, quite independently, have no hesitation in changing what Mark wrote, in whatever direction they feel is required. They did not think that the words of Jesus were sacrosanct and unalterable. They believed he was alive, still teaching and guiding the Church. So they saw nothing wrong in developing the tradition of his words and deeds.[8]

Apologists refuse to be discomfited by having thus to admit that one evangelist is perfectly capable of changing the narrative of another so as to make it mean something different, but proclaim that this merely shows that what the gospels offer is "rich, vibrant and alive", "a whole wealth of interpretation, as people have tried to come to terms with their experience of Jesus, to express it and to understand their new faith in what God has been doing through Jesus".[9]

Stewart Sutherland has conceded (in his 1984 book based on his Wilde Lectures at Oxford) that there is "very deep-seated scepticism and widespread disagreement about almost all of the doctrinally central elements of Jesus's life and sayings", and that "little agreement is to be found between specialist scholars about the historical content of [his] life beyond the barest of bare outlines".[10] If, then, neither the recorded words nor the recorded deeds of Jesus can be taken as authentic, all that is left to make what Vidler called an "enduring impression or impact" is his miraculous birth and resurrection; and these have not survived critical scrutiny. So conservative a scholar as C. H. Dodd attempted but a half-hearted defence of the former, calling the birth narratives of Matthew and Luke a "structure of imagery", with "a basis in fact somewhere behind it all".[11] On the Catholic side, one scholar (Mackey) concedes that these two narratives (which alone in the New Testament provide any evidence on the subject at all) are "of extremely doubtful historical value if taken at all literally";[12] and another (Brown) admits that it is "quite impossible" to harmonize them, and that we have "no reliable information" about the source of either.[13] As for the resurrection, Dodd allowed that "the historian may properly suspend judgment" as to whether "Jesus had in some way left his tomb" (pp. 166–7). Hick admits that the earliest references to the resurrection (those in the Pauline letters) simply allege Jesus to be risen, and that the gospels elaborate this message into a catena of incompatible stories characterized by "progressive degeneration from history to legend", so that we cannot tell whether he did actually emerge from his grave, or whether this was merely an idea based on "a series of visions" of him "as a glorified figure of exalted majesty".[14] Mackey finds that the gospel empty tomb stories are better understood as "imagery and symbolism of resurrection", rather than as "supporting evidence" for it (p. 107). Likewise David Jenkins, now Bishop of Durham, wonders "whether the actual discovery of the empty tomb was one of the preludes to discovering Jesus to be alive or whether the story came to be told as a symbol of the discovery that Jesus was alive".[15] Such concessions have come to be made only because vindicating the actuality of the events on the basis of the New Testament evidence has proved to be a well-nigh hopeless task.

Jesus's resurrection can be pictured in the mind quite concretely as a man coming to life in his tomb, emerging from it and then conversing with his friends. As the Biblical accounts that he was resurrected are full of contradictions and unsubstantiated by external evidence, and as we are today in any case disinclined to believe that anyone can return to life after death, it has become necessary to safeguard the belief in his resurrection by describing the event in words which suggest no such concrete mental pictures. David Jenkins, for instance, maintains that "a series of experiences" convinced apostles that, after Jesus's death and burial, "the very life and power and purpose and personality which was in him was actually continuing both in the sphere of God and in the sphere of history, so that he was a risen and living presence and possibility".[16] A Christian commentator, in a booklet to which the Bishop of London has contributed an enthusiastic preface, notes that this "sophisticated reinterpretation of the resurrection" has "clearly failed to do justice to Biblical teaching".[17] A more serious drawback, from my standpoint, is that it does not stand for any acceptable ideas. Many, however, will charitably assume that it does, simply because it is expressed in full accordance with the requirements of grammar and syntax and in words each one of which is familiar and would, in an intelligible context, be perfectly clear.

Dr. Jenkins is—or was until his appointment as Bishop of Durham—a professor of theology. In the seventeenth century Thomas Hobbes noted (at the beginning of his *Leviathan*), as one of the things that should be amended in universities, what he called "the frequency of insignificant speech". It is difficult nowadays to imagine a university continuing to exist, except as a kind of technical school, if its staff and students were deprived of this ancient privilege.

In our thinking we often have to make do with ideas which are simple compared with the reality they represent. Massive realities, for instance, cannot be mentally represented otherwise. It is easy to speak of 'scientific progress', 'world opinion' or 'juvenile crime', but the realities which these words stand for are thinkable at all only by means of some simple deputy. In this sense our thinking of these realities is effected by means of symbols. If error is to be avoided, there must be a continual return to concrete ideas as a check on this process of reasoning with the aid of symbols.[18] This is particularly true when the symbols in the mind are mere words. But a writer who wishes to make an erroneous proposition look plausible will discourage in his readers this reconversion of symbols into fuller and more concrete conceptions which more faithfully represent reality. This is not difficult, as the task of reconversion is too laborious to be undertaken readily, even if its advisability is realized.

Although it is no longer easy for educated Christians to believe that the power they suppose lies behind the universe has the characteristics of a man, they commonly preserve the emotional relationship to this power that would be appropriate towards a human being. One suspects that really there has been only a verbal renunciation of the human characteristics of God, in defensive argument with critics, and that the believer has not really given them up. Many Christians tend to speak of Jesus rather than of God the Father precisely because it is easier to think of the human virtues in connection with a human figure. We can picture Jesus as a babe in his mother's arms, as a beautiful boy disputing with the rabbis in the temple, and as a tortured figure on the cross. Some apologists have made a virtue of what they take for necessity here. Ernst Cassirer, for instance, wrote:

> By its very nature religion can never escape from the sphere of the 'image', the sphere of intuition and fantasy. From them it derives its peculiar power; it would wither away and die were it not continuously nourished from this soil. On the other hand the image can never be treated as merely a picture, as an arbitrary play of the powers of imagination. The image has a meaning, in that it not only represents the truth but is the truth itself.[19]

This purports to explain why religion is so full of myths. But the explanation must not be supposed to imply any limitation or defect in religion. Oh no. The image is not merely an arbitrary picture, a distortion of the truth; it really *is* the truth. It would follow that when religion presents the picture of hell and heaven, of angels and devils, of incarnations and resurrections, it is not dealing in figures of speech, but must be accepted as true. It is in order to avoid thus committing the believer to such a position that liberal apologists have come to re-interpret the gospel 'pictures' into obscure ideas.

Unlike some other liberals, Jenkins finds that the information about Jesus given in the New Testament is basically reliable. He admits that the four canonical gospels give "often enigmatic and differing presentations of Jesus"; yet these, "taken as a whole", show him to be a unique person, characterized by an "awkwardness . . . reflected in terms of eschatology, of transcendence, of strange otherness".[20] Jenkins's requirement that these presentations be "taken as a whole" has the merit that it precludes any criticism that can be checked. If we are not to be allowed to criticize particular parts, or to quote particular passages to justify our criticisms, on the ground that what the gospels say about Jesus must be taken as a whole, then what can we do? We may of course make general statements about them, as their admirers do, but we cannot justify our statements except by reference to this part or that.

Jenkins claims that "the historical reality of the personality of Jesus is validly and effectively reflected" in these writings. They are therefore not to be set aside as merely "church talk" (that is, as views which spokesmen of diverse early Christian communities put into Jesus's mouth) nor as merely "the culturally conditioned mythical account of a faith experience". Jenkins does not deny that the New Testament includes such talk and such myths, but insists that the talk and the myths "reflect in their own way experiences of an objectively conditioned Mystery with which we are involved and of which we are a part". The phrase "in their own way" is protective (in similar fashion to the phrase "taken as a whole"). It forbids the critic to demur by reserving the retort that the way he understands the myths is inadequate. Jenkins's own interpretation of the 'pictorial' or 'mythological' language of the New Testament is such that, for him, "Jesus Christ points decisively to ultimate reality".[21] His belief in God is not, however, based only on the traditions enshrined in the Bible. We know God also "because he finds us". "In some often more or less hidden, obscure, and only occasionally remembered way we have experienced a presence, a power, a personality who is with us and for us". It is always hard to know how much to rely on such revelations of intimate experience. They are in any case individual, and the attempt to describe them must depend on the psychological notions, often very crude, of the subject. But generalizations can have but little basis if the experiences of many people cannot be compared.

Jenkins's third ground for knowing God is that, by living "in the policy which the tradition suggests to us and in the light of such vision as God has given us", we "find God" in that, "in company with other Christians brought together by the Holy Spirit, we find that life is enhanced in this living, experience is deepened and the tradition is illuminated." Thus "this threefold cord—the tradition, our experience, the policy of common living—assures us that the Gospel is indeed true".[22] All this is unlikely to convince those not already susceptible, and he admits that "we can never finally know, at any rate in this world, that Jesus is the Christ", although his being this is "the definitive fact for the human understanding of both history and cosmos".[23] The second and third elements in Jenkins's "threefold cord"—experience of a "presence" and of enhancement of life in fellowship—are primarily emotional. For him as for Vidler (above, p. 67) this emotional factor is none the less decisive for being linked with but the vaguest of ideas.

A great source of variety in opinion is the insistence of many modern apologists that much of the gospel story, although literally untrue, is symbolical, and that when the symbolism is interpreted, truths are revealed. This kind of exegesis was popularized by Rudolf Bultmann, according to whom the resurrection is "not an event of past history", but nevertheless a "cosmic event", for it tells us the truth that death has been deprived of its powers, so that we need not fear it and thus obtain "the possibility of authentic life".[24] Since there are no generally accepted rules for interpreting the symbols, the 'truths' can be arranged so as to suit the purposes of different apologists. Hick, for instance, says that Jesus as the son of God is a symbol, meaning, among other things, that "he is so far above us in the 'direction' of God that he stands between ourselves and the Ultimate as a mediator of salvation". He implies that the authors of the New Testament books knew that what they wrote was mere symbol, for he says that their statements quickly "came to be understood by the Christian mind not as symbols but as components in literal statements".[25] But is it really credible that the authors of epistles and gospels were consciously speaking in symbols and that the whole Christian Church for centuries afterwards assumed that they were speaking literally? Why should they not have found a direct way of expressing the truths they were trying to communicate, instead of resorting to language which was bound to be misunderstood?

Bultmann too failed to give an adequate answer to this question. He too supposed that the New Testament writers who thought "mythologically" knew quite well that, for instance, God was "transcendent", but were not yet capable of forming this idea, and so formed instead the idea of his heavenly domicile. In lectures delivered at Yale and at Vanderbilt in 1951, he said: "The thinking which is not yet capable of forming the abstract idea of transcendence expresses its intention in the category of space; the transcendent God is imagined as being at an immense spatial distance, far above the world".[26] The actual truth was, then, known to the writers in some way although they could not form the idea which truly represented it. How they could have knowledge of a thing of which they could form no idea is not plain. Again, Bultmann says that the mythological thinker cannot form the idea of "the transcendence of evil", but he can form the idea of "a tremendous power which again and again afflicts mankind", and so he "forms the conception of hell" and locates it below the earth in darkness. A myth is, then, a crude expression of a profound truth, and we who have at our disposal better modes of expression can interpret the myths of our predecessors and disclose the precious truths which they contain. The utility of this is that it does not involve actual rejection, but only reinterpretation of what is stated in the New Testament. The admission that what was taught for hundreds of years is now at last discovered to be untrue will naturally occasion suspicion that the whole thing is untrue from beginning to end; and so it is understandable that every effort is made to retain the verbal form of the beliefs and pretend that the inspired words of the prophet or the sacred book have merely been misinterpreted.

The idea of hell and of its eternal torments is, without such reinterpretation, "morally revolting", in Hick's phrase. He notes too that the simple division of mankind (ascribed to Jesus at Matthew 25:41–6) into the "cursed", who are to be forever tormented, and the "righteous", who are to enter eternal life, takes a totally unrealistic view of "the innumerable gradations of human good and evil". He finds this rigid division a "disconcerting idea" imposed on his source material by Matthew, writing in a "post-apostolic age" for Christians who were suffering persecution and thus receptive to the idea that their persecutors would face a fearful doom.[27] It is, then, not surprising that today we hear little of hell, whereas "at one time no self-respecting preacher could possibly exclude it from public utterance". Sutherland makes this comment by way of noting that, quite generally, elements of Christian tradition which "were regarded as quite central in earlier periods are now given at most a peripheral place" (p. 169). One could really say without exaggeration that the only features of Christianity which have today remained almost unchanged are its buildings.

Apologists who have abandoned so much of earlier doctrine are naturally fiercely criticized by upholders of traditional orthodoxy. William Ledwich, for instance, who organized a national petition against Dr. Jenkins's consecration as bishop—it attracted 14,000 signatures within weeks—complains that "the views of the Liberals . . . are becoming new and formidable wedges between Christians". Ledwich finds that "all the liberal arguments" have long since been "answered"—by John Henry Newman.[28] The opening page of this present chapter gives Newman's own avowal that he did nothing of the sort. On Ledwich's own showing, all that Newman did was to allege that liberals have no right to come forward with any arguments at all against the received teaching.[29]

In June 1986 the House of Bishops of the General Synod of the Church of England published a statement and exposition of *The*

Nature of Christian Belief. According to the *Church Times* (13 June, 1986), it was Bishop Jenkins's controversial pronouncements on the resurrection and the virgin birth that gave rise to this document; and according to Dr. Jenkins himself, as quoted in that issue of the *Church Times*, the document "had been written principally as an exercise in reassurance". It does unequivocally affirm that the resurrection is "an objective reality, both historical and divine". But it allows that, although the canonical gospels report that Jesus's tomb was found to be empty, this story may not be historically true. The risen Jesus may have left his flesh and bones in his grave; for when he appeared to his disciples he was able to arrive within closed doors and vanish at will, and was not always immediately recognizable. Hence the physical nature of his body was "of a very unusual kind". Yet the bishops insist that the empty tomb belongs to the faith and to the historic teaching of the Church, and that it is the duty of bishops to teach the faith. They take the same position regarding the virgin birth, even though (unlike the empty tomb) this is explicitly affirmed as a historical fact in the creeds. As Dr. Runcie, Archbishop of Canterbury (reported in the *Church Times, loc. cit.*) says: the bishops' report embodies "a form of words which . . . does not exclude those bishops . . . who agree with their colleagues over the theological meaning of the Empty Tomb and the Virginal Conception but cannot accept them as historical fact". The journal goes on to record the following comment on the bishops' report made by Keith Ward (Professor of the History and Philosophy of Religion at King's College, London, and an apologist mentioned elsewhere in the present volume):

> What it is saying is: we all accept that this is the faith of the Church of England, we all accept that we are bound to accept and affirm this faith, and we all accept that some of us don't actually believe it. And that, of course, is, I'm sorry to say it, either hypocrisy or perjury, because what they are saying is that some of us should stand up in public and say things we don't actually believe.

To say, with the bishops, that the body of the risen Jesus was "of a very unusual kind" is to gloss over the problems arising from what another theologian, Dr. Paul Badham, has called the "internal incoherence" of the narratives on this issue. These refer to the "flesh and bones" of the risen Jesus (Luke 24:40), who "eats and drinks" with his disciples (Acts 10:41) and invites Thomas to touch him (John 20:27; cf. Luke 24:40). His risen body also has to be strong enough to support clothes, as no one supposes that he manifested himself naked, yet intangible enough to pass through the walls of the upper room. Badham also notes that Paul states categorically that "flesh and blood cannot inherit the kingdom of God" (1 Corinthians 15:50, cf. 2 Corinthians 5:6–8) and so could not have accepted any traditions that Jesus rose in physical body and ate and drank. Finally Badham shows how some of the more absurd elements in traditional Christian teaching have been retracted even in official pronouncements by the Church. For instance, the fourth article of the Church of England affirmed that Christ ascended into heaven "with flesh and bones", where he now "sitteth", whereas in 1962 the then Archbishop of Canterbury's Commission on Doctrine ruled that the physical features of the ascension narratives "are to be interpreted symbolically".[30]

Chapter Four
Theology of Reassurance: Tillich

Beliefs are important for peace of mind, especially where they refer to the future or to anything remote which cannot be easily confirmed or disproved. It is the anticipation of good that raises a man's spirits and of evil that causes dejection. An unforeseen misfortune can cause no distress before it occurs. A feared misfortune may cause great distress even though it in fact never does occur. Hence the psychological importance of reassuring beliefs.

Religion often includes such beliefs—beliefs by which the individual compensates himself for what he may lack in more material ways and which recompense him for ills he cannot escape. No community is intellectually homogeneous, and the more intelligent and more educated individuals often abandon traditional beliefs of this kind. But the need for reassurance, for consolation in trouble, for compensation, is just as great in the most enlightened as in the least. This is the psychological situation in which a great deal of recent theology has arisen— theology which argues that the essentials of religion do not lie in belief in God in any of the senses that that word used to convey, and which tries instead, in the words of J. A. T. Robinson, to "validate the idea of transcendence for modern man".[1]

A typical exponent of such theology is Paul Tillich. Born in 1886, he was a chaplain in the German army in the first world war, and later taught theology and philosophy at a number of German universities until he left Germany for the USA in 1933 to become Professor of Philosophical Theology at New York. He later held similar appointments at Harvard and Chicago until his death in 1965. I refer to certain of his works with the abbreviations Sh and ST which are explained below (p. 244). According to a recent biography, he "expressed himself more convincingly in his sermons than anywhere else" and claimed that they "manifested the 'existential implications' of his theology".[2] In one of them, entitled 'The Depth of Existence' (Sh, pp. 52–63), he defines God as:

1. The infinite and inexhaustible depth and ground of all being.
2. Depth.
3. The depths of your life.
4. The source of your being.
5. Your ultimate concern.
6. What you take seriously without any reservation.
7. The infinite and inexhaustible ground of history.
8. The depth of history.
9. The ground and aim of our social life.
10. What you take seriously without reservation in your moral and political activities.
11. Hope.

According to Robinson, who bases a great deal of his *Honest to God* on the views of Tillich, all this means that God "is not a projection 'out there', an Other beyond the skies, of whose existence we have to convince ourselves." He thinks that Tillich's "great contribution to theology" is this "reinterpretation of transcendence in a way which preserves its reality while detaching it from the projection of supranaturalism". He says too:

> The necessity for the name 'God' lies in the fact that our being has depths which naturalism, whether evolutionary, mechanistic, dialectical or humanistic, cannot or will not recognize.

Naturalism would seem to be any view of things which regards the phenomena of religion as merely one aspect of human culture to be studied and explained in the same way as other aspects. And he goes on to speak of the "nemesis which has overtaken naturalism in our day" as a result of its having tried to suppress these depths. The passage he then quotes from Tillich's sermons (Sh, p. 181) about "the unconditional devotion of millions to a satanic image" shows that they are both thinking of Mussolini, Hitler, and Stalin. And, in elucidation of this passage, Robinson says:

There are depths of revelation, intimations of eternity, judgements of the holy and the sacred, awarenesses of the unconditional, the numinous and the ecstatic, which cannot be explained in purely naturalistic categories without being reduced to something else. There is the 'Thus saith the Lord' heard by prophet, apostle and martyr for which naturalism cannot account.[3]

Unfortunately our psychologists are not very successful in explaining any of our experiences, and it is hardly surprising that they should have failed to deal adequately with exceptional forms of experience. Both Robinson and Tillich wish to suggest that the horrors of recent wars and persecutions have resulted from 'naturalism', although the history of Christendom does not yield evidence that war and persecution have ever been kept in check by religion.

One commentator claims that, when Tillich speaks of God as the 'ground' of life, ground "does not mean cause or substance taken literally, but something which underlies all things in some way or other [!] which we can only symbolically describe as causation or substantiality".[4] All this seems to rest on a scholastic fallacy. As it was supposed that a cow did not cease to be a cow because it had lost an eye, become deaf, or suffered any other 'accident', the problem arose as to what exactly made it a cow; what was the essence or being of a cow, or the basis or 'ground' of its being what it is. Some philosophers believed that there was something occult and mysterious underlying all the familiar and perceptible qualities which constitute the 'real' cow. The philosopher John Locke was concerned to point out that, of that essence, if it exists, we know nothing; that when the word 'cow' is used intelligibly, it means no more than the set of qualities which we have learned to associate with the name.[5] He did not say that the essence does not exist—how can we know whether it exists if we know nothing about it? But since philosophers were inclined to introduce it into their arguments, he thought it advisable to dispose of it once and for all.

We often try to decide what an observed occurrence means, what it portends, what is behind it, what we are to expect to follow it, or what will be the effects of our reacting to it in this way or that. We often put the matter briefly in this form, that we ask what it *is*. Knowing what a thing is normally means that we identify a particular experience with a class of past experiences. When we have an uncomfortable feeling at the back of the nose, we recognize this as the first stage in a sequence which we have experienced before, and we say 'It is a cold coming'. If the sensation is not one we have had before, we shall not know *what it is*. It is a failure to appreciate what this form of words means that has given rise to a great deal of philosophical talk about 'being'. In common parlance, to know what a thing is means to be able to recognize it by certain external appearances, and to have a certain minimum knowledge of how to deal with it. By more minute and prolonged study one may get a great deal more information about it and know it much better. But however prolonged the study, one can only extend one's knowledge and never make it exhaustive. Between the dog's simple knowledge of the cat, which it recognizes from certain characteristics of colour, shape, movement, and smell, and the more elaborate knowledge of the anatomist and physiologist, there are many intermediate stages. It is, however, an illusion to imagine that there is a peculiar and superior kind of knowledge, distinct from the catalogue of facts accumulated by the scientific inquirer, and that this superior knowledge concerns the 'essence', the 'real nature' of a thing. Properties or characters like the feeling in the throat just mentioned are of great practical importance because they are both easy to detect and also diagnostic, in the sense that they are correlated with a large number of others which may be less accessible. This often facilitates scientific classification. One may tell, for instance, from the shape of a vein in the wing of a fly whether it belongs to a certain family, in which case it will possess a large number of characters in common with the remaining members of the family. But it would be arbitrary to say that the shape of the vein was more 'essential' than any other character of the fly. Again, we may say that a cat without a tail is still a cat, but a tail without a cat is not. In relation to any particular purpose it is generally fairly easy to say what is essential and what is not, what matters and what is of no consequence. But the attempt to elevate such relativities into absolute properties results in futility. We do of course find that many properties of a thing are the consequence of a more fundamental quality. Much may be attributed to the temperature of a material, so that if we

Does 'non-being' have ontological character?

know the temperature of the water, for example, we may be able to infer its behaviour in many different cases. This ability to infer several forms of behaviour from one state or property (whether temporary or permanent) encourages the view that we might be able to sum up all the properties of a thing by stating some few fundamental characters which would be the thing itself and not mere properties of it.

A. Thatcher has tried to defend Tillich's statements about 'being' by tracing them to a "profusion of different sources"—he instances Aristotle, Schelling, Santayana, and Heidegger, and says that Tillich has "conflated several possible ways of ontological thinking". But if the whole basis of 'ontological thinking' is a misconception, then this conflation will be no advantage. And Thatcher does admit that it is widely held that a misconception is involved. He quotes Tillich's statement that philosophy "asks the question of what being, simply being, means" and comments:

> The problem here of course is that most philosophers simply do not think that 'being' means anything at all: such a statement is usually regarded as a pseudo-problem, or a consequence of the simple logical fallacy of assuming that the word 'being' corresponds or refers to something describable.[6]

Another commentator has complained that Tillich's thought is altogether vitiated by "the fallacy that the existence of a word means the existence of a thing", and that this fallacy leads him to posit not merely 'being' but also 'non-being' as a real entity.[7] Tillich does in fact affirm "the ontological character of non-being", and on the following basis:

> An anticipated event does not occur. This means that the judgment concerning the situation has been mistaken, the necessary conditions for the occurrence of the expected event have been non-existent. Thus disappointed, expectation creates the distinction between being and non-being. But how is such an expectation possible in the first place? What is the structure of this being which is able to transcend the given situation and to fall into error? The answer is that man, who is this being, must be separated from his being in a way which enables him to look at it as something strange and questionable. And such separation is actual because man participates not only in being but also in non-being. Therefore, the very structure which makes negative judgments possible proves the ontological character of non-being. (ST, I, p. 208)

Wrong assessment of a given situation can be studied, without such metaphysical theorizing, in relation to the behaviour of simpler animals. If a dog or an ape acts appropriately in a given situation, we assume that he has 'understood' it. If he acts in a manner that would be appropriate to a quite different situation, we suppose that he is deceived. There is always a *real* situation and the situation as the animal *conceives* it.[8] The evolution of behaviour from the simpler to the higher animals depends on the data of their senses being worked up, by processes occurring in the brain, into a more and more faithful representation of the real situation. No creature, man included, has immediate access to reality, but depends on his senses first and then on his memories and powers of mental reconstruction. The dog interprets a small black patch, just visible between plants in the garden, as the cat and reacts to it just as he would if the cat were fully exposed. But this interpretation of the situation may be mistaken, as a single sensation of sight or sound may be something that can occur in many different situations. Man, who has a much greater capacity for constructing ideas of complicated situations from very fragmentary evidence, has a correspondingly greater liability to error. In all his theorizing, whether this concerns present or absent situations, he cannot but draw on ordinary experience. His idea of Athens or Moscow, if not based on direct and specific experiences of these towns, is constructed from different experiences of streets, houses and people which he combines in his imagination in a certain way suggested to him by what he has read or been told, or by pictures and maps. It seems more satisfactory to explain his errors on this basis rather than by supposing that he "participates not only in being but also in non-being". Even these ideas are constructed out of his imagination, by a process of abstraction *ad infinitum* of all perceptible qualities.

Let us return to Tillich's God. If God is the ground of all being, no one can be an atheist. "There is no place to which we could flee from God which is outside of God." We cannot "reject and forget God", but only "some distorted picture of Him" (Sh, pp. 40–41). A critic has commented that this amounts to "conversion by definition."[9] Tillich says, in the preface to the collection of his sermons from which I have been quoting, that many in the audience to which they were originally addressed were not Christians. He was perhaps concerned to suggest to such persons that they were not so very far from Christian beliefs and could appropriately participate in Christian worship. That this is what he had in mind appears from his account of Psalm 139. He does not wish to give up such a well-known passage in the Bible because it reveals unacceptable notions about God. And so he reinterprets it, declaring that that psalmist was quite right: our downsitting and uprising are known, our thought is understood afar off, there is not a word in our tongue, but lo it is known altogether, we are beset behind and before. But it is not God as usually understood who knows, understands, and besets the psalmist. "The God whom he cannot flee is the Ground of his being" (Sh, p. 47).

We must not, then, "picture God as a thing with superhuman qualities, omnipresent like an electric power field, and omniscient like a superhuman brain." Astoundingly, he rejects such a conception of a personal, all-knowing God on the ground that it is *too abstract* (his own conception of God as 'the ground of all being' being presumably free from this disadvantage); for he continues:

> Such concepts as 'Divine Omnipresence' and 'Divine Omniscience' transform an overwhelming religious experience into an abstract, philosophical statement, which can be accepted and rejected, defined, redefined and replaced. In making God an object besides other objects, the existence and nature of which are matters of argument, theology supports the escape to atheism. It encourages those who are interested in denying the threatening Witness of their existence. The first step to atheism is always a theology which drags God down to the level of doubtful things. The game of the atheist is then very easy. For he is perfectly justified in destroying such a phantom and all its ghostly qualities (Sh, p. 45).

It is a sound observation that so long as we can keep God out of the category of doubtful things, the danger of atheism is much reduced.

In the very same sermon Tillich argues that we must inevitably hate God:

> God knows what we *are*; and He knows what we *do*. Who does not hate a companion who is always present on every road and in every place of rest? (p. 43)
> God peers into man's ground and depth, into his hidden shame and ugliness. The God who sees everything and man also, is the God who

has to die. Man cannot stand that such a Witness live. (p. 43)
A god whom we can easily bear, a god from whom we do not have to
hide, a god whom we do not hate in moments, a god whose destruction
we never desire, is not God at all, and has no reality. (p. 42)

He even argues that fear of the real all-knowing God turns sinful
men to atheism. Men become atheists because they are afraid of
God!

The protest against God, the will that there be no God, and the flight to
atheism are all genuine elements of profound religion. And only on the
basis of these elements has religion meaning and power (p. 45).

We naturally ask what sort of meaning and power religion does
have where it is based on these somewhat unexpected elements.
And if there were in fact a natural tendency in sinful man to get rid
of his belief in God, one would expect atheism to be more common
in the world than it appears to be.

Tillich also says that the kindly paternal Christian God is an
unacceptable notion, that the prevailing ideas of God among the
orthodox were made in the image of man. God was created by man
in the form that man liked to have him. Disbelief in this old
orthodox deity was justified, and if a man called himself an atheist
because he rejected this idea, then he was right in being an atheist.
But this does not dispose of the real God, the terrible God who
knows our most secret thoughts, whom we cannot but hate from
time to time. Robinson claims that it is the merit of Tillich to have
liberated us from the conception of God as "a sort of celestial Big
Brother".[10] But a god whom we must hate because he knows our
innermost secrets is necessarily just that.

The reason for the contradiction in Tillich's thinking about God
is that, in addition to propounding his philosophical idea of God
as the ground of being, he wishes to play on the fears of his
audience by representing God as a fearsome figure to whom we
must defer if we are to be saved. To this end he employs, perhaps
in true sermon style, alliterative phrases; "Omniscience means
that our mystery is manifest. Omnipresence means that our
privacy is public" (Sh, p. 46). Reassurance is in this case preceded
by creating the fear that it disperses. Tillich's willingness to play
on human fears in the interests of his apologetic is very evident in
the sermon where he stresses the bankruptcy of science and the

abuse of power. "Science, which has closed our eyes and thrown us into an abyss of ignorance about the few things that really matter", is now "atoning for the idolatrous abuse to which it has lent itself for centuries"; for it has revealed man's power to annihilate himself and his world. Atomic physics has at last confirmed the prophecy of Isaiah 24:18–20: "The foundations of the earth do shake, the earth is utterly broken" etc. That such visions have become an actual possibility is "the religious meaning of the age into which we have entered" (Sh, pp. 3,5). If we ask how this possibility gives a "religious meaning" to our age, Tillich will reply that, in the face of the imminent danger of complete destruction, "only two alternatives remain—despair, which is the certainty of eternal destruction, or faith, which is the certainty of eternal salvation" (p. 10). Those who have faith in God know that, when the crash comes, they will be saved when all else goes under. God, then, has been redefined so as to be acceptable to the educated person of today; but he still provides reassurance to those who have faith in him.

In another sermon Tillich discusses sin, which he calls "separation"—of man from himself, or of all men from " the Ground of Being". He adds that this state is the normal condition of everything: "Existence is separation"; and he goes on to call it "fate" and "guilt": "Separation which is fate and guilt constitutes the meaning of the word 'sin' " (Sh, p. 154–5). He then explains that there is also a separation of man from man, namely the want of sympathy of one man for another, the ability to contemplate without too much distress the sufferings of others. Although we read in our morning paper of millions freezing or starving, we can go about our daily concerns as if we knew nothing about it. "Estrangement" in the form of want of sympathy "prevails among all things that live. Sin abounds" (p. 158). Our feelings of compassion are, of course, instinctive, and are naturally aroused by the presence of suffering. Fortunately the bald account of suffering does not have such strong effects as its actual presence, or life would be quite unbearable. We have other instincts which also help to determine our behaviour. To call such lack of keen sympathy for remote suffering 'separation', 'sin', 'estrangement', 'guilt', or any of the other terms which he uses, does not help to solve the very difficult problems which must be solved if we are to do anything to improve the lot of the less fortunate. It seems to be merely a way of suggesting that the Christian religion has still some importance by associating it in a mystical manner with the familiar problems of life and society.

Tillich is concerned to arrange not only ideas of God but also ideas of Jesus so as to suit the modern outlook; and in this sense he speaks of "interpreting the call of Jesus for our time" (Sh, p. 102). He admits that the quest of the historical Jesus has been a failure, that the Biblical picture of him is not historical reportage, and that "there is no picture behind the biblical one which could be made scientifically probable" (ST, II, p. 118). Nevertheless, this picture "has power to transform those who are transformed by it", and "this implies that there is . . . an analogy between the picture and the actual personal life from which it has arisen. It was this reality, when encountered by the disciples, which created the picture" (ST, II, p. 132). It is misleading to talk in this way of 'the biblical picture' of Jesus when the 27 books of the New Testament give very different pictures of him. And according to very many New Testament scholars, the gospels do not give the disciples' pictures of Jesus, but pictures of both Jesus and his disciples constructed by authors who were not personally acquainted with either of them.

In any case, according to Tillich, the underlying historical events do not matter. "Historical investigations should neither comfort nor worry theologians". A historian or philologist for whom the contents of the New Testament are "not a mattter of ultimate concern may be able to interpret the text exactly and correctly, but he will miss the ecstatic—revelatory significance of the words and sentences" (ST, I, p. 144). Tillich's argument at this point depends on his doctrine that, apart from knowledge based on historical fact, on reasoning and on experiment, there is also what he calls "revelatory knowledge", with the help of which we gain access to domains of reality forever closed to science. The advantage of such a theory lies in the opportunity it provides of withdrawing from the criticism of science any beliefs which such criticism might endanger. "Ordinary knowledge cannot interfere with knowledge of revelation" (ST, I, p. 144). If there is only one kind of knowledge, we have to bring all our theories into direct relation with one another, contradictions and incoherence being ruled out; but if there is more than one kind of knowledge, this restriction need not hamper us. The theory that there are independent forms of knowledge is of course a psychological theory, and as much in need of justification as the old theories which explained human behaviour by the invention of a number of independent faculties. I shall return to this important issue in the next chapter.

Tillich faces the traditional problem of Christology, namely how Jesus can at the same time be both fully man and fully God, and yet genuinely one person. Those who do not accept Jesus's divinity will reply that the whole thing is an absurdity; that nobody in his senses should try to solve such a pseudo-problem; that the real problem is how such a contradictory conception ever got into the minds of rational beings, and that this is a problem for the psychologist and the historian. Tillich, however, holds that Jesus was the bearer of "The New Being" in that, unlike other men, he was completely united with the "ground of his being and meaning", and therefore "possessed himself completely" and could in consequence "surrender his finitude", including his "knowledge" and his "perfection" when he sacrificed himself (ST, I, p. 148). Commentators have repeatedly observed that to allege in this way that Jesus was not estranged from the ground of his being contradicts Tillich's doctrine that all existence involves such estrangement ("existence is separation") and so does not solve the problem of Christology but "removes Jesus from the human condition".[11]

In one of his sermons Tillich goes so far as to declare that accepting Jesus requires neither belief in any specific doctrines nor adherence to particular ethical principles:

> Forget all Christian doctrines . . . when you hear the call of Jesus. Forget all Christian morals . . . when you come to Him. Nothing is demanded of you—no idea of God, and no goodness in yourselves. . . . What is demanded is only your being open and willing to accept what is given to you, the New Being, the being of love and justice and truth, as it is manifest in Him Whose yoke is easy and Whose burden is light (Sh, p. 102).

He asks: what are the labours and burdens from which Jesus

interesting

promises us rest (Matthew 11:25–30)? He answers, surprisingly: "The burden He wants to take from us is the burden of religion" (p. 95)—not merely the religion of the Jews of the first century, but religion at all times. Tillich believes that man feels a conflict between his animal needs and his higher aspirations, and that this causes a good deal of "anxiety, restlessness and despair", which in turn have given rise to religion which is to overcome them. But religion demands that man accept as true "things he cannot believe". If he then becomes sceptical, he finds that he cannot live in such "emptiness" and "returns to the old yoke in a kind of self-torturing fanaticism and tries to impose it on other people" (p. 97).

As generalizations these statements are questionable. Many Christians have little difficulty in believing what is required of them; and others have acquired a total indifference to religion and have not returned to it. Tillich seems to invent the facts required for his argument that Jesus frees us from religion by not requiring us to believe anything in particular, and by coming only to bring us peace of mind. The yoke of Jesus "is not a new demand, a new doctrine, or new morals, but rather a new reality, a new being, and a new power of transforming life . . . . It is being, power, reality, conquering the anxiety and despair, the fear and restlessness of our existence" (p. 99). We have only to "accept" it. "The true—namely the truth of our life and of our existence—has grasped us. We know that *now*, in this moment, we are in the truth". We do not, then, know the truth: much better, we are *in* it. And "we know that now, in this moment, we are in the good, in spite of all our weakness and evil". We are, then, "in the good", although we may be no better than before. And not only are we in the good, the good is also in us: "The good of life is in us, uniting us with the good of everything" (p. 100).

Thus, by the use of prepositions meaningless in this context and of all but meaningless abstractions, Tillich constructs his case. Many common words have numerous meanings, for if a different word had to be used to denote every different thing, event or situation, the burden of language upon the memory would be intolerable. In normal intercourse the relevant meaning is clear from the context or situation in which the word is used. But in a context which consists almost entirely of equally ambiguous words, there is no possibility of determining the meaning. Yet the familiarity of the separate words makes the unwary reader suppose that there must be some meaning behind the whole proposition.[12] In the previous chapter we saw something similar to all this in the writings of liberals who 'reinterpret' New Testament narratives into obscure philosophemes (cf. above, p. 70); and we shall meet the same thing again from Bonhoeffer and others later in this volume. We do not know what Tillich is offering us, but we gather that it is a free gift if only we can accept it. None of the consolatory virtue of Christian belief has been diminished, only the logical implications. We can still expect to receive the same benefits, but need no longer try to adhere to any particular code of conduct or to understand the incarnation, the miracles, the resurrection. We can still rely on Jesus to guarantee our future if only we accept him. But what such acceptance implies remains unclear. All this is an appeal to the emotions rather than to the intellect and aims at generating a feeling of assurance and security partly by playing on fear, the escape route from which is acceptance of the beliefs offered. In previous centuries it was primarily fear of hell that was exploited in this way. In an illuminating book on conversion and brain-washing, William Sargant has recorded that, in the eighteenth century, John Wesley

> found it easy to convince large audiences . . . that a failure to achieve salvation would necessarily condemn them to hellfire for ever and ever. The immediate acceptance of an escape from such a ghastly fate was then very strongly urged on the ground that anybody who left the meeting 'unchanged' and met with a sudden fatal accident before he had accepted this salvation, would pass straight into the fiery furnace. This sense of urgency increased the prevailing anxiety which, as suggestibility increased, could infect the whole group.[13]

Earlier in the same century, Jonathan Edwards in America likewise preached hellfire, but "always bore in mind that an escape route, consisting of the main belief to be implanted, should be left open."[14] Today, when belief in hell has dwindled, evangelists can still appeal to fear of death—as when Dr. Billy Graham tells his audience that "in ten years a quarter of you will be dead"[15]—and in particular to fear of death from the hydrogen bomb. Dr. Graham says: "I keep having the feeling that God will allow something to fall on us . . . unless we return to him."[16] Tillich, as we saw, plays on the same fears, even if in less crude a manner.

Chapter Five
Disparagement of 'Scientific Truth': Collingwood

As we saw in the previous chapter, to hold that there is more than one kind of knowledge or truth is of some advantage to the religious apologist, for it means that he does not have to bring all his ideas into direct relation with each other, and so has no need to rule out contradiction and incoherence. In this way he may reach, with the American philosopher George Santayana, the pleasing conclusion that "what is false in the science of facts may be true in the science of values".[1] R. G. Collingwood was a strong advocate of the view that truth comprises separate species. He tried to comfort the Christian and humble the scientist—not by arguing that the latter holds mistaken views, but by urging that non-scientific methods of investigation and reasoning are more appropriate to some of the fields in which we have been inclined to accept the authority of science.

Collingwood put his case in his *Speculum Mentis* (Oxford, 1924). The book achieved some popularity after the second world war and was reprinted four times between 1946 and 1970. A recent commentator describes it as "extremely readable" and as "the best worked out and also the most important" of Collingwood's philosophical works;[2] and so I have taken it as the basis for the following examination of his thesis.

To deny the claims of science as a means of ascertaining truth, and to make a counter-claim for religion, would be to take sides in an old controversy and on very unfavourable terms. Collingwood does not offer us the old conflict between science and religion, but rather five combatants—art, religion, science, history, and philosophy—each competing for "the prize of truth" (p. 42); and he does not present himself as the champion of religion, but as the arbitrator. In his whole discussion, he is careful to avoid falling into statements which could be directly denied and demolished by reference to notorious fact, and preserves the vagueness of abstract and figurative writing. So long as the reader can clearly recognize that essential beliefs are being vindicated, he will not object to incoherence in the supporting argument. Indeed, the more impenetrable it is, the more he is likely to be impressed. What is needed, therefore, is a protective screen of elusive verbiage illuminated periodically by passages of emphatic reassurance whose meaning, to the naive reader, seems unmistakable. Here is some of the verbiage:

> Art is not pure language, but thought failing to recognize that it is thought, mistaking itself for imagination. Religion is not a morbid growth of language, but a dialectical development of art, art realizing that it is not bare imagination but assertion, and then proceeding to misinterpret its own assertions and to suppose itself to be asserting the image or word when it is really asserting the meaning of the word (p. 154).

Whereas this is the merest hocus-pocus, the essential message is contained in passages such as the following:

> It is difficult to see that religion in its essential form can ever achieve anything higher and more ultimately or absolutely satisfying than the twin conceptions of the Incarnation and the Atonement (p. 139).

> Religion is an infinitely precious achievement of the mind and an unfailing revelation of truth (p. 153).

The reader will, however, hardly be able to overlook the fact that such assurances are not made good; for Collingwood finds it impossible to accept many propositions of religion without reinterpretation. He thinks that the assertion that the world was created in seven days was in fact "never really meant to be so understood, but was always a symbol of something else"; and that statements in the New Testament to the effect that the end of the world is rapidly approaching are only "the imaginative symbol of a spiritual event which really did take place" (pp. 147–8). Not Christianity but "some new interpretation of Christianity" is what he regards as "the only hope for the world's future" (p. 38). Hence he has to eliminate religion, and art too, from the contest for the prize of truth—not, however, on the ground that they are erroneous, but because the sacred story, like the work of art, "points beyond itself to some hidden mystery of which it is the symbol" (pp. 242–3). It is science that is the contestant that fares really badly in his analysis. "Science", he says, "asserts not the actual truth, but what would be true if something were true which is laid down as an hypothesis" (p. 183). The theory to which he is gradually working his way is that science is a mere tissue of hypotheses having little or no relation to concrete fact. "Scientific fact", he says, is "a fact purged of its crude and scientifically scandalous concreteness . . . and reduced to the status of a mere instance of a rule" (p. 186). This suggestion that the scientist can see his 'facts' only as exemplifications of general laws is quite untrue. The biologist, geologist, and astronomer, for instance, record events as well as explain them; they seek to find out what happens or has happened. Collingwood, however, insists that the "concrete basis of all scientific abstraction is something which science itself never grasps, namely individual or historical fact" (p. 185). A scholar who has written a very sympathetic appraisal of Collingwood's early writings, nevertheless concedes that here he seems to be "describing something he does not quite know enough about".[3] Collingwood obviously supposes that abstraction consists merely in eliminating certain characters of real objects from the mind. It is true that an insect must have six legs and antennae, whereas an arthropod need not. But since the phylum includes groups other than the class Insecta, when we test propositions which purport to be true of the former, we have more, not fewer particulars to review. The characters common to the phylum and which constitute its definition are few in comparison with the number found in an individual specimen; and if one wishes to use the term properly and understand propositions about arthropods, one must be acquainted with some dozens of different specimens selected from the most divergent types.

Collingwood's misconception is common among writers who, like himself, have tried to distinguish science (as abstract) from history (as concrete). Windelband, for instance, wrote in 1894:

> It is indeed true that the human understanding can represent to itself many things at once only by attending to the common content of diverse particulars. But the more it strives in this way to reach a concept and law, the more it leaves the particular as such behind, forgets and abandons it.[4]

One thing that bedevils the discussion is this assumption that a scientific concept is a momentary configuration, a mental representation of many things *at once*, as Windelband here says. Ernst Mach insisted, against this, that every concept has its sometimes quite long and eventful formative history in the mind, and that its content can be expounded only very inadequately by means of a momentary thought. A word denoting an abstract idea may, he added, call up a particular individual image or memory, but this needs to be supplemented by a host of others which can come into consciousness only gradually and over a period of time. By means of such associative enrichment, the individual momentary representation can gradually develop into a concept.[5]

Mach's views have been further developed by Englefield, who has argued that there is in fact no fundamental difference here between a general and a particular idea; that even the latter consists of a collection of memories. An object familiar to me is known from many different aspects, set against many different backgrounds, in all kinds of positions. Each of these remembered aspects may revive in me any or all of the others, and my 'idea' of the object consists of the whole collection. But this revival cannot occur in an instant, but must be spread over a period of time.[6] A house, for instance, looks very different when seen from the front, side or back; and the view of it from the inside is again different. The real house presents these different *aspects*, but they can be perceived only one at a time. It is the work of the brain to link the memories of such aspects so as to form a *conception* more completely representing the real thing. If every view of the thing which I obtain, every observation of its behaviour, is duly recorded in my memory, it is plain that, when I subsequently think of the thing, any or all of these memories may be revived. But they can be revived only in succession, just as the perceptions were only to be had in succession. My idea of a person, book or place well-known to me is not something that I can recall in its entirety at will and then as easily dismiss, but a many-branched chain of memories which present themselves to my mind in turn, as the accidents of association and the promptings of momentary interest determine.

All this is even more true of ideas of classes of things, but to suppose the contrary has been a common misconception. Locke, for instance, held that "the general idea of a triangle . . . must be neither oblique, nor rectangle, neither equilateral, equicrural, nor scalenon; but all and none of these things *at once*".[7] Thomas Reid likewise insisted that "the contents of a general proposition may be brought forth, ripened and exposed to view at our pleasure *in an instant*".[8] He must have had in his mind some very inadequate substitute for the real generalization and have been misled by it. Hume noted more justly that, although our conceptions often consist of some kind of memory at a particular moment, this single memory is surrounded by a host of associated memories which are available on recall and which thus exist at any rate potentially, "in power", as he put it.[9] William James referred to these background ideas as "the fringe";[10] and at the turn of the century Ribot very topically made the fringe unconscious.[11] It may well be the feeling that an adequate store of memories is in fact available that gives rise to the illusion that an idea really somehow includes them all at the same moment. It is certainly the case that many authors even today betray, when they write of ideas, that they think of an idea as a precise and particular image which can be recalled in a moment and contemplated entirely.

For Collingwood history, because it deals with concrete individual fact, is the intellectual activity which overcomes the abstractness besetting science. Whereas "the abstract concept", the coinage of science, is "confessedly an arbitrary construction", history really means what it says when it points to fact as its object (p. 243). Against this assertion of the superior status of history Englefield has adduced the following example: it is a historical fact that Socrates drank a certain quantity of hemlock and died, and a scientific fact that the plant called hemlock contains a poisonous substance which can be extracted and administered with lethal effect. The scientific fact is known in much greater detail than the historical one, which is accepted only on the evidence of a few old documents. If the two 'facts' were incompatible, it is the historical one that we should discard.[12]

Only with the aid of a large number of scientific facts, in the form of generalizations, can we reconstruct the past. Geology could not begin to describe the history of the earth until geologists had observed, based generalizations on, and projected into the past, processes going on at the present time. Inference is essential to recovering the past, and we can make no inference from recovered pottery to an irrecoverable potter unless we first know something of the normal relationship between craftsman and craft; nor from the ruins of a temple to the forgotten deity that once was worshipped in it without independent knowledge of deities and temples. Such historical reconstructions once accomplished are available to assist in the interpretation of new data; but ultimately all this train of inferences must be based on our knowledge of the contemporary world. Even Windelband admits that it is only in terms of generalizations based on our own experience that we can explain or understand remote events.[13]

I have shown elsewhere that the distinctions between science and history of which so much has been made this century go back to Schopenhauer, and that Collingwood is indebted to him on this matter, although he misunderstood and distorted him.[14] Collingwood and Croce made much of the fact that the major events in history are never repeated and for that reason cannot be made the basis of generalizations. They overlooked that these major events are compounded of approximately recurrent minor ones combined in different ways—the unique Thirty Years' War, for instance, is an aggregate of battles, sieges, negotiations, and so forth, each one of which resembles, to some extent, the others. No two things are exactly alike; two forests or two oaks in one forest may nevertheless, for many practical purposes, be regarded as equivalent. The number of leaves on each of the two oak trees is not identical; and the leaves themselves are not exactly alike, but may be regarded as compounded of certain materials of uniform composition. At each stage of this analysis we accept some constituent as uniform and direct our attention to the differences that belong to the higher grade or level of composition; but we can always detect differences in whatever elements we have for convenience adopted. And what is true of things is equally true of events. The large scale events are hardly to be found repeated, but we can divide them up into repeatable parts. What makes historical investigation so difficult is not any fundamental peculiarity of method but the extreme complexity of its subject matter. Even a simple event, like the fall of a tile from a roof, is not an instance of one general principle or law but the result of the interaction of several such laws. The general processes involved are perhaps not numerous, but the way in which at a particular time and place they combine cannot be foreseen and may be hard to establish even in retrospect. It is true that, where human motives are involved, we might be supposed to be better equipped for the task of both ascertaining facts and explaining them. But the complexity of human behaviour more than offsets this advantage, and those sciences which are commonly called 'exact' are not the anthropological ones.

Collingwood's final conclusion is that not even history escapes completely from the abstractness of science, and that this is achieved only by philosophy. The steps which bring him to this conclusion do not here concern me. What I find astounding is that he declares at every turn that "our enemy is abstraction" (p. 268), that "all abstraction is dogmatism" (p. 288); for his own book can only be called abstraction run mad. He uses, for instance, the word 'art' as if there were some type of activity or product to which it applied, not merely a miscellaneous group of activities with little in common. It may therefore be worthwhile to mention some of the differences between the arts.

The poet composes a word sequence, either completing it in his mind before he writes, or dictating or writing while he is composing. The written work may then be read silently or recited. The painter conceives a picture, paints it and may possibly get it reproduced or published, and then it is contemplated by an audience. The second phase here (execution) has nothing in common with execution in the previous case, as the poet requires no special skill to put his invention into writing. The employment of an amanuensis would not in any way detract from his reputation, whereas the painter cannot employ a draughtsman to execute his ideas and yet himself claim credit for the finished product. The musical composer, like the poet, may compose first and then record, or he may write as he composes, although the process of recording music is quite different from that of writing words and is much less easy to dictate. Furthermore, unlike the painting, the poem must be read and the music rendered; and in the case of music this requires a performer, often many. Sculpture resembles painting except that it is not usually reproduced so easily. Architecture is so different from the other arts that a whole company of expert executants intervene between the creator and the final audience.

I have mentioned only the obvious external differences, but the psychological processes involved (those underlying the act of creation, those of the different types of executant, and the effects of the finished products on the audience) are all different. In as much as they are all human psychological processes they must have much in common not only with each other but with all kinds of other human activities not usually classified as artistic. But that they have anything important in common which distinguishes them as a whole from all other human activities, such as religion, science, politics, and so on, can be regarded merely as an assumption based on the common use of the word 'art' to cover them all.

As for 'science', there are many methods of investigation and scientists employ every one which ingenuity or luck can suggest. It is the merest fantasy to suggest that there is one method for science and another for history. The archeologist does not employ the same technique as the astronomer, chemist, or biographer, but all alike make observations, with the aid of all the appliances that are available, and classify, and generalize and construct hypotheses. It is not only the scientist who employs this method, but everyone who runs a business, follows a profession and conducts his life in an orderly and systematic way. What distinguishes one man from another is merely the accuracy and skill with which he does these things. Collingwood observes like the rest of us; he classifies the data of his observations like any other scientist, only his classes are based on fanciful analogies; he generalizes all too readily, without the restraint and self-criticism that characterize the more successful scientist. And no scientist is more prolific in hypotheses than he. What he wants to do is to classify human intellectual activities—not so much for any practical application, but with a view to enhancing the prestige of one professional activity and diminishing that of another. As a lecturer in philosophy and in history, and later as Waynflete Professor of Metaphysics, he was naturally concerned with the standing of these subjects.[15] He did not realize that the classification of intellectual activities is the concern of the psychologist, that it can be seriously attempted only on the basis of biological investigations, and is therefore as scientific as the science he would fain discredit.

Commentators on *Speculum Mentis* write much on its relation to the views of Hegel and Croce and to other of Collingwood's own works. His very questionable propositions are frequently glossed with others equally questionable, while a few appended reservations suggest competence and independence in the commentator. A recent whole volume of essays on Collingwood exemplifies all this, although it is refreshing to find one contributor declaring that what, according to Collingwood, philosophy has which art, religion, science and history lack, turns out to be "surprisingly thin",[16] and another repudiating his principle that "to abstract is to falsify" on the ground that "without abstraction there can be no thought".[17] It really is rather obvious. I may say that I had chicken for lunch and for practical purposes be understood. But a complete idea of the process of ingestion and digestion could appear possible only to the ignorant.

"It is th merest fantasy to suggest that there is one method for science and another for history'

Chapter Six
Christianity Without Religion: Bonhoeffer

Dietrich Bonhoeffer was hanged in a concentration camp in 1945. His writings in prison in the final two years of his life have repeatedly been called provocative and challenging,[1] and he himself confessed that he often took fright at his own ideas.[2] The editor of a 1967 symposium on him declared that the immense popularity of J. A. T. Robinson's *Honest to God* was "due in the main to the revolutionary power in Bonhoeffer's thought, from which it so freely draws".[3]

Bonhoeffer was a pastor of the 'Confessing Church' ('bekennende Kirche') and lecturer in theology at the University of Berlin from 1931. From the first he opposed Naziism and the 'German Christian' movement influenced by it. As a result, permission to continue his university teaching was withdrawn from him in 1936. He took up an appointment in America in 1939, but with characteristic courage and dedication returned to Germany before the outbreak of war because he could not bear to sit in security while his fellows suffered under Nazi rule. During his imprisonment he affirmed (pp. 129, 173) that he had never regretted his decision to return. In 1940 he was forbidden to speak in public, and in 1941, to publish. He was arrested by the Gestapo in April 1943, and, after the failure of the attempt on Hitler's life in July 1944, documents were discovered which implicated Bonhoeffer as active in the German resistance. He was in consequence transferred from his Berlin military prison to a concentration camp and hanged only days before American forces liberated it. He was undoubtedly one of the bravest and most unselfish men of our time.

In his essay entitled 'Nach Zehn Jahren' ('After Ten Years') written at the end of 1942, when he was still free, he muses on the ten years of Nazi rule, "the great masquerade of evil" surrounding him, and asks: "who stands his ground?" in the face of it. He has no confidence in the efficacy of reason and writes of "the failure of 'reasonable people'", who, with the best of intentions, but naively misjudging the real situation, think that a little bit of reason will suffice to bend the warped timbers back into line" (p. 11). The foolish people who surrender their will to a leader and do whatever he requires are, he says, unteachable. They cannot be saved by education, but only by "an act of liberation. . . . The inner liberation of man, so that he comes to live responsibly in the sight of God, is the only real cure for stupidity" (p. 19). Nor, in Bonhoeffer's view, is moral purity a match for the power of evil; and conscience too is an unreliable guide when evil takes on so many specious and deceptive guises. The only way to defeat evil is "to risk doing a deed purely on one's own responsibility" (p. 12). What he has in mind is that it is sometimes necessary to do things which go against one's conscience and sense of duty. Treason and murder were repulsive to his moral consciousness, and yet subversion, even assassination was needed to cope with the Nazi evil. Reason, conscience, and duty do not, then, suffice in order to resist evil. The only person who stands his ground against it is, he says:

> the man whose ultimate criterion is not his reason, his principles, his conscience, his freedom or his virtue, but the man who is ready to sacrifice all these when he is called in faith and in exclusive allegiance to God to obedient and responsible action: the man who is responsible, whose whole life would fain be nothing but a response to the question and call of God. (p. 13)

While he is perfectly justified in saying that rational argument can do very little to enlighten the obdurate or deter the unscrupulous, nevertheless 'exclusive allegiance to God' in defiance of 'reason', 'principles', 'conscience', 'freedom' and 'virtue' has often led to behaviour of the fanatical kind. And there is the additional problem of how one is to know when one has received the 'call' to 'sacrifice' these things.

He goes on to say that the man of responsibility must above all act in such a way that the coming generation can live, and that this cannot be done by acting on rigid principles. "It is ever so much easier to see something through on the basis of a principle than from concrete responsibility" (p. 16). But this is not necessarily the case. Principles, whether good or bad, may be easy or hard to act on. Probably he means that it is easier to decide what should be done if one has merely to apply an inflexible rule, if one believes that a few rules will cover all cases, instead of trying to determine in each case what action seems likely to bring about the most good and the least harm. If this is what he means, it is true; but the latter course of envisaging the probable consequences of alternative actions certainly involves the use of reason, and it is not obvious that it involves anything else. In the prison letters—as their published title *Widerstand und Ergebung* (Resistance and Submission) intimates—he reflects on "where the boundary lies between necessary resistance to 'fate' and equally necessary submission" (pp. 150–1). He finds that this boundary cannot be drawn from principle. But he does not suggest that reason is to determine the choice between the two alternatives in any particular instance. Caught up in a world war which "90 per cent of all people did not want, and for which they nonetheless sacrifice their property and their lives", he concluded that "the world is controlled by forces against which reason is impotent" (p. 204).

In his 'Nach Zehn Jahren' Bonhoeffer is particularly concerned with the problems then confronting Germans who, he says, had come to believe in obedience to the authorities, in readiness to sacrifice themselves for the sake of their country, and in defending the law. In consequence they could not see that such attitudes could be exploited by the authorities and that it is sometimes necessary to take upon oneself the responsibility and risk the consequences of disobeying authority. He concludes:

> Civil courage can grow only from the free responsibility of free men. Germans are only now beginning to discover what free responsibility means.

One might suppose that discovering this depended on the use of one's own conscience and one's reason. But this is not Bonhoeffer's idea, for he continues:

> It depends on a God who demands the free venture in faith of responsible action, and who promises forgiveness and consolation to him who thereby becomes a sinner (pp. 14–15).

Implicated as he was in conspiracies for subversion, even assassination, he clearly felt that he was a sinner and needed forgiveness. His biographer Eberhard Bethge has distinguished five different stages of escalation open to Germans who resisted National Socialism, from passive resistance to the final step of active conspiracy. Bethge stresses how difficult it was for anyone of the evangelical Lutheran traditions to take this final step, as those traditions did not provide for anything of the kind. In that last stage there was no protection by the Church and no apparent justification of something outside all normal contingencies. And he notes that Bonhoeffer was one of the very few church officials on the Protestant side who nevertheless took that final step.[4] The atheist might say that it is quite rational to kill a monster such as Hitler to save thousands of people and might ask whether there was in fact anything but reason and conscience which prompted Bonhoeffer. The answer is that his belief that he was inspired and supported by the ruler of the universe played a vital part in giving him the strength both to act as he did—mere rational conviction that such action was appropriate would not have sufficed—and to endure the consequences. Hence he reiterated that "Christ makes man not only 'good' but also strong" (p. 267) and that "in every emergency God will give us as much strength to resist as we need" (p. 22). He refers repeatedly to the psychological strains imposed by imprisonment and deprivation: "One gets used to the physical deprivations . . . almost too readily but one does not get used to the psychological burdens—quite the contrary" (p. 117). But he faces up to them with the thought that "this poor Earth is not our abode" (p. 123) and by recalling the doctrine of the bringing together of everything in Christ (Ephesians 1:10)—"a splendid and really consolatory thought" (p. 125). His need for comfort was real indeed:

> I often ask myself who I really am. Am I the man who keeps writhing under these horrible experiences here, and who breaks down into tears, or the man who hits out at himself with a whip and lets himself be seen by others (and even by himself) as calm, cheerful, composed and on top of it all, and lets himself be admired for it? (p. 118)

Bonhoeffer, then, finds that he can bear all things in faith (p. 129). But wherein does this faith consist? He realizes that the average man of today is not worried about immortality: "The individualistic concern for personal salvation of the soul has almost completely disappeared from us all" (p. 184). And he

"Is not justice and the kingdom of God on earth the centre of everything"?[6]

denies that Christianity involves belief in an after-life. It is not a "religion of salvation" in the sense of "salvation . . . in a better beyond" (p. 226). He is particularly drawn to the Old Testament because he finds it lacking such expectations and concerned only with redemption on this side of death: "Is the question of the soul's salvation even raised in the Old Testament? Is not justice and the kingdom of God on earth the centre of everything?" (p. 184). He thinks that the same is true even of the gospels and Pauline letters (p. 226), although some of his fellow theologians have politely but firmly pointed out that such a view of the New Testament is untenable.[5] He, however, thinks that we should read the New Testament from the perspective of the Old (p. 182), for we see in both "one and the same God" (p. 113). As a recent commentator has observed, for Bonhoeffer the Old Testament "guarantees the non-religious interpretation of the cross and the resurrection".[6]

Another aspect of Bonhoeffer's interpretation of the New Testament is his assumption that not merely its ethical teachings but also its record of conflicts long past are meant as references to the position of Christians in the twentieth century. St. Paul had a serious disagreement with Jewish-orientated Christians concerning whether gentiles who become Christians must accept circumcision (περιτομη). Bonhoeffer, as hostile to what he calls 'religion' as was Paul to compulsory circumcision, comments: "The Pauline question as to whether peritomē is the condition of justification means today, in my view, whether religion is the condition of salvation. Freedom from peritomē is also freedom from religion" (pp. 180–1). He does not say here merely that a parallel may be drawn between Paul's question and the question that concerned him, but that, in 1944, Paul's question 'means' the question at issue in 1944. As a commentator has said, he "speaks of religion as the present-day synonym of circumcision".[7]

It is remarkable how many Christian apologists are willing to drop what they call 'religion'. Tillich, we saw, thinks that Jesus "wants to take from us the burden of religion"; and Bonhoeffer stresses that modern man has abandoned not only belief in immortality, but nearly every other belief traditionally reckoned religious. He does not dissent from this modern attitude, but speaks in this connection of the adulthood of the world ("die

mündig gewordene Welt", (p. 216)—a phrase which, it has been
said,[8] is now becoming synonymous with Bonhoeffer's name—
and of the autonomy of man, meaning that "God as a moral,
political and scientific working hypothesis is abolished, overcome" (p. 240). Man has learned to cope with all questions of
importance without such a hypothesis (p. 215). The only way to be
honest is to recognize that we have to live in the world as if God
were not given, "*etsi deus non daretur*" (p. 241). We are, he says,
proceeding towards a time of no religion at all (p. 178). "What has
been the basis of all our 'Christianity' until this day is being drawn
away" (p. 179), and this raises the questions: What is Christianity,
and indeed what *is* Christ for us today? He goes on to moot the
possibility of "a religionless Christianity" and to ask "How can
Christ become the Lord of the religionless?"

Bonhoeffer clearly felt that he could not deny that what
generally passes for religion is outdated and inadequate, but it
seems that he was unable to do without his own emotional attitude to the words in which the traditional religious ideas are
expressed. It is evidently the *words* that are important to him, for
he cannot make up his mind about the *ideas* they represent. He
says, for instance:

> What is meant by atonement, redemption, regeneration, the holy spirit,
> love of enemies, the cross and resurrection is all so difficult and so
> remote, that we hardly dare to speak of them any more. We suspect that,
> in the traditional words and rites, there is something quite new and
> epoch-making, but we cannot yet grasp it and put it into words.
> (p. 206)

He is continually suggesting that it is possible to get rid of all the
generally accepted beliefs and still have something to offer which
may be called Christianity, a non-religious Christianity, as he calls
it. But he cannot say what rites or what ideas will be left, only that
he is giving "much thought" to these matters (p. 182), that he is
thinking over the problem of "how the concepts of repentence,
faith, justification, rebirth, sanctification . . . are to be reinterpreted" (p. 185). Against Bultmann's attempts to discern truths
underlying New Testament 'myths', he declared:

> The New Testament is not a universal truth in mythological guise, but
> this mythology (resurrection etc.) is the thing itself! But these [my-

thological] concepts must now be interpreted in a way that does not make religion the necessary condition of faith (cf. 'peritomē' in Paul) (p. 221).

A critic has justly noted that "try as he might, Bonhoeffer did not get very far with his 'non-religious interpretation of biblical concepts.'"[9]

Whether Bonhoeffer could answer such questions or not, the need he felt for his religious emotion was in no way diminished; and in the conditions in which he was condemned to live, it is understandable that he needed spiritual support, and that he should suppose this need universal. The question for him was, therefore, how could this sustaining emotion be nourished if the old rites, traditions and doctrines were to be foregone. The name of this emotion was 'Christ' or 'God'—he often uses the two words almost interchangeably. In his imagination he saw the whole tangible framework of Christianity swept away, with Christ still illuminating and sustaining the efforts, the hopes, and the tribulations of secular man. That this Christ or God of whom he speaks is an emotional condition, linked to certain words and phrases, he cannot see or is not willing to admit.

That an emotional state is involved is suggested not only by his inability to be clear about the relevant ideas, but also by his statements that he frequently feels drawn by a "Christian instinct" to religionless people, and feels ill at ease when the religious start using religious terminology (p. 181). Many a non-Christian might share his emotions, though perhaps describing them in different terms; but with many Christians he would feel intellectually out of sympathy. We have already seen in the case of other apologists (above, p. 73) that little more than emotional attachment is involved—be it to ritual, to unclear ideas or even to mere words; and we shall be meeting the same phenomenon again.

Although Bonhoeffer frankly avowed that he found God a source of comfort and encouragement in the face of difficulty or disaster, he was equally emphatic that this is not enough (p. 181). God is not to be brought in only where human resources fail. If God is God, He must always be there and His presence must be signified at all times, otherwise He will gradually disappear from human life in proportion as purely human resources are extended.

- God suffers at the hands of sinful man
- God let himself be driven from the world to the cross
- Christians stand with God in his suffering, this is our faith

110   CHRISTIANITY WITHOUT RELIGION: BONHOEFFER

If God is important only where science cannot reach, if we need to resort to prayer only when it is useless to send for the plumber or the doctor, then His importance will go on diminishing as science advances. This feeling is understandable. Too much emphasis on God the comforter, on Christ the saviour, suggests a psychological need as the real source of the God-idea. And so he says that we should not use God as a stop-gap ("Lückenbüßer") for the incompleteness of our knowledge: "We are to find God in what we know, not in what we do not know. He would fain be comprehended by us not in our unsolved questions but in those we have solved" (pp. 210–211). But how do we find God in the problems we have solved? And how do we combine this with living in the world 'as if God were not given', which we must do if we are to live 'honestly'? I can see why he should wish to find another function for God which should not be affected by scientific discoveries. But he does not find it easy to tell us what this function is.

Bonhoeffer stresses, then, that we must live in the world as if God were not given; yet he also maintains that He is at its centre (pp. 211, 241). One student writes in this connection of the "subtlety of his dialectic".[10] Bonhoeffer is able to affirm the importance of the God whom we must, if we are honest, abandon as a working hypothesis, by giving God's absence from the world an alternative meaning—by no longer taking it to mean that man confronts all his problems with purely secular resources. It comes to mean instead that God suffers at the hands of sinful man:

> God lets himself be driven from the world onto the cross. God is impotent and weak in the world, and only because this is so is he with us and helps us (p. 242). Christians stand with God in his suffering. . . . Man is called upon to suffer God's suffering at the hands of the godless world (p. 244).

The only evidence he offers in support of this latter statement is what he considers believers in various narratives of the gospels and of the Acts of the Apostles to have in common. He lists some of the personages who figure there as rich or influential or simply as healthy in body and mind—the magi, the centurion at Capernaum, the rich youth whom Jesus loved, the minister of the Ethiopian queen (Acts 8), the centurion Cornelius (Acts 10), and others—and declares: "The only thing common to them all is participation in the suffering of God in Christ. That is their 'faith'"

(p. 245). And for him it follows that that should likewise be the faith of modern Christians. Here we are no longer asked to live 'as though God were not given', but—as a commentator has said, noting the contradiction[11]—to live in the sufferings of the God who is very much given and at hand.

Bonhoeffer of course claims that this view of God as impotent and weak in the world is substantiated by scripture: "The Bible points man to the impotence and the suffering of God" (p. 242). But even the most sympathetic commentators demur at this. One, for instance, protests that it would be necessary to say more, especially about the record of the Old Testament[12] (in the light of which we are, according to Bonhoeffer, to read the New). Any concordance will illustrate how frequently Yahweh 'thundered' and 'smote'. Admittedly some Old Testament authors, presumably by way of taking exception to such a view, represent Him as "a still small voice". But this shows how impossible it is to regard the Old Testament, let alone the whole Bible, as uniform in this important doctrine.

A. MacIntyre has argued that Bonhoeffer's idea that God is 'powerless' and that 'only a suffering God can help' must be understood from the context in which he lived:

> In Nazi Germany, and in the Europe of the 'thirties, the Christian role was at best one of suffering witness. The Nazi regress to gods of race made relevant a Christian regress to a witness of the catacombs and of the martyrs. There was available then a simple form in which to relive Christ's passion. Bonhoeffer lived it. And in all situations where nothing else remains for Christians this remains. But what has this Christianity to say not of powerlessness, but of the handling of power? Nothing; and hence the oddity of trying to reissue Bonhoeffer's message in our world.[13]

It is the figure of Jesus on which Bonhoeffer draws for his only explicit answer to the question 'what is God?', namely

> Encounter with Jesus Christ, the experience that here a complete reversal of all human existence is given, in that Jesus is 'there for others'. Jesus' 'being-there-for-others' is the experience of transcendence . . . Faith is participation in this being of Jesus . . . Our relation to God is not a 'religious' relationship to an entity that is as exalted, as powerful and as good as possible—that is no real transcendence—but our relation to God is a new life in 'being-there-for-others', in participation in the being of Jesus (pp. 259–60).

This is the foundation on which J. A. T. Robinson built. He wrote:

> Jesus is 'the man for others', the one in whom Love has completely taken over, the one who is utterly open to, and united with, the ground of his being. And this 'life for others through participation in the Being of God' is transcendence.[14]

One can understand what is meant by 'Life for others' but not by the phrase 'through participation in the Being of God'. Bonhoeffer seems to think that there is something specifically Christian about altruism, although in fact it is not even specifically human, as social instincts are always found in gregarious animals (cf. below, pp. 178 ff). He writes that, when an air-raid alarm sounds, "we Christians", unlike others, have other things to think about than anxiety for our own safety; we have, for instance, to help others around us keep calm. The moment that happens, "the situation becomes completely different" (pp. 209–10). Of course it does. An emotion such as fear is almost intolerable when one has to sit idly awaiting events. If one has a task to perform, the accumulated energy which goes with the emotion can find an outlet, so that the tension is relieved. And that the task envisaged by Bonhoeffer is altruistic in nature does not necessitate a religious basis for it. If a normal person observes another in difficulties, he has a natural impulse to go to his assistance (even when to do so involves definite risks), and the existence of such an impulse implies some instinctive tendency (cf. below, p. 179). The act of coming to the aid of somebody or some animal in apparent distress is pleasurable, it resolves the tension which has determined the action, just as eating and drinking resolve the tension of hunger and thirst.

My quotations have shown that Bonhoeffer's faith is essentially Christological. He wrote in 1940, while he was still free:

> To speak today of God's love for the world brings difficulties to those who are not content with mere formulas. It is clear enough that God's love for the world does not consist in making an end of wars, or in taking away poverty, need, persecutions and catastrophes of every kind.[15]

He adds that we are to find the love of God only in Jesus Christ. Hence his statement in the prison letters that, "if Jesus had not lived, our life would be meaningless, in spite of all the other people whom we know, respect and love" (p. 266). Well ac-

quainted though he was with New Testament scholarship, he
would presumably not have been prepared to admit that the 27
books of the New Testament contain not one but several different
Christologies. On the contrary, as we have seen apropos of his
views concerning an after-life, he interprets the New Testament in
the light of his own convictions. And although the life of Jesus
meant everything for him, he shows an almost total unawareness
of the problems his fellow theologians have experienced in
authenticating any given incident in that life as it is recorded in
the gospels. Only at one point in his prison writings is this issue
raised, namely apropos of Jesus's prayer in Gethsemane. Bonhoeffer expresses his surprise as to how the evangelists were able
to record it when, according to their own account, there was no
one present to overhear it, and when immediately afterwards his
disciples fled and left him, without returning, at his arrest.
Bonhoeffer helplessly asks his correspondent: "Can you make
some sort of comment on this for me?" (p. 137). It has been justly
noted that his "New Testament exegesis was . . . conservative",
quite unlike Bultmann's, which was "extremely sceptical".[16] He
praised Bultmann's intellectual honesty in giving wide publicity
to the destructive impact of liberal Christian scholarship on
traditional Christian tenets. Bultmann, he said, had let the cat out
of the bag, "the liberal cat out of the confessional bag", and cannot
be adequately answered simply by taking refuge in faith: "I find
Pharisaism of faith, which is drummed up against this by many
brethren, simply frightful". One must expose oneself to the
draught of fresh air that Bultmann has let in; nevertheless, the
window must then be closed again, otherwise susceptible Christians ("die Anfälligen") will catch cold.[17]

Bonhoeffer's influence will be obvious (as was Tillich's) to any
reader of *Honest to God*—to mention only one work of one author
who was beholden to him. Robinson there wanted to suggest a
meaning for the word 'God' which is acceptable to the modern
educated person. At the same time, unlike Bonhoeffer, he did not
want to discredit older and more traditional ideas of God. "If the
image of a God 'up there' . . . makes him real for people, well and
good".[18] So it does not matter what sort of 'image' we form of God,
so long as it makes him real for us. In other words—and here
Robinson is on common ground with Bonhoeffer—it is the

emotion linked with the word that matters, not the idea, as, for Robinson, the idea can be varied indefinitely. This is a weakness of theological apologetics that I am much concerned to stress in this book. However, the importance of emotion in Bonhoeffer's religious thinking is understandable in the light of his situation, even though emotions cannot serve to vindicate ideas. The course of action on which he embarked in order to resist National Socialism was so appallingly difficult that it could not have been sustained without the impelling force of strong moral emotion. The extent of his commitment makes it entirely appropriate that the authors of a recent study of the Christian Churches in Hitler's Germany have given him special mention, while—equally appropriately—insisting that his struggle against Hitler should not make us oblivious of the many men and women whose struggle in the same cause has left no record.[19]

Bonhoeffer's ideas have elicited an enormous amount of comment. The secondary literature listed at the end of the 1971 detailed study mentioned in note 7 of this chapter fills 20 closely printed pages. Bethge has noted that for many in the west he is "a menace to Christian identity and a destroyer of the Lutheran doctrine of the two separate kingdoms of Church and State"; whereas his 'religionless Christianity' is more popular in eastern Europe, as it offers Christians there a philosophy which they feel does not entirely cut them off from the officially approved attitudes in their societies; it delivers them "from the temptation to brick themselves up inside an ecclesiastical ghetto of defiance".[20]

What will remain permanently impressive about the letters from prison is the author's dispassionate and lucid account of the psychological processes that go with imprisonment. He observed and recorded what went on in the minds of his fellow-sufferers and in his own mind without a trace of self-pity. (He uses this English word (pp. 122f.) to designate a weakness to which he was determined not to succumb.) And all the time he tried to think out how what he had learned of the psychology of imprisonment could be applied for the relief of a future generation. To all this the following moving passage about Christmas in prison bears eloquent testimony:

At midday on 24th a dear old chap always comes here of his own accord and plays some carols on a wind instrument. But sensible people have found that the only result is that the prisoners break down, so that this day is made even harder for them to bear. . . . In earlier years quite a few of them are said to have started whistling and kicking up a row, presumably just so as not to be overcome by emotion. I'm quite sure that, with the misery that prevails in this institution, a more or less superficial and sentimental reminder of Christmas is inappropriate. A good personal message or sermon would be the right thing. Without something of that kind, music by itself can be positively dangerous. Please don't think that I have any fear of it myself. . . . but I'm sorry for the many young soldiers helpless in their cells. I suppose that one can never be quite rid of the pressure which weighs upon one because of the unpleasant experiences that every day brings. And probably it is right that it should be so. I am giving much thought to a fundamental reform of the penal system, and hope that one day my ideas can be put into effect. (pp. 126–7)

His was indeed a 'being-there-for-others'. He thought there could be no greater happiness than to know that one meant something to other people. This, he said, was no cult of the human, but simple fact: "What to me is the loveliest book or picture or house or estate compared with my wife, my parents, my friend?" He adds—and all this was written after the failure of the attempt to assassinate Hitler in July 1944, and thus at a time when he could no longer reckon to leave prison alive:

> Admittedly, only he who has really found people in his life can speak in this manner. . . . We must feel great happiness that, in our lives, this experience has been richly bestowed upon us. (p. 264)

Many of us can endorse this, quite irrespective of any metaphysical or religious beliefs we may or may not hold.

on Bonhoeffer:- "he thought there could be no greater happiness than to know that one meant something to other people"

Chapter Seven
Humanist Religion: Julian Huxley

Today we are familiar with Christians pleading for a revised Christianity which is much less precise than its predecessor. God in heaven has, as we saw, been converted by Tillich, followed by J. A. T. Robinson and others, into "the ground of all our being". Some humanists have likewise sought to replace traditional religious beliefs with what they call humanist religion; but have they thereby provided an acceptable alternative? Examination of the late Sir Julian Huxley's *Religion Without Revelation* will help to answer this question. It was first published in 1927, but my references will be to the revised edition issued in 1967, seven years before the author's death.

Huxley finds that the hypothesis of God has ceased to be scientifically tenable and is becoming a burden to our thought. But although we must give up God, this does not, he adds, mean abandoning all religion; for we may retain "divinity". "The stuff of divinity out of which God and all gods have grown and developed remains" (p. 4). He thinks that the hypothesis of gods was proposed to account for man's experience of the "quality" expressed by the term "divine". This quality seems to be simply mysteriousness:

> Some events and some phenomena of outer nature transcend ordinary explanation and ordinary experience. They inspire awe and seem mysterious, explicable only in terms of something beyond or above ordinary nature.

It is well-known that different things are mysterious to different people. Huxley is quite aware of this for he adds that "such magical, mysterious, awe-inspiring, divinity-suggesting facts have included wholly outer phenomena like volcanic eruptions, thunder and hurricanes", and "biological phenomena such as sex and birth, disease and death" (pp. 4–5).

Mystery, then, is relative to knowledge, and as Huxley later notes (p. 57), the more ignorant man sees nothing mysterious in many things which puzzle the man of science. The suggestion that primitive man found birth, sickness and death mysterious may perhaps be questioned. They were familiar enough and could in many cases be predicted. Indeed, men had or believed they had control over these things, and the mystery arose only when they did not happen in the usual manner. Certainly it was not such things as these that gave rise to the belief in gods or spirits. The normal behaviour of human beings was so completely taken for granted that it served as the model for all kinds of explanations of non-human phenomena.

Huxley finds that most of the phenomena he has listed as having been once mysterious have ceased to be so "as far as rational or scientific explicability is concerned" (p. 5). However, he adds that "many phenomena are charged with some sort of magic or compulsive power, and do introduce us to a realm beyond our ordinary experience." Such events and such experiences he calls "divine". This definition is very obscure. What does he mean by "compulsive"? And does he here use "magic" in the sense that anthropologists use it, that is to say of beliefs and practices erroneously adopted by ignorant folk on the ground of mistaken analogies for the purpose of controlling people and events?[1] It is obvious from what he says on later pages that he does not speak as a believer in magic. The distinction is important. Thus if we say that certain things are accomplished by witchcraft, we may refer to the real effects of a false belief, as when people, supposing themselves bewitched, fall sick and die; or we may be referring to the effects which the witch doctor claims to be able to produce. As Huxley accepts that magic is merely a primitive and erroneous set of notions, then it is clear that there are no 'phenomena charged with some sort of magic'.

It seems then that by "magic" he here means no more than 'inexplicable', 'awe inspiring'. And he in fact goes on to say that the divine is "what man finds worthy of adoration, that which compels his awe" (p. 5). Why should man adore what he does not understand? Moreover, adoration and awe are not the same, and Huxley shows awareness of this when he later says that awe has, as ingredients, "fear, wonder and admiration" (p. 56). Awe, then, goes with a sense of one's own helplessness or insignificance that may be linked with any of these three emotions, none of which constitutes adoration. One may be moved to awe by the eclipse or the comet, or even by the wonted spectacle of the starry heavens without adoring them. Furthermore, unless all men find the same things worthy of adoration, Huxley's definition fails and would have to be replaced by 'what John Smith or what Sir Julian Huxley finds worthy of adoration'. Otherwise what is divine for you is not divine for me. Much of the rest of Huxley's book is built up on his notion of the divine, and so we must try to be clear as to its meaning. He says:

> Much of every religion is aimed at the discovery and safeguarding of divinity in this sense, and seeks contact and communion with what is regarded as divine (p. 5).

Divinity, then, is a quality attaching to certain things, to things with which men seek contact and communion. But men in fact seek contact and communion with other men or other animals, not with vegetables or inanimate objects, unless they first suppose them alive and possessed of an essentially human nature. The magician seeks to control nature in all its forms, but he exerts his power so as to force obedience. If this is to be called seeking communion, then the engineer seeks communion with the river when he diverts its course and the physician seeks communion with the bacteria of disease when he tries to destroy them. Some kind of person must be the object of this desire for communion and contact. Hence if there is this desire to be in communion with the things which are divine, then these must be divine persons. The religion of the humanist, says Huxley,

> needs divinity, but divinity without God. It must strip the divine of the theistic qualities which man has anthropomorphically projected into it, search for its habitations in every aspect of existence, elicit it, and establish fruitful contact with its manifestations (p. 5).

Let us rewrite this passage according to the definition that the divine is that which man finds worthy of adoration:

> The religion of the humanist needs something worthy of adoration, but not an anthropomorphic god. It must seek and elicit the habitations in every aspect of existence of that which man finds worthy of adoration. And contact must be established with the manifestations of such things.

This seems to mean that we must, by hook or by crook, find something to adore, search everywhere for the adorable. Then how do we know when we have found it? Are the things worthy of adoration always mysterious? Why did men 'adore' the lightning, the earthquake, the pestilence? Did they become less adorable when their causes were better understood? If adoration is taken to mean an act of self-abasement in the presence of a powerful enemy, then the answer is perhaps 'yes'. But one cannot really adore an abstraction. The attitude of adoration, as that word is normally understood, can be adopted only towards another human being or some being supposed to have something at least analogous to the principal psychological attributes of a human being. As a Christian critic of Huxley has noted: "Surely we require a living object for devotion and sense of dependence".[2]

What Huxley says about prayer well illustrates his position. He sees no room in the religion of the humanist for what he calls "petitionary prayer", but he sees "much value in prayer involving aspiration and self-exploration" (p. 7). But while the expression of one's aspirations and exploration of one's nature can be, and in certain traditions has been regarded as a prayerful exercise, it is a very limited aspect of what is understood by prayer, and if—as in the case of what Huxley is recommending—it is to be unaccompanied by any belief in God, it can be conducted without being in any sense prayer at all. It is surely by now becoming obvious that he is among the many writers who wish to keep the outward forms of religion without being expected to accept all their usual implications. "A humanist religion", he says, "will have to work out its own rituals and its own basic symbolism" (p. 6), and "will of course continue to celebrate the outstanding events of personal and national existence" (p. 7). So there will still be wedding and burial services, and presumably humanist priests to conduct the ceremonial and preach the sermon.

Huxley claims that Christianity has "released vast human forces which have largely shaped the Western world as we know it." He supposes that a humanist religion could "release even vaster human forces", although he admits that he has not yet completely worked out the details of such a religion, and that there will have to be a preliminary period of "discussion and ferment" (p. 7). In fact ideas tend to canalize and direct forces, rather than release them. The energy which appears in the form of human behavior is released anyhow in one way or other. The function of the brain and nervous system is to direct this energy into forms of behaviour which are profitable to the animal or his species. How has Christianity directed the energies of western man? Huxley is aware that morals do not depend on religion (p. 64). He nevertheless claims that "the greatest change wrought by Christianity" in "the ethical history of man" has been "the dethronement of many . . . primitive values and their replacement by love, mercy, sacrifice and humility" (p. 142). Students of Church history will find this claim to be excessive, and can also point to the want of constancy in the weight attached to the several ethical principles proclaimed by Christians, which have also frequently been totally disregarded in historic practice. Westermarck noted that Christianity, like many other religions, has a far from uniform influence either on moral beliefs or on conduct. Religion, he said, "has inculcated humanity and charity, but has also led to cruel persecutions of persons embracing another creed. It has emphasized the duty of truthspeaking, and has itself been a cause of pious fraud. It has promoted cleanly habits and filthiness . . . "[3] One of the most prominent ethical principles enjoined by Christianity through the greater part of its career was the duty of belief; and in view of the emphasis laid on faith in a great deal of the New Testament, this is understandable. Westermarck recorded, following Buckle, that in the seventeenth century the Scottish clergy taught (presumably on the basis of 2 John 10) that food or shelter must on no occasion be given to a starving man unless his opinions were orthodox.[4] On the other hand, there is Paul's insistence in 1 Corinthians 13 that love is greater than faith; and there is the argument in the epistle of James—surely *pace* Luther no epistle of straw—that faith without works does not profit.

Huxley's account of "the realities on which religion is based" (p. 43) leads him to conclude that "the essential religious reality" is "the sense of sacredness" (pp. 49f.). "The normal man", he says, has an innate capacity for experiencing sanctity in certain events, "just as . . . he has for experiencing . . . fear, disgust or desire . . . , love or hate" (p. 55). There is thus a specifically religious emotion, which he refers to as the "religious sense or sentiment". He shrinks from saying that this "religious sentiment" is an instinct. "It is not", he says, "inherited as such, although certain inherited capacities, like fear and reverence, enter into it" (p. 108). But every emotion surely has an instinctive basis; for an emotion arises when an instinct is excited and has not yet been satisfied. If there is no religious instinct, religious emotions must be derivative in the sense that they may be traced to non-religious ones related to obvious instincts. For example, the devotee may feel towards his god the emotion appropriate to a trustful son in relation to his father. The religious form of the emotion may possibly be stronger since the imagination may have constructed an object superior to any real object of the emotion. Many of our ideas are necessarily dependent on the constructive work of the imagination. To be able to form some notion of the plague in Athens, we need not have witnessed it, nor any plague anywhere else. But the description of Thucydides is composed of many details each one of which recalls to memory some experience, and the work of piecing these together constitutes the act of imagining the scenes described. Those who have witnessed such an epidemic will the more easily appreciate the description, but anybody who is familiar with the human body and its common reactions will be able to form some conception of the total event from perusing the verbal description (cf. above, 84). Similarly, for my idea of a remote historical character of whom I have read or heard, I have to draw on my actual experience of persons who have the qualities which I suppose him to have had. Conceptions which men form of their deities can be constructed in the same way. The sense of humble dependence and complete trust, which is natural in the child toward a parent, may be inapplicable in the adult to any part of his natural environment. But the attitude can persist, and, if an ideal object can be provided, the attitude is ready and available for use.

The emotions involved may be composite, resulting from the combined effect of more than one instinct. Fear and respect may be involved, as well as the emotion associated with being under somebody's protection. Psychologists have discussed the matter often enough. William James, for instance, mentions fear of the supernatural as one variety of fear, and with the example of fear of ghosts. This, he says, can be evoked by a combination of loneliness, darkness, inexplicable sounds, especially of a dismal character, and

> a vertiginous baffling of the expectation. This last element, which is intellectual, is very important. It produces a strange emotional 'curdle' in our blood to see a process with which we are familiar deliberately taking an unwonted course. Any one's heart would stop beating if he perceived his chair sliding unassisted across the floor. The lower animals appear to be sensitive to the mysteriously exceptional as well as ourselves.[5]

Our instincts like our organs have been evolved in relation to our needs or to those of our ancestors; and it is clear from the above passage that James was able to see the relevance of an analogous instinct in other animals besides man.

When we speak of an emotion, it is profitable to consider the situation which excites it, and also the reaction (or at least the will to react). When an animal is attacked, the aggressor is the exciting situation, the defensive act or counter-attack is the natural reaction, and the emotion is anger or fear. In the case of sexual stimulation, the exciting situation is given by the aspect of a suitable mate, the reaction is pursuit and embrace, and the emotion is what is familiarly called love. It would be hard to say what the specific nature of any emotion was apart from the ideas and situations linked with it; for it is only these that can be clearly expressed. An emotion which is linked to them can be judged by various means as to its strength, but by no independent method as to its specific nature. Now Huxley maintains that there is a religious emotion. The exciting situation is anything which is held sacred—and this, he admits (p. 56), can include almost anything—the reaction, if any, is presumably religious behaviour, not clearly defined; and the emotion is a feeling of the sacred. This is really all too vague to serve as an explanation of anything. We all know that religion exists, that men do all kinds of things in its name and are stirred by powerful emotions in relation to the objects they worship and the rites which they observe. These differ from one religion to another, and the emotions are also extremely variable and range from elation to depression. When Huxley speaks of religious emotion he has in mind emotions such as fear, wonder and admiration which are characterized by negative self-feeling. But religion very often nourishes self-esteem by constructing an imaginary world-order in which the believer will be rewarded.

Some writers speak not of a religious instinct but of what they call 'religious needs'. If this is taken to mean the general psychological features which lead to the formation of religious beliefs and practices, we may regard it as the first thing that needs explanation. What are these needs, how do they vary in different individuals or in different times and social conditions; and what is their biological origin? What is sometimes called the religious instinct is often merely the instinct of a social animal which relies on its fellows and feels secure only when united with them, or at least with some of them. It is human support, human company and friendship that the human being instinctively seeks. And it is the human characters of the gods which make them an acceptable substitute. Considerable sophistication is required for belief in the Anglican Church's God 'without body, parts or passions'.

The religion advocated by Huxley has evolution as its "central hypothesis" (p. 5) and entails the "remodelling" of existing religious ideas: "In place of eternity we shall have to think of enduring process; in place of salvation in terms of attaining the satisfying states of inner being which combine energy and peace" (p. 7). Later he says that "evolutionary humanism" has taught him that "man's mind is a partner with nature; it participates with the external world in the process of generating awareness and creating values" (p. 188). In this connection he mentions his work with UNESCO, of which he became the first Director-General in 1946, saying that this was one of the contexts in which "the importance of this idea of participation, of co-operative partnership in a joint enterprise", had been brought home to him. He restated these ideas in the introduction he wrote to the English version of Teilhard de Chardin's *The Phenomenon of Man* (London, 1959). P. B. Medawar's review of this work includes severe criticism of what he calls Huxley's "mistaken belief that the so-called 'Psychosocial evolution' of mankind and the genetical evolution of living organisms generally are two episodes of a continuous integral process." Medawar finds that Huxley's conception of evolution is altogether "so diluted or attenuated in the course of being generalized as to cover all events or phenomena that are not immobile in time." He finds it ridiculous to attribute "cosmic significance" to such an imprecise idea.[6]

I have tried to show that Huxley can justly be charged with imprecision, and (returning now to his *Religion Without Revelation*) I would suggest that one reason why he is prone to it is his conviction that conceptual thought, of which in his view man alone is capable (p. 79), is free from images, and that these characterize only the lower grades of thinking (pp. 96–7). Without wishing to dogmatize about the nature of adequate thinking,[7] I merely suggest that the holder of such a view is more exposed to the danger of believing that ideas to which reality very imperfectly corresponds are adequate than is the thinker whose ideas consist of what Huxley calls "a succession of images and symbols" (p. 96).

A recent commentator has noted that, while Huxley's interpretation of his own "mystic and ecstatic experiences" as a religious transcending of the everyday world satisfied Huxley himself, his proposals for a new universal religion without God have found practically no acceptance.[8] My account has shown that, for Huxley, it is the emotions linked with words such as 'divine' or 'sacred' that matter, not the ideas these words stand for, as the ideas are vague and almost infinitely variable. It will be apparent to my readers that here he is on common ground with some recent Christian writers. Huxley wants to drop God but retain religion. Bonhoeffer wanted to drop religion but retain Christianity (without making plain what of Christianity will be left when religion has been disposed of). In both cases powerful emotions are linked with a word of indeterminate meaning. In like manner J. A. T. Robinson argued that it does not matter what 'image' we form of God, what we take the word to mean, so long as this image makes him real for us (cf. above, p. 113). Tillich, we saw, even declared that no idea of God at all is required of the believer. Most recently, Cupitt has argued, in effect, that we may construct our religion as we will. The gospel portraits of Jesus, he says, present us with "a challenge to religious creativity", and "the more diverse religious thought becomes the better." He says too:

> Christian faith is not an ideology, but a form of life, a passionate commitment to the quest for deliverance from the world, for salvation and spiritual perfection. Religious teachings prescribe the itinerary;

they show the course of the Path . . . Understood spiritually they become the means to inner liberation. God becomes our Saviour in so far as religious doctrines no longer constrain us externally but inspire and guide us inwardly.[9]

Such views, imprecise as they are, seem to have a powerful appeal to the many men and women, Christians and humanists alike, who have rejected traditional beliefs yet cannot accept that the universe is indifferent to man and his fate.

Chapter Eight
Miracles and the Nature of Truth

Discussion about miracles is bedevilled by the ambiguity of the word.[1] If a miracle merely means an event contrary to the normal order of things—something unusual, or something we cannot explain—then no one can deny that miracles occur. We are surrounded by so many things which most of us do not in the least understand that we become accustomed to the inexplicable, and that it *is* inexplicable becomes the last of reasons for discrediting an alleged happening. The most intelligible belief in miracles that is not merely belief in the occurrence of unusual or inexplicable things is belief in activities of invisible beings (spirits, demons, gods) who possess powers far superior to those of man. This belief is usually accompanied by the further belief that men can league themselves with these spirits (both with the good and the bad ones) and so borrow some of their powers. That views of this kind are still entertained by religious scholars is clear from the argument of Professor C. F. D. Moule that Jesus's "unique degree of unity with the will of God" effected his resurrection; "for it seems consistent with all we know of God" that "perfect goodness of character cannot be held by death".[2]

The practical question which allegations of miracle pose is: are we justified in disbelieving apparent facts or statements of them? For what reasons, apart from the question of the credibility of witnesses, are they definitely incredible? An example will help to explain the force of this question. I hear my father's voice outside the door, but only yesterday I saw him off abroad; and so I infer that what I took for his voice was a hallucination, or that someone is hoaxing me. Even if he walks into my room, I may believe myself to be dreaming rather than abandon the assumption that it is an illusion. At length his voice, his face, his manner begin to convince me that he is really there. My memory of yesterday's events is in conflict with my present experience, and I ask myself whether I actually saw him on the boat as it drew away from the quay, or whether he might have come ashore again without my knowing. My perplexity continues until the explanation is given which reconciles my two apparently irreconcilable experiences; for such contradiction is intolerable, and it is our nature to make every effort to remove it by means of hypotheses.

The majority of what are loosely called facts are really hypotheses, in that a large part of what we observe is supplied by our imagination, and what we supply depends on our knowledge and our habits of thought. This is true of mammals generally. For instance, the dog reacts to the small black patch in the bushes exactly as he would if he could see the whole cat (cf. above, p. 84). The fragmentary data given to the dog suffices to evoke in his mind an idea of the cat—an idea which consists of many memories of cats and of his dealings with them. Likewise, when a shadow flits across my table, I can infer that a bird has passed my window. If I am quick in getting to the window, I may see the bird sailing across my neighbour's garden. This is a fresh hypothesis, based on a new set of sense data, and is compatible with the first. What we call the evidence of our senses, then, consists in fragmentary data from which we infer the presence of objects. Some of these inferences are so well established that we have lost the capacity to doubt them. When some contradiction is presented to us, we have to revise our hypotheses. The compatibility or otherwise of two hypotheses can be recognized only if there is some means of bringing the two into relationship with one another. The more general their scope, the more likely they are to be involved with each other. Scientific investigation often consists in an effort to bring different hypotheses together to test their consistency. But this is a relatively recent sophistication. The primitive forest-dweller is prepared to revise his stock of hypotheses to fit every new experience. If there is an eclipse of the sun, he supposes that the moon has simply devoured it. If ten minutes later the reappearance of the sun gives the lie to this theory, he as readily explains that the moon has vomited it up again. This new theory reconciles all the observed facts for the moment, and that is all that matters, for it will be forgotten before it has the opportunity of becoming an obstacle in the way of further essays in explanation. Thus, for primitive man a 'miracle' was simply a remarkable occurrence and did not involve any inconsistency with nature. Such marvels might be explained quite simply as the acts of unseen superhuman personages, and were therefore perfectly explicable. The conception of a miracle as an event conflicting with natural laws is comparatively modern; miracles could not possibly be regarded that way until men had first conceived the notion of 'natural law'.

The savage, then, explains from hand to mouth, and, having little knowledge of the experience of others and still less record of the past, he is seldom troubled by the difficulty of making his different explanations harmonize with each other. Even when his theories do conflict he may be unperturbed, being not fully aware of the rational necessity to fit them together into a consistent system. I must not exaggerate the advance which civilized man has made in this respect, for it is not rare to hear today, from the same person on different occasions, explanations which go ill together. Nevertheless, I would suggest that, in historical times among civilized peoples, the need to organize one's beliefs into a coherent system without contradiction has been more clearly recognized; and that it has distinguished the wiser and more gifted persons of all ages.

Educated medieval people did not make up momentary hypotheses like savages, but constructed coherent systems of beliefs. They relied upon the truth of certain written authorities (e.g. the Bible, the Fathers, some writings from Antiquity), and they tried to harmonize them when they appeared to clash. They were probably not by nature more credulous than people of today, but their authorities gave them 'facts' and their system allowed inferences which are today unacceptable. Medieval zoological handbooks described not only familiar household animals, but also many fabulous ones, such as unipeds—men with one enormous foot which they used as an umbrella by lying on their backs in the rain. The Vikings found unipeds in North America, and the chronicle of Erik the Red's voyage records such sightings. The reason is that Erik and his crew believed that unipeds were likely in distant places, so they thought it quite reasonable to assume that the things they saw were unipeds.[3] Later navigators would have interpreted the data differently, and, certainly, the Pilgrim Fathers saw no unipeds. What we say we see depends, then, on what we expect to see, and if a number of people have the same habits of thought, they will supplement what is given to their senses with the same interpretive elements and so give the same report of an event. The number of witnesses, even their intellectual quality, counts for little in such cases.

This tendency to organize beliefs into a coherent system is biologically quite intelligible. It arises out of a need to understand phenomena so as to guide our behaviour. To achieve our various goals we need to predict the outcome of our actions, and our only basis for such prediction is our observation of the general pattern of consequences as experienced in the past. In the case of immediate goals, acting on false beliefs will normally lead to ineffectual behaviour and so to the prompt correction of the beliefs. But when our goals are relatively remote from our familiar environment, the tendency to organize our beliefs may result in the construction of fantastic ideologies. This can be illustrated by the rise and decline of the craze for persecuting witches. Witches were accused of leaguing themselves with evil spirits, in particular with the Devil, in order to harm or even kill man and beast. Persecutions did not assume craze-proportions until the publication (with papal support) of the first great encyclopedia of demonology in 1486. Society had long been conscious of a certain amount of non-conforming behaviour (social or religious) among its members, and this new systematic mythology about demons and their dealings with mankind seemed to explain all oddities of this kind in terms of an overall theory, just as Newton's theory brings together, under a single generalization, such superficially unrelated behaviour as that of the apple and the moon. The fear which was a concomitant of the wars of religion—Catholic and Protestant alike seeing the influence of demons in any beliefs but their own—meant that the whole system of demonology was not generally and seriously questioned until these wars came to an end in the mid-seventeenth century; and from that time, witchcraft trials ceased to be common. Our ancestors can hardly be supposed to have wished witchcraft to be a reality. Their belief was encouraged, rather than discouraged, by their fears.

Today it seems absurd that courts of law accepted evidence that old women were carried hundreds of miles in a few minutes on broomsticks, or by any other means the Devil might select, to join him in obscene frolics. But it was precisely because such beliefs were not capricious aberrations, but had their place in a coherent and consistent cosmology, that they appealed to the finest and most cultivated minds of the time. Bodin is a striking example. Contemporary critics of the witchcraft trials, repelled by the cruel judicial torture, might argue that some of the confessions on which victims were burned could not suffice to identify them as witches. But the central doctrine of the kingdom of Satan, and its war on humanity by means of demons and witches, was rarely impugned—for, as H. R. Trevor-Roper says, there was at that time "no substitute for such a doctrine".[4] He goes on to show that the witch craze ceased when the new philosophy of Bacon, Grotius, Selden, and—in particular—Descartes changed the whole concept of nature and its operations. Descartes' universal, mechanical, laws of nature made demons unnecessary.[5] Of course, the whole European population did not read Descartes. But the new philosophy was influential on those sections of society which wrote and read the books and furnished the judges. Trevor-Roper justly concludes from all this that "rationalism is . . . relative to the general intellectual structure of the time" (*op. cit.*, pp. 123, 176). Bodin and his like were being perfectly 'rational' in bringing their views on witchcraft into line with their general philosophy of nature. Such rationalism looks like madness to us, not because the inferences involved are illogical, but because the fundamental premisses have long since been abandoned. Once this had begun to occur, the evidence for witchcraft dwindled, and the defenders of its reality were hard put to explain how the miraculous signs of Satan's presence, formerly so abundant, could have so completely disappeared.

This seventeenth-century controversy shows that one cannot destroy belief in miracles by direct arguments; for there is no means of defining, by *a priori* rules, a credible belief. A belief is credible if it accords with an agreed understanding of nature. As man's understanding of nature changes, so different kinds of belief become (or cease to be) reasonable. Apart from our current picture of nature, our fears and desires may also influence us towards belief or scepticism. We tend to believe what we intensely fear (as we have seen in the case of beliefs about Satan), but where there is no such fear we may believe what we passionately desire. Under the stress of a stong emotion, our faculty of reason may lose control of the mind; belief is then determined by the emotions which work upon the material stored in the memory.

The importance that fear sometimes has in determining belief can be illustrated by reference to ideas about ghosts. The human—indeed the mammalian—brain is able to supply unperceived elements of a situation, to enlarge the aspect of the situation that is perceived by the senses, so that the animal's response may be adequate to the real situation, and not merely to the perceived aspect. When we are sitting in a room silently with other people whom we cannot see, we are nevertheless aware of their presence. We have formed an idea which represents all the environment (including the parts of it that are behind us). If we speak and get no answer, or turn round and find out that our companion is not there, we experience a shock. When in this way a man (or an animal) knows that there exists a certain feature in his situation, although it is not accessible to any of his senses, he nevertheless has a kind of awareness that can easily be described as a sensation. It is especially in the dark that our ideas of the general structure of the situation play a conspicuous part in our behaviour. In daylight we are constantly surveying our surroundings and so correcting our ideas, but in the dark we have to rely much more on our ideas as they remain from earlier experiences. Every sound or glimmer of light is utilized to correct our ideas, but if we greatly fear (or greatly desire) the existence of a particular event, we are easily led to infer its presence from the incomplete suggestions of a few sensations.

The history of the decline of belief in miracles seems to have taken the following course. There was originally no distinction between the normal and the miraculous, because the unsophisticated savage has no system of co-ordinated beliefs by which he can test probability. The concept of 'abnormal', 'miraculous', arises as such generalized systems arise, and is a consequence of applying them. When the system is unclear, then the distinction normal/miraculous is correspondingly unclear. As experience and knowledge grow in certain fields, some general principles come to be recognized within these fields, and systems of belief begin to develop. The power of comparing propositions and determining their consistency is slowly developed in relation to the most frequently repeated daily operations. The everyday affairs of life, by their more continual operation, their constant opportunity for testing and experimentation, form the nucleus of what may be called the secular attitude, where man foresees the consequences of his operations and feels surprise when his expectations are not fulfilled. It coexists for a long time with the religious and magical attitude, but reigns over different spheres of life. As the secular sphere extends with the increase of knowledge, that other region of incalculable events becomes isolated and specialized. It becomes separated in thought as the realm of the miraculous. Gradually it comes to be associated with certain special occasions or aspects of life. More and more, miracles acquire a religious significance. And when religious philosophy begins to take shape, miracles are regarded as the special medium of divine revelation.

Now as long as divinities were merely tribal appurtenances, there was no tendency to claim any monopoly of marvels. But when rivalry between different religions begins, the miracles of the rival have somehow to be discredited. The first stage in this direction consisted in admitting the reality of rival miracles, but declaring them diabolical rather than divine. The next stage consisted in a denial of the authenticity of any miracles save one's own. The Protestants in Europe denied the reality of the Catholic miracles, and the Catholic enemies of the Jansenist Port-Royal refused to credit the miracle of the Holy Thorn.[6] Mutual criticism on the part of the champions of rival faiths tended to undermine and discredit the whole system of miracles. Attention was more and more directed to the possibility of error and fraud. Even those who could see no reason for rejecting miracles altogether could not help noticing their growing infrequency. This was sometimes explained by supposing that they ceased to be necessary once Christianity had gained definite ascendancy in the world.[7] From the eighteenth century, many apologists have gone even further. They reject ecclesiastical miracles from the second century onwards, and defend only the miracles ascribed to Jesus and the apostles. As J. M. Robertson noted, this thesis "is the childish one that in an age in which all cults claimed miracles, and none scrutinized them, we are first to accept Christian prodigies and reject all others, and then to reject all post-apostolic Christian prodigies but stand firm to the earlier".[8]

The attempt to reject superstitious beliefs on grounds of scientific incredibility is not an exclusively modern undertaking. Lucretius, moved by horror at the cruelties resulting from superstition, tried to dispel by rational criticism all fear of the mysterious powers of the world. In order to dispose of the innumerable magical and miraculous beliefs, he tried to build up a complete and satisfying picture of the universe which should serve as a model and a criterion for the checking of all reports. That which should be reported contrary to this scheme of things was incredible and worthy of instant rejection.[9] Thus he insisted that the gods lived in tranquillity remote from man and his world, and would certainly not interfere in his affairs. From this premiss, events alleged to be miraculous are inconsistent with the nature of the universe, and so do not merit belief. But this inconsistency can be certainly recognized only by one who is perfectly acquainted with the constitution of the universe.

Had Lucretius been able indeed to tell us what can and what cannot come into being, perhaps we should have heard no more of miracles—always supposing that everybody had heard and understood him. But this was of course beyond his power, and every attempt to discredit the belief in supernatural manifestations on earth was always met by the argument that, nothing being certain, we cannot be sure that this thing did not occur. The improbability of an event may be admitted, but this does not justify our confident rejection of it. One must have, the argument goes, an extraordinary confidence in one's own conception of the universe to be able to determine without regard to the evidence that the report of an event—however remarkable or even miraculous—is false.

Hume, facing the same problem, was less optimistic than Lucretius, though he too supposed that he had found an argument which really did dispose of beliefs in miracles.[10] All belief, he says, is founded on experience, and we believe human testimony only because we know from experience that it is in the main to be relied on. But our knowledge of the natural determinants of things and events is also founded on experience. When we are presented with an incredible report, there is a contradiction between that impulse which bids us accept the testimony and that other which bids us believe our memory of the normal processes of nature. Our experience of natural events is opposed to the acceptance of the report. Our experience of human testimony may be opposed to the rejection of the report. Hume says that in such a case we can only balance the opposed forces and follow the stronger impulse. He then compares in a general way the amount of experience which underlies on the one hand the trust in human testimony and on the other the belief in natural law. And he comes to the conclusion that "no human testimony can have such force as to prove a miracle and make it a just foundation for any system of religion". His point is that we have so much evidence that nature runs a uniform course,[11] with phenomena determined by natural antecedents, that, in any given instance, it is more likely that men should deceive or be deceived, than that supernatural determinants should be responsible for an alleged break in nature's uniformity.

The way in which our reception of a report depends both on our premises and on our familiarity with the phenomena reported is well illustrated by two examples which Hume gives. If, he says, all authors in all languages were agreed that, from 1 January 1600, there had been total darkness over the whole earth for eight days, then the fact ought to be accepted as certain and its causes sought. But if all historians of England agreed that, on the same 1 January, Queen Elizabeth had died, was seen by her physicians and courtiers both before and after her death, and, after being interred a month, again appeared and reigned for a further three years; then we ought to reject this testimony and hold that she did not really die in 1600 at all, but that the "knavery and folly of men" led to the report that she did.

Now there is an enormous difference in the weight of testimony in these two examples. In the first, the phenomenon is attested by the whole of mankind, in the second by a limited number of courtiers. Again, in the first example the witnesses need only to be aware of the difference between night and day, and so error could be due only to definite hallucination. A large number of people in the same circumstances, under the influence of the same emotions, may suffer from the same hallucination. But it is not possible that the whole race, scattered over the globe, ignorant of one another's doings, exposed at any given moment to a multitude of different conditions and emotions, should simultaneously be afflicted by a delusion of a kind seldom heard of even in cases of definite mental aberration. In the second example, however, a crucial item in the report is whether the queen was really dead. Even modern physicians are sometimes mistaken in this matter; courtiers and doctors of the past might easily have been.

But let us equalize the testimony by supposing that some remote settlement of people in the sixteenth century reported that the sun had set an hour before its time. This gives two improbabilities— that of some irregularity in gravitation, and that of a person being restored to life. It is obvious from Hume's remarks that he is too sceptical about the existence of supernatural entities to countenance supernatural influence in either case; and that, being relatively ignorant of celestial mechanics, he is prepared to entertain rather imprecise natural causes to account for an alleged gravitational irregularity. (There is, he says, considerable evidence for "the decay, corruption and dissolution of nature"). On the other hand, he is equally confident that resurrection from the dead cannot be effected by natural determinants but would constitute a "signal violation of the laws of nature". In this case, he not only disallows supernatural influence, but his greater familiarity with the phenomena of life and death has led him to assume that the relevant laws of nature are completely and finally known.[12] And being also well acquainted with the human character, he felt justified in attributing the report to "knavery and folly".

It is instructive to compare Hume's hypothetical example of a gravitational irregularity with the real irregularities in the movements of planets which were observed by Newton, and which he could not explain by means of his law of gravitation. As a theist, Newton did not hesitate to explain the phenomena by supposing that God intervened from time to time to put the planets back into orbit. Laplace later showed that the irregularities in question are not cumulative but self-correcting, and that there was therefore no need for any religious hypothesis. In all these examples, the reasoner's attitude to the phenomena has depended on his familiarity with them and on the premisses from which his reasoning proceeds.

As a final example I mention the explanation that Newton's contemporary, the philosopher John Locke, gave of the Flood recorded in Genesis. He accepted this event as established fact and looked for some additional fact, not recorded in history, which would account for it. In his essay *Some Thoughts Concerning Education*, he suggested (§192) that God "altered the centre of gravity in the earth for a time" and caused it to move in a path round the centre of the earth so as to make the deluge universal. He clearly thought that the Deity will have created the Flood by recourse to the same kind of mechanical and mathematical sophistication which, so the evidence suggested, underlay his creation of the universe. He will have nicely calculated the path along which the centre of gravity needed to pass so that in due sequence every dry region of the globe should be engulfed for sufficient time to ensure the drowning of all its inhabitants. One can only comment that a Deity of such sophistication might perhaps have found a fairer way of disposing of his wicked people. Was it really necessary to destroy the plant and animal worlds (apart from the few individuals taken into the ark) in order to punish mankind?

Some years ago there was considerable discussion of the allegedly miraculous recovery of John Fagan, a Glasgow docker, from cancer following prayers to the Blessed John Ogilvie, who was hanged in 1615. T. M. Parker, writing on this subject in the *New Statesman* (9 April 1976, p. 469) dismisses Hume's arguments against miracles on the ground that this "18th-century philosopher . . . believed that he lived in a tidy and uniform world, all the mechanisms of which had been explained by Newton". Hume in fact believed nothing of the sort. He wrote: "The essence and composition of external bodies are so obscure, that we must necessarily, in our reasonings, or rather conjectures concerning them, involve ourselves in contradictions and absurdities".[13] Parker also (23 April 1976) dismissed Newton as "a believer of a rather naive sort, to judge from his attempts to elucidate Biblical prophecies". Newton's total work surely shows very clearly that what is needed is independence of tradition, combined with strict dependence on fact and experiment. In his mathematical and physical inquiries Newton was original in that he broke with tradition, but he was rigidly conservative in his slavish dependence on experimental facts. In his writings on the prophets he seems to have been faithful to the tradition. It is of course true, as Dr. Mary Hesse has recently reminded us, that in science Newtonionism has been replaced by the quantum theory, "whose laws are not deterministic but statistical; that is, they do not determine occurrences of single events, but only proportions in large classes of events . . . According to quantum theory this is not merely a question of [our] ignorance . . . but of irreducible indeterminism in the events themselves". Contrary to what is often supposed, this does not make miracles more plausible, and Dr. Hesse is herself quite clear on this.[14]

I will attempt to summarize. Many beliefs are hypotheses which determine our behaviour. In this sense, a hypothesis is a rule for action; it tells us what must be done if a certain desired result is to follow. When I hear a familiar voice in the next room, I am acquainted with the actual sound of it, but I judge that it is the voice of E. This means that, if I now experience those muscular and other sensations which I should describe as 'going into the next room', I should thereafter experience those further sensations which would be described as seeing E. Thus knowledge of a truth is knowledge of what sensations follow other sensations, and a true belief is distinguished from a false one through being confirmed by experience. Furthermore, a true belief must be consistent with my other beliefs. If I assume the presence of E in the house to explain the voice, I must not at the same time assume that E is in the garden to explain the noise of the lawn-mower. Either E is indoors or not. I may not assume it for one purpose and not for another. Experience informs me that inconsistency in my beliefs has serious disadvantages for various important practical operations.

I am unable, perhaps, to go into the next room to verify my belief directly, but later I find a note there, written by E. My general conception of the order of nature informs me that this note, or the visual sensations which I describe in that way, is to be accounted for by the same hypothesis as that by which I accounted for the sound of the voice. If I had not a general conception of the order of nature, if I did not believe that things happen in a certain way, that some events are to be expected and others impossible, then I should not be able to judge the compatibility of one hypothesis with another. When a belief is said to be coherent with others, it is really only the accordance of them all with our notion of the natural order that is being asserted. And a given individual's conception of nature is merely the result of his experience.

It follows that the quest for an absolute truth, one which is final and not subject to any possible revision, is vain. What we regard as true is relative to our understanding of things. A proposition appears true in proportion to the degree of its coherence with the general system of nature, as understood and codified by the experience and endeavours of the race. Its truth depends, therefore, on its relation to the established view of nature, and on the extent and elaboration of the latter. Since human experience has not yet come to an end, the established view of nature is never final, and every accepted truth may be revised as a result of future discoveries.

A sound hypothesis, then, is one that is reliable as a practical guide to behaviour, and which is consistent with all others which fulfil this condition. We rapidly and readily construct hypotheses from multitudinous sense data: the voice, we say, means the proximity of an acquaintance, the shadow a passing bird. The frequency with which we make these inferences from sense data makes us very expert at the business so long as we work in a comparatively constant environment—although it is easy to put any animal into an environment in which the evidences of his senses deceive him. But there can be no universal rule for the acceptance or rejection of hypotheses. We try to build up as large a body of well-confirmed and mutually consistent hypotheses as possible, continually comparing the different departments of our knowledge to make sure there are no discoverable inconsistencies. Where two hypotheses are both apparently adapted to the facts and nevertheless conflict with one another, a careful investigation will sometimes lead to a more general hypothesis which replaces both. But all this requires a great deal, and so it is not surprising that strange ideas, even about witchcraft, continue to flourish among the unsophisticated.

Serious scholarly defence of belief in miracles today comes only from those who make religious beliefs their fundamental pre-misses for interpreting their whole experience. Thus the theologian G. F. Woods says, of the Biblical miracles: "It cannot be denied that the evidential value of the miraculous is closely interwoven with the metaphysical views of those to whom the evidence is offered. Those who reject theism and do not believe in the divinity of Christ have many alternative interpretations of the reported miracles".[15] And R. Swinburne notes, in similar vein, that whether one is convinced by evidence for a miracle depends to some extent on one's overall 'Weltanschauung' or 'world-view'.[16] Each of us tries to fit his views and experiences together into a coherent system, so that they do not contradict each other, and we must all judge the credibility of any given report according to the system of beliefs by which we live.

Finally, what of the miracles recorded in the Bible? A. R. Vidler noted that, "since no historical truths can be demonstrated, obviously miracles cannot be".[17] This is cunningly put: for if the miracles recorded in the gospels were as probably true as the assassination of Julius Caesar or the death of Mohammed in AD 632, the question of their historicity could be regarded as settled. Most, but not all theologians argue for the authenticity of at any rate some of the miraculous deeds ascribed to Jesus in the gospels.[18] Thus although W. Trilling concedes that no particular one of them can be proved true, he claims to infer "with certainty from the testimony of the gospels as a whole that Jesus performed some miracles". Particular details cannot be vouched for, but "the New Testament writers deserve in general a high degree of credibility".[19] To insist on taking the gospels 'as a whole' (or 'in general') is a good way of blunting criticism, which is bound to refer to particular incidents (cf. above, p. 72). Theologians have repeatedly shown that what gospel writers give us is very often tendentious fiction; and Trilling himself does not dispute that Jesus is represented as curing those who have exceptional faith in him (p. 100). The easy inference is that such stories were concocted in order to underline the virtue of faith. Trilling, however, sees that, without the miracle stories, very little of the gospels remains, and that if the miracles were invented, we may as well admit that the whole is fiction.[20]

H. C. Kee has been able to show in two recent books that many scholars, because they find miracles intellectually embarrassing, have been reluctant to admit their dominant role in the gospels and in the Acts of the Apostles. Kee shows that miracles fulfil ever-increasing functions in later strands of the New Testament traditions. For Mark they serve to indicate belief in the defeat of evil powers, his apocalyptic world-view seeing the cosmos as the place of struggle between God and his opponents; Matthew and Luke add the further idea that miracles are portents or evidence that an overall divine purpose is being worked out in history; and later New Testament traditions introduce additionally magical notions apropos of miracles, as evident in the stories in Acts of the expected therapeutic effects of Peter's shadow and the actual efficacy of Paul's handkerchief (Acts 5:15 and 19:11–12).[21]

Chapter Nine
German Metaphysics as a Refuge from Scepticism*

(i) The Origin of Our Ideas and the Quest for Certainty.

De Wette was saved from scepticism on religious matters by acceptance of Kantian metaphysics. Later, Hegel's metaphysics kept Strauss within the faith, if only for a while. Let us therefore study the kind of help that these German philosophical systems supplied.

The central element in Western religion and philosophy has been the immortal human soul, without which there can be no belief in a future life where the wicked will be punished and the faithful rewarded. It was once believed that the better world would be the result of a revolution on earth, but this, so often prophesied and as often postponed, has been given up (except by such sects as Jehovah's Witnesses) and replaced by a 'spiritual' resurrection.

The notion of a soul, as the invisible principle which distinguishes the living body from the dead, is very ancient and widespread. The soul has been identified with the blood and with the breath, but when the machinery of the human body and of other animal bodies began to be a little understood, the material properties of the soul were given up and it became airy and imperceptible. The term 'spirit', which had originally meant merely air, came to denote something immaterial, something which had none of the measurable properties of ordinary matter, unless that of localization. The adjective 'spiritual' has come to be

*Kant's *Kritik der reinen Vernunft* is conveniently available as edited by R. Schmidt (2nd edn., Hamburg, 1930, reprinted 1956) where A and B are used to mark the pagination of the original edition of 1781 and the second edition of 1787 respectively. My references use this same notation. Thus B 20 means p. 20 of the second edition. An English translation (by Norman Kemp Smith) is currently available in paperback (published by Macmillan Education).

used as the opposite of 'material', though the positive qualities of spirit have never been defined; but since ideas and thoughts are not material, they have been held to be the proper functions of the soul. The emotions are obviously related to the body; the acceleration of the heartbeat, the trembling of the limbs, the erection of the hair, the altered rhythm of respiration, the perspiration and other bodily manifestations betray them as a function of the body, whereas the calm unfolding of reflection seems to be without any effect on the body.

What, then, of our ideas? Locke undertook in his *Essay Concerning Human Understanding* (1690) to investigate how the thinking process was in fact conducted, what it consisted in, why it sometimes produced useful results and at other times seemed impotent. This was essentially a psychological investigation, and was chiefly defective through the absence of any account of the relation of thought to the emotions and purposes and motives. He said that all ideas were derived from the elements of sensory experience. The simple sensations of vision, hearing, touch, and so on, revived in different combinations, constituted ideas. Objects, he said, are known to us only by the sensations they excite, which are compounded of the simple sensations of colour, warmth, smell, sound, and so on. His manner of analyzing the complex into the simple sensations is based rather on abstract qualities than on true sensory elements, and this error was continued long after.[1] But it is not important for my immediate purpose, which is to point out that he analyzed the ideas in his mind to find out what information they could be supposed to give on the subject of the real world. He found that most of the *things* in the world to which we give distinct names are not represented in the mind by distinct ideas, but rather by clusters of simple ideas combined in a great many different ways. He maintained that the things themselves are not known to us except in the form of such complex groupings of simple ideas.

Now if all our ideas come to us through our senses, none of them, and no combination of them, can claim any authority higher than that of our eyes and ears. Locke was careful not to say anything which might expose him to charges of heresy, but it can hardly be questioned that his whole method, consisting as it did in an analysis of the elements of human knowledge, and in the reference of these elements to the natural operation of the senses which men possess in common with other animals, was bound, as soon as it came to be seriously reflected on, to undermine some of the fundamental dogmas of Christianity. Stillingfleet, then Bishop of Worcester, did in fact complain to Locke that his book had given occasion "to the enemies of our faith to take up your new way of ideas as an effectual battery, as they imagined, against the mysteries of the Christian faith".

In 1787 Kant published the second edition of his *Kritik der reinen Vernunft* (Critique of Pure Reason) and it was hailed as a crushing retort to the scepticism of Locke and of his successor Hume. In the preface to the first edition of 1781 he had suggested that the results of his inquiry would not be likely to gratify the orthodox; but his preface to the second edition made claims which were more likely to recommend the book to a wider circle of readers and stated, for instance, that his critical philosophy could cut the roots of materialism, fatalism, freethinking unbelief, fanaticism, and superstition—the two latter being as distasteful to a settled orthodoxy as the others. He added that governments should not worry if philosophers who achieve such things destroy, incidentally, some "cobwebs". He meant, presumably, that as long as philosophers support public morality by defending the doctrines of God's existence, of free-will and of immortality, no notice need be taken of their unorthodoxy in relation to the Christian doctrines of original sin, redemption, etc.

Locke, we saw, insisted that ideas depend on the sensations the individual receives from the external world and from the interior of his own body. But they depend also on his brain. Ideas represent things, and in consequence they are much more than a copy of sensations. Two men may have the same sensations and yet not by any means the same idea. Even a dog may have the same sensations as a man, but can hardly have the same ideas. The idea, then, is a highly organized system of memories derived from sensations, and the extent and range of such a system depends very much on the capacity of the individual brain. Two questions then arise: is it possible to say which elements of an idea depend on sensations and which on the organizing power of the mind?

And is it true, against Locke, that some ideas depend entirely on the mind and owe nothing to experience of anything outside it? Kant answered both these questions affirmatively. He held that many ideas and many pieces of knowledge are *a priori*, meaning that they owe nothing to experience. (The term used in the opposite sense, to indicate dependence on experience, is *a posteriori*).

Kant raises these questions by reasoning on the following lines. When we say that the boiling of the water is caused by the heat applied to the kettle, we suppose that, given such application of heat, the boiling always must occur. But experience, says Kant, can tell us only that whenever we have put the kettle on, the water has boiled, not that it will always, nor must always. These notions of the universality and necessity of the connection between the application of the heat and the boiling of the water are, therefore, in some sense supplied by the mind. Does this merely mean that the mind is apt to feel confident that what has happened before will happen again under like conditions, or is this confidence fully and completely justified because the notions of universality and necessity lie *a priori* in the mind? Kant came to this question, so crucial to him, from reading Hume, and we must study the basis of Hume's view before proceeding to Kant's criticism of it.

Hume maintained that "all the laws of nature and all the operations of bodies without exception are known only by experience".[2] That gunpowder explodes and loadstone attracts, he says, "could never be discovered by arguments *a priori*". One might, perhaps, object that gunpowder and loadstone were used before any general knowledge of chemistry and physics was available, and that for this reason their properties were known only as isolated facts; but that, now that we are better acquainted with the general nature of explosive substances, it is not impossible to prepare compounds in the laboratory and predict their explosive character in advance of experiment. Once general principles are known, particular happenings can often be predicted with great precision. But this does not invalidate Hume's general principle. The facts of atomic structure on which chemical predictions are now based are discovered by experience or represented by theories based on induction (induction being the process whereby we infer, from a limited number of observations, a general law). The particular case can, sometimes, thereafter be deduced. One may, then, distinguish between a purely empirical formula and one deduced from a principle. But Hume's position implies that deductive reasoning only consists in referring to wider generalizations already established inductively, empirically.

Many philosophers had resisted this conclusion, and had insisted that we really know some things to be necessarily true. Leibniz, for instance, had said that the astronomer knows "by reason" that it will be day tomorrow, even if the layman's expectation that day will follow night is merely empirical, that is, based on his experience that the sequence has never failed.[3] The argument is that the sequence seems necessary to the astronomer because he can refer it to certain observed motions of the earth in relation to the sun. But how, one must ask, does he know that the motion of the earth will continue? Only because it is in accordance with an observed law of motion. And such laws are expected to hold good tomorrow only because they have never failed. The real difference between the astronomer and the layman is that the former's 'rational' law is based on a much greater array of observations than the latter's empirical law. By rising from an empirical law to a more general one we can make our predictions more accurate. The law that night follows day does not hold in the Arctic regions. Furthermore, in an aeroplane, we may remain on the dark side of the earth indefinitely, if only we travel fast enough. But the law that describes the motions of the earth accounts for the sequence of light and darkness at all places on the globe and enables us to predict the length of daylight at any place or time.

It is perhaps worth pressing the implications of Hume's position with further examples. We say that eating oranges causes recovery from scurvy. Hume would hold that this simply means that the two are correlated in our experience, and that we therefore expect the one to follow from the other even in cases where we have not tried it. Supposing we next find that drinking orange juice from which the vitamins have been removed is not followed by recovery. We may then feel that we understand *why* patients who eat normal oranges do recover. We now understand, so it may seem to us, not only *that* they recovered, but that they *necessarily* did so, given the constitution of the oranges on the one hand and of their bodies on the other. We seem now to have found not merely a correlation, but a necessary connection. Hume would reply that we have in truth found nothing of the sort; that we connect the absorption of the vitamins with the health of the patient only because we find them correlated in experience. And his position implies that however far we carry our analysis, we never find anything more profound than this. Let me illustrate the implications of this, taking a different illustration.

(1) The pilot was burned to death.

Why?

(2) Because the petrol caught fire.

Why?

(3) Because petrol is a highly inflammable substance.

Why?

(4) Because it consists of a complex combination of hydrogen and carbon which at a certain temperature is very unstable, its components readily combining with the oxygen of the atmosphere.

Why?

(5) Because of the electrical composition of matter and the structure of the carbon, hydrogen and oxygen atoms.

Proposition (1) appears fortuitous (contingent) if viewed in isolation, but necessary if we have knowledge of proposition (2). But proposition (2) appears equally contingent in itself and seems necessary only given knowledge of proposition (3). And so on. Thus none of these propositions is necessarily true in itself. The appearance of necessity arises from perception of its relation to a more general proposition, and when we have reached the most general proposition to which chemistry has yet attained, there will be no further one in the light of which it will appear necessarily true. At the end of our analysis, then, we are left with a correlation between facts which appears just as fortuitous as the correlation in proposition (1) with which we began.[4] It was surely considerations of this kind which led Wittgenstein to declare categorically: 'Der Glaube an den Kausalnexus ist der Aberglaube' (The belief in the causal nexus is . . . superstition).[5]

Many philosophers have argued that we must know *a priori* that everything has a cause, since otherwise we could never begin to look for particular causes. For instance, W. S. Jevons asked (in criticism of John Stuart Mill's view that the idea of universal causation is derived from ideas of particular causes, and is in fact a sophisticated and far from obvious generalization from such ideas): "How in any particular case [do] we know that a phenomenon has a cause, we being supposed ignorant of the universal law of causation?"[6] Mill would have replied that we do not in fact begin with knowledge that something has a cause; that we have merely "a tendency, which some call an instinct and which others account for by association, to infer the future from the past, the known from the unknown". This "is simply a habit of expecting what has been found true once or several times, and never found false, will be found true again".[7] This habit, he intimates (p. 215)—even though he wrote before Darwin—is characteristic of all vertebrate behaviour. All the more highly organized animals act at times in anticipation of events. The scent of a lion makes the herd of buck change its course. The sound of the cracked twig sends the snake back to cover. Things are linked in experience. When the one happens, the other is looked for. Looking for causes is a relatively sophisticated form of this basic animal behaviour. The ideas associated with the word 'cause' all seem to be derived from this observed connection between distinguishable events. The underlying attitude of regarding one event as a warning or symptom of another is so universal among vertebrates that it may be presumed instinctive in man. In this sense only may one say that the idea of 'cause' is *a priori*, a character which has a basis in our nervous system and which is, in a physiological sense, prior to the stimuli to which we respond. Thus Sir Karl Popper, criticizing Hume, notes that "we are born with expectations, with 'knowledge', which although not *valid* a priori, is *psychologically* or *genetically* a priori, i.e. prior to all observational experience". And, he adds, one of the most important of these expectations is that of finding regularities.[8] Nevertheless, the biologist would insist that this applies only to man as he exists today, not to all his ancestors, who *acquired* the character in question in the course of evolution. The point is well put by Konrad Lorenz: "In the phylogenetic sense, transcending individual persons, the forms of our perceiving and our thinking are just as much of a *posteriori* origin as those of our organs".[9]

The animal's brain organizes its memories automatically. Every new experience is superposed on the accumulated traces which past experiences have left. Similar experiences deepen an existing trace. If his reaction to a certain situation has been appropriate (if it has led to the satisfaction of some desire or the avoidance of some danger), then the reaction becomes linked in his mind with the situation. And so when a new situation is presented, the reaction evoked is that which is linked to the trace which most closely resembles this new situation. If the situation is very novel, the animal's only resource is to try out his repertoire of responses until he finds one which is effective.[10]

Animals, then, adapt themselves by recognizing recurrent situations where they occur, and resorting to trial and error otherwise. Recurrence presupposes a degree of uniformity in nature. Hume says that, if we could not assume that like conditions produce like results, we could explain nothing, infer nothing[11]—even, one might add, describe nothing. Nature's uniformity is such that, in a restricted environment, an animal can with much confidence adapt his behaviour at least to his immediate future. But as he extends his experience and widens his horizon, he comes into contact with complex conditions in which the uniformity is more often masked by complexity. This condition reaches its maximum in man, and it required considerable scientific sophistication for him to reconcile apparent aberrations with the principle of uniformity.

It is possible to hold that the philosophical idea of universality of causation is the result of generalizing *ad infinitum* this expectation of uniformity. We learn to reinterpret phenomena so as to recognize uniformities where at first sight there were none; and on this basis we may be led to the illegitimate generalization *ad infinitum* that, if only we interpreted phenomena suitably, all irregularities would vanish. It is surely a mistake to suppose that science requires such a hypothesis of universal uniformity.[12] Scientists merely seek uniformities where they can be found and make the most of those which they discover. Some have been well established, others are merely suspected. Nothing is certain in the philosophical sense, but all that matters to us is that we should be confident. But because some things can obviously be relied on more confidently than others, some philosophers carry the idea to an extreme and suppose that there must be some things *absolutely* sure.

Nevertheless, the uniformity of nature must be considerable, if not absolute; otherwise the evolution of animal life would not have been possible. The fish was able to acquire effective habits because the properties of water remained constant.[13] Man is descended from a long line of animals, and his nervous system has been evolved in relation to the terrestrial and solar environment over a period during which nature has apparently remained uniform. This same nervous system has accordingly been evolved in adaptation to a uniform nature. That reasoning man should now have some confidence in the continuance of a uniformity which has been the experience of all his ancestors is, at all events, in accordance with our notion of evolution, however unsatisfactory a metaphysical basis this confidence may have.

In sum, we trust to experience because we believe in the uniformity of nature, and we believe in nature's uniformity because we have found it uniform. This, as Hume points out, does not prove that it will remain uniform. We may, then, be said to know the uniformity of nature not as a certainty, but as a probability. But do we really know anything as a certainty? Is there any line of distinction between absolute truth and high proba-bility? Does the thrush know with absolute certainty that worms can be dragged from the earth and are good to eat, or does it merely expect and hope? Psychologically there can surely be no differ-ence between certainty and high probability.

(ii) Causal Connection—an Idea of Limited Usefulness and Empirical Origin

If looking for causes is a relatively sophisticated development in man's behaviour, it is nevertheless one which has largely ceased to be appropriate in his even more sophisticated science. What in popular discourse is termed the cause of an event is no more than one of the conditions for its occurrence, usually one over which we happen to be able to exercise control. Artificial respiration is said to be the cause of a man's recovery from near-drowning. The oxygen in the atmosphere and the man's general physiology are not less necessary, but are taken for granted. Or, when I put a match to the fuse on a train of gunpowder leading to a mine, an explosion may occur. If the train of powder is damp or discontinuous, or if the connection between the train and the mine is defective, there will be no explosion. I may choose, for practical purposes, to isolate any one detail (the match, the dryness of the powder, etc.) as the cause of the explosion. But a scientific account would involve a complete statement of all the properties of matter from which, if they are known, the present case can be deduced. It is merely a special instance which is included in the statement of these laws, which themselves are but generalizations. There was a tendency, when the first successes of scientific method became generally known, to think of scientific law as analogous to human legislation, as something imposed on things from outside, whether by God or by some more abstract legislator. There is still a tendency to regard scientific laws as 'irresistible' or 'inexorable', as some kind of force which makes things behave as they do. But in fact a law is not a force and has none of the attributes that a force may have, such as irresistibleness. A law is an observed order or regularity to which manifestations of a force (such as the force of gravity) conform. Events, then, are determined by their conditions, and the law consists in a general statement concerning the correlation of the various definable and recurrent phenomena which constitute the conditions.

In order, then, to state the cause of a phenomenon, in the scientific sense, we have to state the law or laws which it exemplifies; and such laws can be established only by a multitude of observations and experiments. So when we state a scientific cause, we merely say that this event occurs because it has been constantly observed that under the given conditions it does occur. A law may consist merely of a statement of a certain correlation between two recognizable phenomena; or it may be a more

complex statement involving the correlations of many phenomena. Or it may be a complete statement involving all the
aspects and phases of a certain limited system. To this latter
possibility I shall return. But for the moment my concern is to
allege that all scientific laws are empirical. The only difference
between the particular law and the more general law is that the
evidence for the latter is more extensive. I may carry my analysis as
far as I like, but I can never get beyond a law which tells me that in
such conditions such things happen and may therefore be
expected to happen. And the explanation of any particular
happening is just the statement of the relevant law. One may go on
forever asking 'why' something happens, but must expect no other
kind of answer.

For the practical purposes of life, for which incidentally our
brain and thinking apparatus have been evolved, no other answer
could be of greater value. It is of great practical importance to be
able to infer B from A, and if we can rely on such inference, it does
not matter whether A precedes or follows B, or whether they are
simultaneous. Because we are so often concerned to predict or
anticipate coming events, we like to have A's which precede the
B's, so that we can take steps in preparation for B. But in many
cases, as in the investigation of past events, we are concerned to
make retrospective inferences. And there are innumerable cases
where we rely on symptoms. (The situation which we have to
investigate is only partially accessible, and we have to infer the
hidden features from whatever we can manage to observe or test.)
In all cases, the important thing is merely the inference from the
observed to the unobserved. What are called cause and effect are,
then, two aspects of a space-time structure. The structure being
known, either aspect can be deduced from the other. Where the
two aspects refer to the same or nearly the same space coordinates
but different times, the earlier is called the cause and the later the
effect. But this practical distinction loses its point when the matter
is generalized (that is, when we are not thinking of inferences from
what comes earlier to what comes later, but of inferences in any
direction in space-time).[14] What science does is to establish
complexes in space and time, and to enable us to infer from one
observed part of the complex to another.[15] Scientifically, then, the

idea of cause and effect is less useful than the conception of correlation or condition. And if the former is used at all in science, it is understood in the sense of the latter. "The cause", says Mill, "is the sum total of the conditions . . . , the whole of the contingencies of every description; which being realized, the consequent invariably follows" (p. 383. 'Follows' is here ambiguous and would be better replaced by 'occurs').[16] The determining conditions may be co-extensive with the world, or indeed with the universe. But for practical purposes, since many of these conditions remain constant in our corner of the world, we need attend only to a restricted number of them, and this selection is often thought of as 'the cause'.

One of the standard objections to this view that cause and effect are simply correlation which permits an inference from one thing to another is that we do not say that night is the cause of day. Schopenhauer thought that this in itself suffices to refute Hume's view of causation.[17] Mill discusses the objection (p. 391), but not wholly satisfactorily. But really the answer to it is at hand from his own premises; for he holds that the cause of a phenomenon is *all* the conditions, and the presence of night cannot be called all the conditions of day, even if it is any one of them. Hence it is not perplexing that nobody regards the sequence of night and day as a case of cause and effect. A cause is an event which is not always present. We say that A is the cause of B when in the *absence* of A, B does not occur. But nobody ever supposed that if night *failed* to return, day would not follow. The one is simply the absence of the other. Hence, in this case, if A failed to occur, B would not fail to occur but would *ipso facto* be produced. In other words, in order to have any reason for calling night the cause of day, men would have to have had, or to have imagined, cases where night had been absent and as a result there had been no day. So that it is not sufficient to say that A is the cause of B if it is invariably antecedent to it. There must also be the possibility of observing the consequent when the antecedent is not present (as in fact is explained by Mill in a later chapter on the methods of establishing the causes of events).

Another reason why we do not call night the cause of day is that, because the sequence is so regular, we do not find that the occurrence of the one helps us to anticipate the other. It is not from the fact that I am now awake that I infer that I shall go to sleep again, nor from the fact that I am alive that I shall one day die. If the sequence included several possibilities, then the unexpected appearance of one event might give us warning of the imminence of the other. My point here is that we do not usually speak of causes where the entire sequence is familiar. We do not regard each particular segment of the earth's orbit as the cause of that which follows, nor the position at any moment of the hands of a clock as the cause of their position at the next. To say that night is the cause of day would be as absurd as saying that the new moon is the cause of the full moon. We explain such sequences by means of a general law from which we can infer the position at any time, or the time for any position.

It is only in mechanics that we have succeeded in establishing anything like complete laws. The moon, for instance, is so far away that we observe its general motion, not its minor eccentricities. We see its path as an ellipse and find that this is in accord with observed laws of mechanics which apply to objects on the earth. Given these laws, and given, at any moment, the motions of various neighbouring planetary bodies, we can say where the moon was at any moment in the past or will be at any moment in the future. In such inferences we assume that the conditions of the motion remain unchanged. If they do change and we are aware of the change, we can make allowance for them. Such prediction is possible not only because of the relative stability of the conditions but also because the phenomenon of the moon's motion is capable of adequate description in quantitative terms. We can state a law in terms of time and space. Once such a law is stated it can be applied universally. By means of it we are able to infer both forwards and backwards in time just as we are able to infer both up and down in space. If the astronomer can predict an eclipse a thousand years hence, then he can with the same mathematical apparatus and by a process of exactly the same kind retrodict an eclipse of a thousand years ago. The very same equations serve both purposes. It is only necessary to substitute a minus sign for a plus sign. The relation between the relative positions of the earth and moon today and their relative positions at any time in the past or future is established by the same mechanical laws. You may, if you wish, say that their position and motion today are the cause of their position and motion tomorrow. But you might equally well reverse the propositions and say that their position and motion tomorrow are the cause of their position and motion today and yesterday, or a million years ago. But in reality there is no purpose served by speaking here of cause at all. The idea of cause is only practically applicable when the law of the process is not completely known, and where we observe only disjointed fragments, as it were, of the process, which we recognize as correlated without being able to express such correlation in the precise and complete form of a mathematical equation.

In sum, the question 'why' something happens, or the statement that it happens 'because' of some other thing, is very useful in the analysis of phenomena which are both complex and little understood, but becomes more and more inadequate as our analysis advances; and in the final stages such a question or such a statement becomes almost meaningless. In the nineteenth century, the idea of cause was refined, for scientific purposes, into the idea of correlation or conditioning, and it came to be realized that it is arbitrary (however indispensable for the practical needs of ordinary life) to select nameable items from a complex and call the one cause and the other effect.[18] In this way, the idea of cause was, for many scientific purposes, dropped.[19] It is still convenient to speak of the cause of an epidemic or of a misunderstanding; but to answer the question 'why does the earth travel round the sun', we should have to give a complete account of the principles of dynamics, and indeed of relativity physics.

Now if, as Kant supposed, the idea of cause were *a priori*, it would not have a history; one would not be able to trace its gradual refinement into the idea of correlation. Only persistent reflection and the accumulation of experience made this refinement possible, and this historical development of the notion shows that it is empirical. Ernst Mach has put the point forcefully:

> Causality has not always been understood in the same way. The way it is understood has changed in the course of history and can change still further. All the less ground for believing that one is here dealing with an idea innate in the mind.[20]

Hume still thought in terms of cause and effect, not in terms of correlation or conditioning. Furthermore, because he was concerned mainly with cases where what is called the cause precedes what is called the effect, he readily supposed that scientific inferences always work in this one direction in time; and so he defined cause as invariable *sequence*.[21] But it is obvious that there is a difference between events which are said to be causally connected, and those which are merely coincident. Hume gives no clue by which we may decide whether two events which commonly accompany or follow one another are causally connected or not. High tides accompany the full moon, but how long did men take to discover the 'causal' connection. And what exactly is it?

The limitations of Hume's account are understandable. He was not concerned with scientific reasoning for its own sake. He sought merely to dispose of the metaphysical conception of cause, and to him it did not matter how one decided to pick out the causes and determine the effects. What he insisted on was that the connection between them was recognizable only from experience and habit. It is only, he says (*Enquiry*, section 4, pt 1), because our experience of motion following impact has been so often repeated since our birth that we feel we have not learned it from experience at all, but have come into the world already knowing it. In other words, it is because our experience concerning certain elementary and universal physical relations is so old, so continual, and so uniform, that we are tempted to think that we know them *a priori*.

There remains, however, the question; what is the origin of the idea—erroneous or not—of necessary connection between cause and effect? It is obvious that the phrase 'necessary connection' has a natural meaning based on limited experience. If two objects are connected by a rigid rod, any motion of the one 'produces' a motion in the other. Similarly, the motion of the cart is 'connected' with that of the yoked horses; the motion of the bucket with that of the rope. Again man (and other mammals) find that they can move an object if they can establish physical contact with it (either directly with their own limbs or indirectly, by means of a stick or other tool in their hand). They know that if they can establish no such connection, they are powerless to move it. Now when sophisticated men look for a 'necessary connection' between events, they are really looking for this rigid bond (the bar, stick, or rope) along which the power of the agent may be transmitted to the other object. This, perhaps, is the psychological source of the idea of necessary connection, of the idea that the cause has power to produce the effect.[22] The idea depends, of course, on experience— man has had to learn what he can achieve with or without sticks— and to this extent Hume is right in his general contention, even though the experience is very old and may be assumed to be instinctive in man. But this idea of mechanical linkage can serve only in a very limited number of cases. The bucket is pulled to the surface by a rope, but it is vain to look for something analogous to the rope in the case of the magnet drawing the iron, the earth retaining the moon, and other cases of attraction. The correlations established by science include the familiar cases of mechanical linkage long known and relied on in normal behaviour; but they also include a great deal else. And Hume's argument (although he does not make this point himself) enables us to see that the simple model of transmission of power through mechanical linkage will not serve for all cases of correlation.

(iii) Kant Versus Hume. Religious Implications

I have given my reasons for regarding the idea of cause as empirical; but what of Kant's arguments to the contrary? What he says on the matter well illustrates two things which repeatedly obtrude themselves in philosophers' reasonings: first, that the desire to get beyond the empirical laws of nature to principles whose truth is altogether beyond question is responsible for most metaphysical theories; second, that there is often in the background the fear of reaching some conclusion that does not accord with what is accepted as religious truth. Hume's view of cause is certainly religiously dangerous. Religious philosophers had argued that to explain a man's ideas or emotions in terms of chemical processes or movements in his brain is inadequate, because we cannot discern any necessary connection between movements of particles and ideas or emotions. To this Hume replies that the only explanation we can give of *any* phenomenon is to show that it is constantly conjoined with others, that the whole idea of 'necessary connection' is an illusion.[23] If Hume is right, then the physiologist will be able to claim that he has explained an idea or emotion (in the only sense in which explanation is possible) if he can show that it always occurs when certain physical or chemical occurrences take place in the brain, and never occurs in their absence.[24] Accordingly, we may expect those philosophers who find such claims distastefully materialistic to defend the traditional idea of cause (impugned by Hume) with some fervour.

In order to discredit Hume's scepticism, Kant wishes to show that there are some things we know with absolute certainty. For this purpose he points out that the nature of our receptor apparatus determines to some extent how objects appear to us; and he alleges that some characters of objects are known to us *a priori* because these characters derive not from the objects, but from our apparatus. This, he says, includes a faculty of "understanding" (Verstand) which possesses a number of ideas by means of which it pigeonholes or categorizes objects. One such idea is the idea of number; for we always experience things as one or many, as a unity or plurality. Another such idea is the idea of cause. The mind, he believes, imposes this idea on to what it receives in order to make sense of this material that is given to it from without. It is not that, in the world in which we live, things are caused, but that we have to impose the idea of cause on them in order to experience them at all. If this is true, then there is no difficulty in understanding 'cause' as a universal and necessary connection. The mind cannot but supply the idea of cause, in this sense, on all occasions when material is presented to it. The alternative is always at the back of Kant's mind: if there were nothing in our mental apparatus that made the law of universal causation (and other laws of nature) inevitable, if they prevailed merely as a matter of fact, then we should have no reason for our feeling of unshakeable conviction in their truth save the fact of repeated observation. Yet (I must object) if this is so, why should this feeling of conviction be generated by the invariable recurrence just because one condition of it lies in our own body or mind? It is the invariable recurrence in either case that establishes the conviction.

Kant does not suppose that only philosophers or scientists impose the idea of cause on their experience, but that everyone must do so, that one cannot but regard everything in one's experience as caused. In fact, of course, relatively few unsophisticated people have ever embraced such strict determinism, and today even scientists have to some extent abandoned it.

Schopenhauer alleged (p. 90), in support of Kant, that we can conceive the law of gravitation suddenly ceasing to function, but not that it could do so without a cause. If anyone were to reply that he can imagine such a thing quite readily, and that he has often known cases where some change suddenly occurred, apparently spontaneously, and that nothing prevents him from supposing that these changes are in fact spontaneous—for what is the use of this word except to denote such things?—Schopenhauer would presumably reply that he simply deludes himself.

One reason why Kant and Schopenhauer are so confident that causal propositions are necessarily true is that they think that necessary truths are well established in other fields; and so the necessity of causal propositions is, for these two philosophers, merely a further example of a kind of truth that is already quite familiar. One of Kant's examples of necessary truth is the propositions of mathematics. The argument goes somewhat as follows. However many times I have watched the sun rise or the tide come in, I can never be quite sure that it will rise, or come in, again. If, then, I have an invincible conviction that $2 + 2 = 4$ not only always has proved true but always will do so, then I cannot have learned this from experience. I have therefore some other means of recognizing truth which does not depend on any process of learning by experience. Hence mathematical truths are *a priori*; and Kant claims (B19–20) that Hume could not have denied that there are *a priori* ideas (involving necessity and universality) had he looked further than the idea of cause; for he would then have discovered that, on this view, there could be no pure mathematics.

I cannot here attempt any adequate discussion of this view of the origin and nature of mathematics, which today still has many supporters.[25] I will, however, note the following points against it. (i) Even some Euclidean proofs of equality depend on the concrete operation of picking up a triangle and superposing it on another.

(ii) An algebraical proposition such as $(x+y)^2 = x^2 + 2xy + y^2$ may not look as if it owes anything to ordinary experience, yet is obviously derived from the observed area of a square of side $(x + y)$, as the following diagram illustrates:

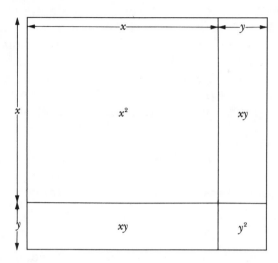

(iii) Kant's own language sometimes betrays that simple mathematical ideas are empirical. He proves, for instance, that only one straight line can be drawn between two points by drawing 'in his thoughts' all sorts of lines between the two points, and discovering that only one is identical with itself throughout its whole length.[26] But how could he draw such lines in his thoughts if he had never done so with his hand? Why should he suppose that the mental act was independent of experience? Again, when he admits that inspection (Anschauung) is necessary to discover that the sum of 7 and 5 is 12 (B15) he is really declaring the proposition to be empirical. Mill argued that if such simple arithmetical propositions seem less empirical than, say, propositions about the sun, this is because numerical relationships are learned so early in our experience, and confirmed so continually by it, that we cannot contemplate their falsity without having to reconstruct our interpretation of all our experience. The rising of the sun can be observed by a man only about 30,000 times if he lives to a ripe old age and never misses one opportunity. But that $2 + 2 = 4$ he may experience and confirm without having to get up early in the morning, and independent of the weather, as often as he opens his eyes or handles separate articles. I know that many philosophers now treat Mill with what R. J. Halliday has aptly called (in the preface of his 1976 book on Mill) "enormous condescension". But I have tried to show elsewhere that the criticisms of his account of the empirical origin of mathematics are much less convincing than is generally supposed.[27] Mill has a powerful ally in Ernst Mach, who shows in one chapter of his *Erkenntnis und Irrtum* that geometrical notions are empirical, and in another that even the irrational idea of $\sqrt{-1}$ was interpreted by means of geometrical applications of algebra (pp. 331, 421).

Kant is so confident over this matter of necessary truth that, in some passages, he deals with Hume simply by alleging that 'cause' *does* imply a universal and necessary connection:

> The idea of a cause quite plainly includes the idea of a necessary linkage with an effect and of a strict universality of the rule.

But this is precisely what Hume had questioned, and simply to allege that it is so is to beg the point in dispute. Nor are we reassured when Kant continues:

> The idea of cause would be completely lost if we were, in Hume's manner, to derive it from frequent association of what happens with what precedes, and from the habit, thence originating, of linking ideas with merely subjective necessity (B5).

The very notion of 'cause' would (he here says) disappear if we adopt the view of Hume. The argument seems to be that, since we have the notion of cause as a universal and necessary connection, and since we like this notion, we cannot allow it to disappear. But there is really no question of the notion disappearing, any more than all the other primitive notions which are no longer useful to science. The notion will survive, but will no longer be regarded as a very reliable representation of reality. Some people will even continue to accept it as reliable. Many erroneous notions long survive what might be supposed to have been the *coup de grâce*.

Kant next asks: "whence could our experience itself acquire certainty, if all the rules on which it depends were themselves

empirical and consequently fortuitous?" This is somewhat mud-
dled, as his basic position is that what we learn from experience is
not certain.[28] But some truths seem more certain than others, and
Kant selects what seem to him to be the most certain and declares
that these cannot have been acquired from experience. Then how
else can we have come by them? The question is artful, for it is
only he who assures us that the certainty of a proposition is
enough to exclude all possibility of origin in experience. If we do
not accept his assurance, then this question of his—how else we
came to know such a proposition—does not arise.

(iv) Kant's Fantastic View of Mind

When we subtract from our idea of an object all that, according
to Kant, is supplied *a priori* by the mind, all that is left, as raw
material given from without, is a kind of splodge, a "manifold"
(Mannigfaltiges) as he calls it (B129), without form or coherence of
any kind. One implication of all this is that we cannot know what
things are really like in themselves. We can only know how they
appear when they have been processed by our apparatus of
perception. The biologist supposes that man has a better idea of
the world than the codfish. He believes that the evolution of the
nervous system has enabled the more complex animals to know
more about their real environment.[29] Yet, according to the Kantian
view, there is no reason for such belief. The real world is, for Kant,
entirely unknowable, and so the human view of it can be no more
authentic than that of any other creature. The information received
from the senses is arranged and ordered by the faculty of
'understanding' (Verstand, cf. above, p. 159) in a certain manner,
and man, observing these arrangements, supposes that that is how
the world is. He supposes that nature is subject to general laws,
and on the strength of this he predicts events. If the predictions are
verified this only means that he is predicting the behaviour of his
own 'Verstand". As Kant puts it:

> The highest legislation for nature must lie in ourselves, that is, in our
> understanding (*Prolegomena*, § 36)

Kant does not, of course, suppose that all natural laws are known to us a priori—only the most general ones, such as 'substance endures' (ibid., § 15), formulated in the Critique (B17) as "in all changes in the material world the quantity of matter remains unchanged". One can only comment that if such a law were known a priori to be true, it could not have been (as it has been) almost universally denied. Did not common experience long suggest that the whole pageant of existence is an endless sequence of coming to be and passing away?[30] Men have never had any difficulty in believing that matter could be created or destroyed, and in alleging that we know the permanency of matter a priori Kant is confounding Lavoisier's recent experimental conclusion[31] with a necessity of thought. The conservation of matter is a principle that was only gradually and recently established, and it was not long before it was subsequently abandoned. Study of the history of the idea, as in the case of cause, shows that the notion is in fact empirical.[32] Sir Karl Popper, who approaches Kant with great sympathy, has noted that his dictum "our intellect does not draw its laws from nature but imposes its laws on nature" is correct only in the sense that certain attitudes (particularly the expectation of finding regularities in nature) are innate in man (cf. above, pp. 149f.). It is not, says Popper, correct in the sense that Kant supposed, namely that these laws are necessarily true, or that we necessarily succeed in imposing them on nature. "Nature", says Popper (p. 174), "very often resists quite successfully, forcing us to discard our laws as refuted: though we may try again".

Kant also supposes that our conceptions of time and space are a priori; that objects do not in themselves exist in time, or in space, but that the mind supplies them with a time-space context in order to be able to experience them at all.[33] And by space he means Euclidean space. That space has three dimensions, and three only, is for him a necessary truth which we know a priori. Again, I must object that if we were obliged, by some unalterable mechanism in our receptor apparatus, to regard space in this way, modern scientists could not have succeeded in abandoning the idea.

The biologist is not embarrassed by this kind of radical change in our manner of looking at things. According to him (see, for instance, Lorenz, p. 106) man's way of looking at the universe has been acquired, in the course of evolution, in the struggle to survive, and has helped him to survive only because it does do justice at any rate to some of the real and important characteristics of the universe. But as man increases his experience, ideas which served him perfectly well for a very long time are found to be no longer adequate. And so, as Lorenz has observed, although Euclid's idea of space is perfectly satisfactory for most practical purposes, the work of Einstein and others has shown that it does far from full justice to the reality of space; and that likewise "the way of thinking in terms of causality, seemingly so compelling and so logically impregnable, . . . is adapted to things but clumsily, and merely at the statistical level" (p. 102; cf. p. 110). The biologist can also show that it would be harmful to man for his outlook to be unalterably determined by a priori factors. Simple animals living in a fairly constant environment are specifically adapted to it and cannot survive any radical change in it. Others are able, in the course of their individual lives, to adapt themselves to a greater variety of conditions. Yet others—man in particular—live in such a variable environment that it would be fatal for them to acquire unmodifiable habits. They must react appropriately to the new situations constantly confronting them, and the thinking process is of great biological importance in this connection. If this thinking process were guided by unalterable a priori conceptions which do only very imperfect justice to the real complexity of external reality, the animal would be heavily penalized.

The innate apparatus which Kant postulates for the processing of the raw material of experience is certainly elaborate. It includes not only 'Verstand', but also other faculties which are lower or higher. There is, for instance, a faculty which Kant is pleased to call (B35) "reine Anschauung a priori" (pure perception a priori). "Anschauung" is a vague word which may mean the ideas someone forms of a thing, or the sensory experience (sensation) he has in its presence. This faculty supplies a time-space context to sensations of colour, hardness, etc., and they are then passed on to the 'Verstand' which imposes its various a priori conceptions such as cause. If the work of the 'Verstand' is thus preluded by that of another faculty, it is superseded or completed—in some way that is not quite clear—by the labours of yet another, namely 'reason' (Vernunft). Schopenhauer justly complained (in his *Kritik der Kantischen Philosophie*) that Kant does not discuss the function of 'Vernunft' adequately, but gives only occasional hints that are not consistent. Some passages suggest that Kant felt he needed 'Vernunft' as the source of his knowledge of the nature and function of all the other faculties. Thus he says: "Reason is the faculty which supplies the principles of knowledge *a priori*" (A11). Whereas, then, 'Verstand' deals with ordinary experiences, 'Vernunft' enables us to ascertain what is going on in the mind independently of all experience. And in matters of 'pure reason', he says, there are no unanswerable questions: "The key lies within ourselves and in our pure thought" ("pure" meaning 'independent of experience'), so we can supply an answer; whereas in studying nature we have to answer questions about what is outside us, often unsuccessfully (A476-481). It seems almost as if Kant supposed he had *a priori* knowledge of all the psychological apparatus that he posits. As so little was known about the mind, he was in fact free to divide it up into as many faculties as he wished, and to assert of each whatever seemed convenient.

There are two obvious criticisms to make of this apparatus of faculties: first that it has no relation to physiological facts and has never been found helpful in psychology, although the distinction between 'Verstand', and 'Vernunft' has proved useful to religious apologists.[34] And second that each of Kant's faculties seems to be able to think and feel like ordinary mortals. He talks of the 'Verstand' "becoming aware" of something, of "desiring" something, of "seeking to usurp" the function of 'Vernunft'. 'Vernunft' in its turn, is a prey to definite emotions, dissatisfaction and hope deferred.[35] I shall no doubt be told that all this is mere metaphor, and that Kant does not really represent the faculties as agents which do things, as if they were men or animals. But that he is not altogether clear as to the status of these faculties is strongly suggested when we find him sometimes speaking of them not as living agents, but as apparatus worked by some manikin or homunculus behind it. There is a common tendency among speculators on human psychology to invent an apparatus of faculties and then to provide an animating principle endowed with all the very qualities the apparatus is supposed to explain.

Kant speaks of 'Vernunft' and 'Verstand' as instruments, and says (A53) that there are rules for their use, as there are for the use of typewriters and slide-rules. So we have to imagine a homunculus working the levers. Often this homunculus appears in the disguise of a personal pronoun: there exist bodies outside *us*; *we* know them through the idea (Vorstellung) which their influence produces on our senses (Sinnlichkeit). The sense organs are here conceived as a medium through which *some observer* becomes indirectly aware of the external world. At every turn we see the homunculus surrounded by a staff of secretaries and bailiffs, the faculties, who bring him news. There is an 'I' or 'me' at the centre, to whom the senses or the understanding or the reason report. But it is just this 'I' or 'we' that psychology has to analyze. It must not be allowed to take a hand in the process.[36] This is something that was perfectly clear to Hume, who implies that the consolidation of all those elements in the field of consciousness which constitute the 'subject' into a more or less permanent group is not essentially different from the consolidation of other elements which constitute possible 'objects'.[37]

The queerest disguise in which Kant's homunculus appears is the expression "our subject". Kant uses 'Subjekt' in the sense of the perceiving consciousness, as against the object perceived. This distinction between consciousness and its object is clear. But at times he speaks of "our subject" as if there is a 'we' or 'us' which in turn has a 'Subjekt', as the ego of the ego.

What, all in all, is Kant's contribution? It is often claimed that he established once and for all the decisive part played by the mind in our knowledge of external reality. But this is a generous assessment of the position. What he in fact says is that the forms which things assume in our mind are the result of (1) the nature of the things (in themselves) and (2) the nature of our receptor apparatus; and that whereas philosophers had tended to exaggerate the former factor he proposes to try exaggerating the latter. The following passage (from the preface to the second edition of the *Critique*) shows that this is no caricature:

> It has hitherto been assumed that all our knowledge must conform to the things [the objects perceived]. But all attempts to ascertain anything about the things *a priori*, by means of our conceptions, whereby our

knowledge would be extended, have been frustrated by this assumption. Let us therefore see whether we do not succeed better with the tasks of metaphysics if we assume that the things must conform to our knowledge. This at least accords better with our desire for some possibility of *a priori* knowledge of things—of knowledge which shall settle something about them before they are given to us [in experience]. This procedure is exactly similar to the primary idea of Copernicus. He, finding that he could make no progress in explaining the celestial movements by assuming that the whole array of stars revolves round the observer, tried to get on better by letting the observer revolve and the stars remain at rest. In metaphysics one can make an experiment of the same kind in regard to the perception [Anschauung] of things. If perception were to have to conform to the nature of the things, then I do not see how we can know anything about their nature *a priori*. But if the thing (as an object of our sense organs) conforms to the nature of our faculty of perception, then I can easily conceive the possibility of such *a priori* knowledge.

In the two final sentences he draws a distinction between things or objects on the one hand and perception (Anschauung) or the faculty of perception (Anschauungsvermögen) on the other. He has in mind the distinction we make between the world around us and our ideas of that world (as, for instance, when we say that one man's idea of a thing may correspond closely to the thing itself, whereas another man's idea of it may be much sketchier). Kant thinks here of the 'Anschauung' as what is given to us in consciousness directly; and of the object as what is given to us only indirectly through the 'Anschauung'. He says that unless we *assume* that it is the nature of the 'Anschauung' (the nature of our 'Anschauungsvermögen') that determines how objects appear to us, we shall not be able to know anything *a priori* about their nature.

The limitations of Kant's whole approach have often been stressed by scientists who, for all their respect for his philosophical labours, have not taken kindly to accepting as necessary truths scientific generalizations which rapidly proved to be obsolete. For instance, in 1873 the mathematician W. K. Clifford noted that Kant had asked: are there any properties of objects in general which are really due to me and to the way in which I perceive them, and which do not really belong to the things themselves? Kant, says Clifford, had tried to answer this question by finding what are those characters of experience which we know to be necessary and universal, and concluding that these are characters of me. This method of answering, says Clifford, is wrong because it requires some infallible way of judging what characters are necessary and universal, whereas in fact judgements of this kind may very possibly be mistaken. The answer to Kant's question, he adds, must not be sought in the subjective method, in the conviction of universality and necessity, but in the physiological method, in the study of the physical facts that accompany sensation, and of the physical properties of the nervous system.[38] Ernst Mach made the point somewhat more tartly, saying (p. 281): "It is not philosophical edicts but actual psycho-physiological research that can settle what is innate".

(v) What is Innate?

In an essay of 1790 Kant replied somewhat touchily to a critic who had accused him of regarding certain ideas as innate. He there says that nothing is innate but the mind's "receptivity, when it is affected in sensation by something, to obtain in accordance with its own nature, a representation (Vorstellung)"[39] He thinks of our sensory and nervous apparatus as a kind of framework to be filled, a neutral scaffolding on which the scenery of experience must be hung. We cannot know what experience will bring, but we know in advance that it must fit this framework. According to Kant, the framework includes all the *forms* of our sensations, only their *matter* reaching us from without (B34). But if, as he supposed, the experience which we call 'seeing the cat' owed all its form and coherence to us, it is hard to understand why our idea of the cat (whatever configuration in the brain represents the cat) should be excited by so many different visual patterns; for one and the same cat, seen from different angles, at different distances and against different backgrounds, presents very different appearances.

That Kant is not altogether clear about what must, from his premises, be regarded as innate is suggested by his discussion of the faculty of reason (die Vernunft) which, we saw, he distinguished from that of understanding (der Verstand). He held that, while it is the function of the latter to supply information about things which depend for their existence on various conditions, reason is not satisfied with this and seeks knowledge of the unconditioned, of what is not dependent on anything else. Reason, he says, has three ideas which are independent of experience: ideas of the unconditioned soul, or free self; of the unconditioned world (the absolute whole of all possible experience, constituting the totality of knowledge); and of the unconditioned entity we call God. Apropos of God, he says that reason cannot actually know him, but must posit him, because it can never rest satisfied with explaining one thing in terms of another, which is all that the faculty of understanding can accomplish.

Kant distinguishes these 'ideas' (Ideen) from 'concepts' (Begriffe) such as cause, by means of which the understanding 'categorizes' the material it receives from the sense organs (via the faculty of "reine Anschauung a priori": cf. above, p. 165), and these again from 'representations' (Vorstellungen), which are our ideas of the things and situations in the world we experience. It would seem to follow from all this that the 'ideas of reason' are innate, although he studiously avoids this word, saying:

> As the understanding needs categories for experience [in order to make sensations into experience of objects and situations], so the reason contains, in itself, the ground for ideas, by which I mean necessary concepts, the object of which can however not be given in any experience. Ideas lie in the nature of reason, as do categories in the nature of understanding (*Prolegomena*, paragraph 40).

It is clear that he thinks of reason as functioning in a kind of cockpit, bounded by a sensory screen which divides what he calls phenomena (things as we experience them, that is, as processed by our sensory and nervous apparatus) from what he calls noumena (things as they really are). It seems that reason can find a crack in the sensory window through which to get a glance at the noumenal world; for Kant writes of reason moving up to the boundary and seeing "an empty space" beyond it—empty space in which it can "think forms for things but no things themselves" (*Prolegomena*, paragraph 59). We have only to ask what kind of process this is—thinking forms for things in an empty space—to realize that Kant is less than clear, or even less than candid, concerning what his theory requires to be innate.

It is of course true that, with man, a great deal is innate. Our capacity as humans to grasp certain principles is innate, even if the principles themselves have to be learned; and this relation between learning and innate capacity was probably in Kant's mind when he said that only the mind's 'receptivity' is innate. Unfortunately he had other purposes besides the straightforward one of explaining scientifically the working of the human mind, and so he invented his hierarchy of faculties with their elaborate protocol. Schopenhauer, who in many respects followed him, nevertheless complained that he had degraded the ordinary reasoning process by assigning it to a relatively low faculty (Verstand) and had reserved the name 'reason' for a purely imaginary capacity which is supposed to open onto the supernatural world a little window through which man may receive in finalized form all those truths which reason as hitherto understood had tried in vain for so many centuries to determine.[40] That this criticism is not unjust will emerge when we study Kant's views on ethics in the next section of this chapter.

(vi) The Problem of Free-Will

Kant insists that man knows right from wrong without resort either to experience, or to instinctive promptings, or to divine instruction, because reason reveals such matters to him (A480); and reasons supplied by the faculty of reason ("Gründe der Vernunft") "give rules to actions on the basis of principles, without any influence on the part of time and place" (*Prolegomena*, paragraph 53). A moral law is thus always and everywhere valid, quite apart from any variation in the circumstances. Man's 'Vernunft' can initiate an action, and the action occurs in the 'phenomenal' world (the world of experience); but the initiation does not, and stems from the free 'noumenal' human psyche. In this same context Kant calls the "natural" causes of an action—ordinary vulgar motives such as fear, desire or hunger which man shares with animals—"subjective determining factors", quite different from "objective" ethical motives, which are noumena. It is all mere assertion, but the language of this paragraph 53 is almost impenetrable and encourages the reader to think that Kant has demonstrated his case, not merely stated it.

Such views proved very popular, and the poet and dramatist Friedrich Schiller, in an essay where he avowedly followed Kant, called reason "absolute consistency and universality of consciousness", and insisted that "when the moral consciousness declares something shall be so, it decides the matter for ever and anon".[41] If this were true, mankind would still be enforcing barbarous practices by appeal to moral intuition, and revision of any ethical code would be out of the question (cf. below, p. 191). Kant's views were felt to be more in accord with the dignity of human nature than those of Hume, who had said that any theory by which we explain the operations of the mind, or the origin and connection of the passions in man, "will acquire additional authority if we find that the same theory is requisite to explain the same phenomena in all other animals" (Enquiry, section 9). According to Carlyle, this kind of writing had come to be regarded in Germany as a threat "to destroy whatever we value most".[42]

De Wette attached particular importance to Kant's doctrine of freedom of will and believed that such freedom elevates man above nature.[43] Kant seems to have shared the common but as I have shown elsewhere,[44] quite unjustified belief that, if the will were not free, it would be impossible to hold a man responsible for his actions and unjust to blame or praise him for what he did, in which case there would be an end of all morality. But a candid study of the conditions and motives of human behaviour leads to the conclusion that, when heredity and education and the surrounding conditions are all taken into account, a man is as much determined in his actions as any other animal or inanimate object. Kant's solution to this dilemma is based on his doctrine that all that we see, hear, smell, taste or feel constitute phenomena, or objects of experience, but that behind these phenomena are the real things, the things in themselves or noumena of which we know nothing. He says in the preface to the second edition of the Critique that, if we do not make this distinction between things as objects of experience and things as they are in themselves, then "the principle of causality, and, by consequence, the mechanism of nature as determined by causality, would have absolute validity in relation to all things as efficient causes;" whereas, thanks to the

Critique, we can say "of the human soul that its will is *free* and yet, at the same time, subject to natural necessity, that is, *not free*, without falling into a palpable contradiction"; for in the former case we take the soul as a thing in itself, and in the latter as an object of experience. The *Critique*, then, teaches us that "an object may be taken in two senses."

In the pre-Kantian days, philosophers would hardly have allowed that an *object* can be taken in two senses. It is words and not objects which have senses, and it is true enough that a word may have any number of senses, in which case it denotes many different objects, one for each sense. If that is what Kant means, if he means merely that the will is a word having two meanings and thus referring to two different things, then it will be seen that we have not gained very much by this piece of legerdemain. What we should like to know is whether a man's behaviour is determined or not, whether what he does at any time is the consequence of all the antecedents or is independent of them. Kant says that there are two things, both called the will, but not further described, one of which we may call free and the other determined. Our question remains unanswered, but we have the satisfaction of punishing the malefactor and at the same time the scientific gratification of explaining why he inevitably acted as he did. Kant was a man of science and believed in the universality of what he regarded as the law of causation. It would have been distasteful to him to have to give up so settled an opinion. On the other hand it was distinctly awkward to find this law applied to human beings, for that might be held to free them from all responsibility for their wickedness.

Kant's influence on ethical theory has been enormous. In 1969 the Cambridge University Press saw fit to publish an attempt, on Kantian lines, to base ethics on man's "innermost being", as distinct from his biological inheritance. I refer to Paul Roubiczek's *Ethical Values in the Age of Science*, the avowed aim of which is to prevent the application of scientific method to the study of human morality. Roubiczek believes (p.3) that acceptance of a biological view of morality must diminish the feeling of personal responsibility—as if by explaining the origin of a function we were to abolish it. He contends against determinism that it represents thinking as "completely determined by men's physiological and psychological make-up", which would logically imply that "men were not free to change their views" and that all argument is therefore futile. But animals, which I presume Roubiczek does not credit with free-will, are capable of changing their views. They certainly learn from their experiences. The supposition that a man may be affected by threats, cajolery, prohibitions, advice, or persuasion obviously seems to Roubiczek quite incompatible with determinism. The determinist would reply that his doctrine is that human behaviour, like any other behaviour, is determined by antecedents, and that when someone is criticized or advised by his fellows, his knowledge of their views represents a new antecedent which may modify his whole behaviour. Roubiczek would not agree that, when we call someone responsible, we mean no more than that he is susceptible to certain socially approved motives.[45] Although he would not deny that men are prompted by emotions and guided by motives and reasonings, he seeks the source of moral behaviour in a kind of transcedent ego that is above such influences, and which as such is the guarantor of free-will and responsibility. His aim is to resist the "prevailing tendency to assume that all our actions are effects of causes upon which we had no influence" (p. 6). The 'we' in this sentence is a transcendent ego, further described as an "embodiment of ulti-mate reality" (p. 13). He makes great play with this word 'reality'. Having posited "two ways of thinking"—one for ethical and another for scientific matters—he insists that "reality as such is not divided into two, but must be one" (p. 111). Hence "ethics is . . . based on a transcendental reality which remains outside external and internal reality, although internal reality can open approaches to it" (p. 190). As the reader can attach no clear idea to the word, it is impossible to argue whether reality is (or 'must be') one, inside this, or outside that.

Roubiczek finds that, without all this apparatus, he cannot explain the commanding voice of conscience (p. 16). He is not prepared to attribute it to an inherited social instinct which prompts all normal persons to consider the interests of their fellows (cf. below, p. 178ff). Nor would he allow that a dog—presumably not an embodiment of ultimate reality—can be as loving, as courageous and as self-sacrificing as any human being. Conscience is, for him, the voice of the absolute which enables us "to know absolutely what we ought to do if we want to do the good" (pp. 14, 158). Roubiczek's experience must have been very different from mine if he has never doubted what in given circumstances ought to be done. He allows that there is such a thing as ethical progress, but, he insists, only up to the stage represented by the ethics of the Decalogue and the Sermon on the Mount, the precepts of which remain absolutes for all time (pp. 61, 94f, 155f). Yet although "thou shalt not steal" is thus an "absolute law", he has to allow that under certain circumstances (for example, to save a starving child) theft may be perfectly justified. He alleges that such instances represent a conflict between absolutes which does not make them relative!

A more recent apologist, Richard Swinburne (Professor of the Philosophy of the Christian Religion at Oxford) has noted a number of facts about the universe, including its orderliness, the pervasiveness of religious experience and—what is relevant to the present context—the existence of "conscious beings capable of responsible action". He thinks it appropriate to "account for" these facts "in the simplest possible way . . . by supposing one being controlling the evolution of the universe and bringing it into being".[46] In this chapter I have tried to show that accounting for anything by picking on one cause is not defensible; and in the next chapter I shall return to the question of responsible action. My principal concern in this one has been to note the important and continuing influence of metaphysics as an aid to devotion. Theologians commonly allude approvingly to German metaphysical theories and look askance at the British empirical tradition in philosophy. But it was Schopenhauer who, although himself firmly within the German tradition, insisted: "I cannot too often repeat that all abstract ideas are to be checked in the light of experience".[47]

Chapter Ten
Morality, Religion, and Reason

(i) Egoistic Instincts and Social Instincts

Every tendency in man and every kind of behaviour that admits of description rests finally upon a small number of definable urges which are common to the whole species (although the practical problem in each case is to determine the other factors). These urges include egoistic, parental, and social instincts. Those instincts which are concerned with feeding, shelter-seeking and defence against injury may fitly be called egoistic because they have the function of preserving the individual in isolation, while the primary function of the parental instincts is to preserve the race, and of social instincts to adapt the individual to life in some kind of community.

Egoistic instincts are obviously vital to an animal; for every creature must look after itself. If somebody treads on his tail, he must not adopt an impartial attitude, but bring teeth and claws into action, or at least yelp. If his nervous apparatus were not adapted for this basic need of self-protection, it would be hard to understand how his species had survived.

With man we find a great extension in his mind of that portion of the world which constitutes his vital sphere of interest. His self spreads out to embrace not merely his own body and his family, but his friends, his property and even his opinions. Everything that is interpreted as an injury to this enlarged self awakens the same aggressive impulse elicited by an injury to his own body. Pride, vanity, and contempt refer to different forms of satisfying the tendency which aims at establishing his own superiority; humility, shame, and envy are emotions associated with its non-resolution.

Apart from material contrivances, advance in civilization consists in the progressive repression of the cruder and more direct methods of satisfying the egoistic instincts, and the substitution of complex indirect processes which enable them to be satisfied with less social conflict. Since man cannot exist without society, and since the existence of society depends on the suppression of the more violent forms of conflict, the function of this change is evident. But the fundamental instincts are not altered. They still provide the motive force.

Ethical systems cannot be constructed without reference to the needs of the community. The anchorite in the wilderness has only his own peace of mind to consider and may regard as right anything which wards off evil dreams and gives him a sense of superiority or saintliness. But in society every member must pay regard to the interests of his fellows, and that is the real foundation of ethics. The practical difficulty lies in knowing what kind of conduct can be prescribed for all (or at least for all the members of a sub-group or class: this much is implied by prescription).

Society, then, as Westermarck says is "the birthplace of the moral consciousness".[1] He goes on to imply that there is no clear line of division between the social and the solitary animals. At first a number of individuals of the same species live in the same neighbourhood because the conditions are favourable and the food supplies ample. In such cases an important part of each animal's environment consists of other members of his own species, and he must adapt himself to this part of his environment as well as to the rest. In time, when this adaptation has been accomplished, he no longer feels at ease in an environment in which he is isolated. Aggregation in a social group involves, then, a special adaptation, and human culture (including morals) results from it.[2]

As no community can survive unless its members restrict, for instance, their sexual, acquisitive, and revenge impulses, enlightened self-interest may lead them to such a course. But the individual is also prompted to behaviour which benefits the community by social instincts, which are always found in gregarious animals. It is not only domestic animals that are capable of affectionate, self-sacrificing, and loyal behaviour. Darwin mentions Brehm's account of a baboon which went alone to rescue a young one surrounded by dogs, and monkeys which hastened to the assistance of one member of the troop when he was attacked.[3] Even animals of different species can live on friendly terms when they are brought up together or become familiar. In human communities there is similar readiness to do what is good for the community, even though it is fatal to the individual. Such behaviour does not benefit the individual directly, but each individual stands to benefit if such impulses are present in the species. All mammals seem to possess to some extent what may be called a sympathetic instinct, which makes them react more or less specifically to the behaviour of other members of their own species. Not only does the mother defend her baby, the male his mate, but the individual is concerned more widely with what befalls other members of his group. It is *as if* he were able to experience in a lesser degree what happens to his companion. His companion is attacked and he reacts as if attacked himself. The immediate object of the sympathetic instinct is at first the group of persons of the same kin and living together. With the growth of states and the increased contact between people of different kin and even of different race, the sympathetic impulses have a more general effect on behaviour. Other tendencies (particularly fear or hatred) may counter them, and when a man's companion offends him he retaliates. The sympathetic instinct is all too readily suppressed, but it is possible to suggest the kind of situation which excites it, namely one involving another member of the species, and more especially a familiar member. "In the late war", wrote Gilbert Murray in 1939, "how many thousands of men—not particularly selected or high-minded men—risked their lives eagerly to save a companion wounded in No Man's Land? They did not ask or know why they did it. Some may have alleged motives of religion, or motives of ambition in the form of medals or promotions. But the basic motive was probably more or less the same all through; that instinctively they could not see a mate lying there wounded and not try to help him".[4]

In mammals, what we call 'conscience' is the impulse to act in accordance with the social instinct when it is in conflict with some other more immediately effective impulse. In domestic dogs the conscience consists in an impulse to win the approval or reward of a human being, or to avoid his anger. When the human being is present and watching, the impulse is much stronger than when nobody is there.

All social animals are, then, ethical beings in the sense of creatures which have an innate impulse to behave in a certain way generally beneficial to their race or community. These instinctive impulses do not always prompt the animal to social behaviour because the conditions of life are apt to change before the instincts can be modified appropriately. This is particularly the case with man, who is so sensitive to environmental changes that his adaptations become rapidly obsolete. The character developed among conditions of nomad life was scarcely likely to suit conditions of settled agriculture, or life in cities. And apart from unsocial promptings from the social instincts themselves, these instincts are often countered by the egoistic ones.

If justice prevails in a community, this can only mean that in all disputes a compromise is reached in accordance with agreed rules, unaffected by the special power or influence of one of the parties. Such justice seldom exists unless there is some central power to enforce it. This does not mean that men are essentially egoistic, but rather that the instinctive basis to social behaviour is not generally sufficient to enforce it. A community in which there existed a strong tendency to self-sacrifice would soon change its character, since the more egoistical would be the only ones to survive.

How social instincts originated in mammals has been discussed by Darwin and by Westermarck (op. cit., chapter 34). Instincts can be regarded as merely well established and heritable habits. If the habits of conduct acquired by experience in the group in the end become heritable, there would then exist an impulse to certain kinds of conduct or a repugnance for certain acts. These tendencies might be rationalized, but they would be effective without this. And just as repugnance was felt for committing the action, so indignation might be felt at witnessing it. Social instincts will of course have been favoured by natural selection: communities whose members practised proper reciprocity would be more likely to survive.

When the social instinct requires conduct which conflicts with the self-regarding instincts, a new adaptation to resolve the conflict can be achieved by sublimation. But this is possible only in the case of instincts which do not serve imperative needs. No sublimation can long divert the energy of the feeding instinct. At least if it does, the animal will die, and this is not a biological solution. But those instincts which may be satisfied by beliefs do admit of sublimation. By a mental process, the social behaviour is made to appear favourable to the general objects of the self-regarding instincts. When, for instance, self-denial is imposed on the individual by the needs of the group, sublimation occurs when he persuades himself that self-restraint enhances his importance more than self-indulgence. This sometimes results in alterations in the ethical system. A moderate degree of self-restraint would suffice for society; an excessive degree of self-mortification is required by self-esteem. Thus moral codes become exaggerated. Whatever the particular origin of a code, there is always the possibility that saints will arise who push its maxims to the absurd for the better exhibition of their own excellence.

If morality originates in social instincts, then in every inquiry into the basis of morals we come finally to a sentiment or bias which cannot be further analyzed. Westermarck shows in his opening chapter that moral ideas are in fact based on instinctive tendencies to approve or disapprove certain acts. He explains that, although men may attempt to find an objective criterion for moral actions, they must measure the reliability of the criterion by reference to their own or other people's feelings. The fundamental fact is the emotional attitude to men's behaviour. But because we are all more or less alike we all tend to react in the same way to similar actions. If we were exactly alike and always reacted in exactly the same way to like behaviour, then different types of behaviour would be precisely correlated with certain types of reaction, and it would be a matter of indifference whether we classified the behaviour or the reactions, for the same classification would of necessity be applicable to both. But because we are not the same and do not all react in the same way to similar behaviour, it is impossible to find an objective criterion which will correspond with everybody's feelings of what is right and wrong. This recognition that right and wrong are relative does not mean that I lose my sense of right and wrong. To this I shall return.

The basis of all ethical systems must, then, be the common reactions of approval and disapproval on the part of the members of a society in general towards the actions of individuals. These common reactions determine the laws and customs of the society. Since each individual may stand to profit from the social behaviour of his neighbour, he naturally tends to emphasize the importance of such behaviour when not thinking particularly of himself. Thus codes of behaviour always stress the duty of the individual to his neighbour and generally take note of his duty to himself only indirectly, as affecting his usefulness to the community.

In small, primitive, and isolated communities, a relatively small number of rules and customs may suffice. In a settled community whose circumstances and institutions have been long stable, these special rules may become very comprehensive. Then all actions seem to fall into definite categories, as right or wrong, and doubtful cases are uncommon. But when conditions change, when migrations and conquests and the mingling of cultures introduce new relationships, it is found that the old rules do not suffice for the cases which arise. In modern civilized societies the question 'What must I do?' has many meanings. There is the law. If I would avoid fines or imprisonment, I must act legally. There is custom and convention, by which I must abide if I would not be regarded as a boor and an outsider. These maxims are less precise than legal enactments, the judges are all my neighbours, the judgement rather more arbitrary, and the penalties less distinct. But in both cases a certain code of conduct is prescribed with sanctions. Again, there is prudence. If I would avoid ill-health, accidents and impecuniosity, I must follow certain lines of conduct. The penalties in this case are inflicted by the impersonal forces of nature or by social effects not deliberately intended by individuals. Finally, there are moral principles. If I would have my conscience at rest, I must observe yet other rules. All these factors—law, convention, prudence, and conscience—have in common that they often run contrary to the immediate impulse. In a more primitive state of society they cannot be distinguished.

The social instincts of man prompt him to seek the good of his neighbour in the same way that other instincts make him seek food or shelter, in that in none of these cases is calculation involved. Reason comes in only when the question arises how best to achieve this natural desire. But it may happen that a man is kind or generous to his neighbour, not because he is prompted by any social instinct, but because he has reached the rational conclusion that in certain circumstances he will reap some worthwhile benefit. Such behaviour may be said to be prompted by a different instinct, namely that of self-preservation or self-enhancement. One may say that a human being has a duty to his neighbour, whom he must, in indulging himself, avoid injuring; and that this 'must' has two sources: social instinct, which is stronger in some than in others, and social pressure. As in the natural environment man learns to behave under the guidance of natural rewards and punishments, so in the social environment he is guided by the rewards and punishments of his fellows. These social rewards and punishments are, initially, merely the normal reactions to his behaviour (approving or disapproving it) of other members of the group. The parental education is of the same kind. The human parent does not contemplate some ultimate benefit to his off-spring, but merely acts in accordance with his own instinctive promptings. The offspring adapts his behaviour to the presence of the parent and learns thus some useful lessons that may serve in a larger group. The members of the social group, in administering their rewards and punishments, are not deliberately defending the interests of the abstract group. They too are merely following their instinctive bent.

At some stage in the development these unreflective sanctions, applied by the impulsive and instinctive reactions of other members of the tribe, are supplemented by sanctions deliberately contrived. Retaliation was replaced by punishment. This means that at some stage men became partially aware of the process. It was the same with communication, as Englefield has shown.[5] To begin with, communication occurred as the natural consequence of impulsive reactions, as in animals. The natural, spontaneous and unreflecting reaction to a potential intruder would be a threatening gesture; and the equally natural reaction of the intruder would be a tendency to withdraw. When the process becomes 'conscious'—that is to say, as soon as some individuals can see the essential factors in the process and imitate them—then a new stage begins, and communication is replaced by language. A secondary but important result was that language was complicated by mendacity, just as punishment was by oppression. So long as communication was not deliberate, there could be no deliberate deception. So long as social sanctions were impulsive and instinctive in character, there was equality of treatment. But when it was realized that a man's behaviour could be modified by threats and promises, each individual would be apt to employ the technique for his own advantage.

(ii) Religion and Social Behaviour

If there is an instinctive basis to social behaviour, one does not need a theist's creed in order to sympathize with one's neighbour. Because a few sound maxims are to be found in sacred books it is not reasonable to credit religion with their dissemination; they were recognized in the most primitive societies because they were based both on instinct and on social necessity. There are certain precepts held in common by religious and irreligious persons, and these almost universal moral principles are, as it were, generic characters, established in the course of social evolution. We can all observe in ourselves natural promptings to kindness, generosity and self-sacrifice which have no relation to any religious or metaphysical beliefs. Nor does theistic creed at all ensure sympathy with one's neighbour. The state of mind we call faith has often been correlated with hatred for the large majority of mankind, and it is very doubtful whether devoutly religious people are in any way better citizens, friends, or parents than people who have deliberately rejected religion.

Religious arguments in favour of moral behaviour sometimes depend for their effectiveness on sublimation; the reward or sanction is postponed. It is the idea of the consequences of the actions which determines the behaviour, and when the idea has gained this power of control, it is only necessary to postpone the reward or the sanction indefinitely. For instance, the child learns to perform the right action for the sake of his mother's word of praise and smiling approval. Usually this follows the action without delay, but the interval may be gradually prolonged. As the child grows older he may act in the approved way even though he knows that it may be long before his merit can be appreciated. At last the mere thought that the action would be approved if it were known may suffice. The approving parent or beloved teacher exerts influence at a distance. A man may even act in a certain way because he knows it would be pleasing to a deceased friend. The mere remembered image of the revered or beloved person has a potency only a little weaker than the presence of the person in the flesh. In some cases this presence is felt. There may be a genuine belief in the spiritual presence, and in that case the effect will be the same as that of the bodily presence. But without this there may be a strong feeling of obligation to act as the departed one would have wished. Thus a lively idea may function as a real presence, and we can understand in this way those forms of conduct, especially religious, which are guided by an ideal imagined as the will of a superior being, whether supernatural or not. On this basis, belief in an omniscient and all-powerful deity, who will in an after-life punish selfish actions, can help to keep selfish tendencies under control. The special advantage of sanctions beyond the grave is that they cannot easily be discredited.

In considering the way in which behaviour is controlled by ideas, it is relevant to bear in mind that man, like other social animals, is able to subordinate himself to a leader. It was long ago discovered that there can be no orderly regulation of human affairs unless, at certain times or for certain purposes, certain individuals are invested with an overruling authority. Furthermore, man has developed a more powerful imagination than any other animal, a greater capacity for representing in his brain situations (real or imaginary) other than the one facing him at any given moment. Thus a man may subordinate himself to an imaginary leader of immense authority and power, and will perform any action if he believes it in accordance with this leader's will. Ethical systems framed by such reliant persons will vary according to the nature of the leader; and since often he exists only in the minds of his followers, there is hardly any limit to the variety of resulting precepts. There is enough evidence to show that a man who believes himself to be obeying the commands of his God will often have courage and strength to accomplish anything. And what he regards as the will of his God will be determined by all kinds of independent conditions.

It is, then, clear that the effect of religion on behaviour is really one part of a larger question, namely how far behaviour is affected by ideas—for instance, by fear of consequences, or by the example, precept, or command of a leader. Where the consequences are not clear and the leader not conspicuous, the most important determinant of behaviour (other than instinct or habit) is the common example: what others do, we do—or rather, what we believe that the majority of our fellows do, we either do or pretend to do. Religion influences behaviour just in so far as it introduces one or other of these conditions or motives, namely fear of consequences, obedience to a leader and the common example. And it is not only religion which exerts such influences. Fascism, Naziism, and Communism are powerful forces that affect behaviour, both through fear of punishment and hope of reward, and because of the influence of a leader; and when they have become widespread, they affect the individual by example and suggestion. It has often been argued that, as the early Christians were prepared to face martyrdom for their religious convictions, these must have been securely based. In fact such behaviour shows only that the convictions were strongly held. Fascists, Nazis, and Communists, among others (including Islamic Fundamentalists), have shown a like readiness to sacrifice their lives for their faith.

The contention that Christian belief necessarily promotes moral behaviour fails to take account of the want of any consistency in the ethical system proclaimed by Christians save in those principles that are universally accepted (cf. above, p. 121); and it also fails to take account of the record of the Church during periods when belief was almost universal and much more strongly held than today: the forcible conversions under Charlemagne, the persecutions under the Inquisition, the Crusades (at home as well as abroad), the Spanish and Portuguese conquests in America, the witch-burning, Jew-baiting, and dogged opposition to all kinds of progress in knowledge. If any religious belief might be expected to deter men from sinful projects, it would surely be the fear of eternity in hell. Yet most humane Christians seem today to have given up this belief.[6] In so far as religion does promote moral behaviour, there is nevertheless an obvious danger in making it the basis of ethics: namely that, as Margaret Knight has repeatedly observed, if people lose their religious beliefs, they may then come to think that there is no sanction for moral behaviour except the criminal law.[7]

Theists commonly complain that atheists undermine the simple religious faith which is a necessary support for many people in this complex and stressful world. The argument implies that, since religion fulfils a useful function, it should be valued whether it is true or untrue, and the argument is commonly heard from those who deplore any appeal to 'utility' in ethical questions. But surely it is better to find the truth and proclaim it. In the long run, it may be impossible to hide it; and instead of shutting our eyes, we may more wisely use our ingenuity to exploit it, for every real remedy for our troubles can come only from knowledge and not from ignorance. Moreover, the consolatory character of a creed is not valid universally. Like clothes, creeds must be made to taste and measure. The illusion which affords comfort to one man here today may elsewhere lack or later lose its charm, and lead also to ill-adapted courses with evil effects that far outweigh the benefit to the believer. The consolations of religion are also sometimes efficacious against terrors religiously inspired in the first place; and indeed the effect of religion is sometimes the reverse of consolatory. The truth, then, however painful, is the indispensable instrument for the remedying of ills. The bitterness lies in this, that in discovering how to cure our ills, we also discover which are incurable.

Nobody really admits that it is a good thing to be deceived, and this is one reason for the claim (discussed in chapter 5) that there is more than one kind of truth; that, for example, religious truth is quite distinct from scientific truth. Although this is nonsense, I do not mean to contest that, in individual instances, the truth is better concealed (although it must be admitted that one cannot conceal it without knowing what it is). Bacon asked:

> Doth any man doubt that if there were taken out of men's minds vain opinions, flattering hopes, false valuations, imaginations as one would, and the like, but it would leave the minds of a number of men poor shrunken things, full of melancholy and indisposition and unpleasing to themselves?[8]

Obviously a doctor will think twice before telling a patient that he is terminally ill. But the systematic inculcation of highly suspect doctrines is another matter.

Those who criticize Christianity are often asked what they would propose to put in its place. But it is absurd to assume, in the manner of Julian Huxley, that new *institutions* ought to be proposed to replace those discredited. And as for the underlying beliefs, you cannot drive out a belief without giving another belief in its place. J. M. Robertson once observed that theologians themselves "are just as much 'unbelievers' as anybody else". Their creed took its rise by way of disbelief in another creed.[9] He added (p. 26) that although religious people "speak much of the pain caused to them and their like by attacks on their beliefs, they say little of any pain they have felt on finding that they had denounced the bringer of a new truth".

(iii) The Relativity of Moral Principles

What is meant by saying that moral rules are either absolute or relative? An illustration will help. Suppose that a man has sought refuge in my house knowing that the police are seeking to arrest him on a capital charge. Suppose further that I know he is innocent, yet that circumstantial evidence is likely to lead to his conviction and execution if he is arrested. If a policeman then calls, and asks me whether I know where the man is, my reply may depend on the relative weighting I give to three obvious moral rules, the first two of which conflict with the third:

1) That maximum co-operation must be given to the authorities who enforce the law.
2) That the truth must be told.
3) That a fellow human being in danger must be assisted.

When one or other of these rules is said to be absolute, what is meant is that it must always, in these or any other circumstances, be given priority over others which conflict with it. On the other hand, when all ethical rules are said to be relative, the meaning is that there is no moral rule which can invariably be given this priority.

Insistence on absolute standards is often defended by appeal to Kant, who wrote contemptuously of the kind of grocer who merely on prudential grounds does not cheat children, instead of being honest without regard to any consequences. But Kant is in fact in no better position than this grocer. Kant argues that, to act ethically, we must be able to will that the rule we are acting on should be followed by all other people. If, for instance, a man makes it a rule to seek revenge for every injury, he yet cannot—so Kant says—will that everyone else should do so. But why not? Only because that would mean that others would always be taking revenge on each other and on him. When he pays his debts he can, however, says Kant, will that everyone else should follow his course. Now this is plainly an explanation of moral law in terms of utility; and Schopenhauer was able to quote a number of passages where Kant in effect concedes this: e.g. "that I cannot will that there should be a universal law permitting lying, because people would then no longer believe me or would pay me back with the same coin".[10]

In an essay of 1798 (entitled, in English translation, 'On a Supposed Right to Lie from Altruistic Motives'), Kant pretends to dispense with utility, and argues that a homicidal maniac must be told the truth, even if this guides him to one of his chosen victims, because the principle 'Thou shalt not lie' is an absolute that must be upheld irrespective of consequences.[11] But when he had occasion to advise on a human problem that was more likely to fall within his own practical experience, he no longer took his stance on absolute veracity; for in his treatise on *Religion Within the Bounds of Mere Reason*, published in 1793, he expressly advised that pastors who do not believe in the inspiration of the Bible, or in the truth of miraculous narratives which are devoutly believed by their congregations, should nevertheless go on using the Bible in the usual way because it is a good means of edification.[12] Altogether, study of real human situations seems not to promote rigorously absolutist views of ethics. It was Macaulay, as historian, who, for instance, said, apropos of the situation in England in 1687:

> A nation may be placed in such a situation that the majority must either impose disabilities or submit to them, and that what would, under ordinary circumstances, be justly condemned as persecution, may fall within the bounds of legitimate self defence.[13]

I take this to mean that political measures draw their virtue or viciousness from the circumstances of the time, and that to say that tolerance is always and in every circumstance a good, and intolerance an evil, is to base political justice on an unconditional imperative as elusive as that on which Kant professed to base individual morality.

How difficult these questions are can be seen not merely from Kant's adherence to utility while professing to repudiate it, but also from the absolutism which sometimes informs the arguments of professed utilitarians. They know that it is vain to tell men that they must calculate the future effects, throughout all eternity, of their actions; and so they would fain show that certain simple maxims may be relied on always to produce desirable effects. Thus J. S. Mill, in his *On Liberty* (1859), would like to show that licence to express any views is always ultimately beneficial. This he could not show, even if he made it plausible. But because he wants a general rule that can be applied without continual reference to the fundamental utilitarian principle, a rule of action that need not involve laborious investigation of probable consequences, he tries to prove too much. All he is really entitled to say is that, on the whole, or on the average, freedom of expression is more helpful to society than hurtful.

Belief in absolute right and wrong has often been supported by appeal to the fact that in many cases the moral character of an action seems immediately evident; and how can this be so if there were not something other than calculation of consequences to guide us? The answer is that we have certain instinctive promptings, and that these lie at the root not only of our 'lower' impulses, but also of the 'higher' ones.

One disadvantage of such appeal to moral instinct as a standard independent of all utilitarian tests is that it is futile from the point of view of moral persuasion. The Scottish army officer Macpherson would not have brought (as he did) the Khonds of India to abandon infanticide and human sacrifice by expressing horror at and revulsion from such practices. They would have found their own moral instincts and promptings as much entitled to respect as his. He succeeded, as J. M. Robertson noted, by asking them what evidence they could offer to support their conviction that, for instance, sacrificing a human victim secured a good harvest, and by then showing that this evidence was in fact inadequate.[14]

Moral instinct, then, is as readily resorted to in a bad cause as in a good. It is because the assumption that man always knows the right by the light of nature (or of revelation) has set up so many conflicts and perplexities that resort to the utilitarian test has become so common. Another serious criticism of intuitional ethics is that it exempts ethical codes from revision. Such relatively civilized codes as exist today have been reached by constant revision of more barbarous ones; and without it, blood-vengeance (once felt to be a sacred duty), heretic-burning, witch-burning, slavery, religious persecution of every kind, human sacrifice, capital punishment for all manner of offences would have gone on unchanged, and none of the religions which are now founded on as codes of right would have been allowed to come into existence. It is, of course, easier to condemn in accordance with inflexible rules of behaviour, but it is also easy to be very inhumane in applying such rigid standards. Belief in absolute moral values is apt to be associated, for instance, with an uncivilized attitude to punishment.

While the intuitionists claim that there is a clear distinction between good and bad actions which has nothing to do with their consequences, the utilitarians, on the other hand, say that there is no way of defining right and wrong unless with reference to their consequences. The practical problem for the individual is to know at each moment what he ought to do. He must either memorize a complete code of behaviour which covers every possible case, or judge each case as it arises by reference to some general principles. It is often important to find out quickly what is the right thing to do, as the occasion may soon go by and whatever is done or left undone can no longer be altered. It is therefore very useful to have as complete a set as possible of particular maxims which may be applied without hesitation when needed. But however complete such a set may be, the occasion will inevitably arise when applying the appropriate maxims brings about disaster. There is therefore a real difficulty underlying this fundamental ethical controversy. To say, on the one hand, that on every possible occasion there is a clear line of duty, unmistakable and immediately evident, which the individual must follow, is to imply that there exists an exhaustive list of maxims which can be memorized by every man, or that there is a simple principle which may be immediately applied as soon as the question arises. Experience shows that neither of these is possible. Those who are most convinced that they have acted rightly will often harm themselves and their friends and do no good to anybody, however good their intentions. On the other hand, to say that the rightness of an action can be determined only when we have ascertained all its consequences and weighed the good against the bad is to paralyze all action. For how can we ever do this? It is, then, in the nature of man to wish to help his fellows but it is often very hard to know how best to do so.

We may nevertheless form a reasonable estimate of the probable usefulness of certain types of behaviour (drunkenness, lying, and so forth). A certain and definite answer to ethical problems is never possible. Here, as elsewhere, we have to be content with the relative, and judge that 'on the whole', in general, and apart from special cases, etc., it is a good thing for this or that community to abide by a certain rule of conduct. Once the rule has been established or imposed on that community, each individual will be regarded as virtuous or otherwise according as he observes it or not, and his own conscience will on the whole reflect the opinion of the community.

In real life, as opposed to ethical theorizing, we compromise. We have a number of useful maxims which we apply without hesitation, and a number of general principles of limited scope which can be referred to when necessary and which are simple enough to serve our purpose in most cases. In really difficult cases we have to take a chance. But when we reflect on human behaviour more generally, and without immediate reference to anything we have to do ourselves, we are free to consider the validity of the maxims on which we rely or which happen to be current. This is where utilitarian principles are important. Men act from instinct, from habit, from impulse, but when we seek to draw up *rules* of behaviour, we can find no basis but that of the utilitarian. He does not, of course, claim that a virtuous act must be based on a nice calculation of consequences—for the act is commonly performed on the spur of the moment, when there is no time for such investigation. The man of virtue must take the majority of his maxims for granted. He has made for himself a set of rules and his virtue consists in obeying them consistently even when it is inconvenient or painful. It is this recognition of paramountcy in the moral maxim, the categorical imperative, that makes the 'intuitive' moralist reject utilitarianism. But where do the rules come from? And on what ground do we compare one set of rules with another and determine their respective merits? The history of morals reveals one thing clearly, and that is that there is no common set accepted by all mankind. Intuition cannot choose between such rival systems, but utilitarianism can, and when we set about constructing our rules, we must depend on the utilitarian principle—otherwise we shall merely accept the impulses which we find in ourselves as divinely inspired. Both points of view—intuitionism and utilitarianism—are fully justified if their application is properly understood.

(iv) Innovation and Stability in Society

The investigator naturally asks himself whether it is permissible to raise doubts about the foundation of our moral principles; for if society depends on their general acceptance, we should avoid doing anything to weaken belief in their sanctity. On the other hand, the tendency to defend old traditions and established authorities under conditions of social change can lead only to the existence of obsolete and harmful customs. If customs are to be modified to suit changed conditions, there must exist in the community some possibility of questioning traditions and discrediting those which have become obsolete.

In the so-called 'free world', parliamentary democracy is one mechanism which serves this purpose. It is an attempt to avoid both anarchy and authoritarian rule by enabling the people, if they are so minded, to dismiss their rulers, peacefully and constitutionally, at regular intervals, and replace them with others. The problem of devising an organization where the conflicting forces of individual opinion can be gathered up and canalized into definite decisions and actions was a very difficult one even in the little states of ancient Greece. It was soon found that more can be accomplished under the consistent leadership of one individual than where everybody gives his opinion and a decision has to be reached by agreement; but it was also found that sooner or later the individual or group to whom power was entrusted tended to use it to its own advantage. Rulers also tried to establish a dynasty, or at any rate appoint their successsors, and disorders which accompanied disputed successions led many people to assent to this proceeding.

The advocate of democracy has no need to revolt against the principle of authority as such. There must be leaders, not only in times of crisis, because law and order at all times depend on authority. The problem is to have the kind of authorities which inspire general recognition of the need to have them and, in consequence, make the majority desire to defend them. The democrat will argue that all political systems that do not represent merely the tyranny of power are devised with a view to selecting the most able rulers; and that if we are to select them other than by parliamentary elections, we shall need to know what qualities are most important in persons to whom the legislation and administration are to be entrusted. It is clear that intelligence alone is not sufficient. No intellectual qualifications in a ruler compensate for the presence of inordinate ambition, love of luxury or want of integrity. The democrat argues that men so simple-minded and public-spirited that they can resist the temptations associated with arbitrary power are too rare to be counted on; and that it is better to suffer the inconveniences of responsible government depending on the uninstructed opinion of the whole adult population than to risk the consequences of autocracy.

As we saw, all social animals have impulses which prompt them to do what is useful to the community, even at considerable cost to themselves as individuals. However, even when the promptings of these social impulses are strong, they are frequently countered by those of egoistic ones. Hence, as the individual must have some motive in order to act consistently, he will acquire social habits only if he reaps external rewards from them, or if he is insightful enough to appreciate that to press the claims of an individual or party too far will be fatal to society as a whole (which cannot cohere if all are rebels) and hence to the individual who depends upon society. Whether people in general can be prompted to hard work and self-sacrifice for the sake of preserving their society, without the expectation of any other reward, is doubtful. The chief other reward to which they will look is the approval of their fellows, and this, coupled with fear of censure, is one of society's chief integrating forces. An individual desires to be respected because, if he is assured of this, he feels more safe, and may expect to obtain more easily whatever he wants. The desire for approval is thus prompted by the desire for power, perhaps the most important human drive after hunger and love. But if desire for approval and fear of censure are to be effective as socially integrating forces, there must exist a climate of opinion, a common attitude of approval and disapproval toward certain forms of behaviour. If this attitude is not universal, or nearly so, its influence on the individual is much diminished. In a democratic society, dissent, criticism and unconventional opinions are encouraged. Everything is, or can be, put in question, the climate of opinion becomes unsettled, and certain acts are no longer universally approved or disapproved, with the result that the ordinary man's main motive for social behaviour is very much weakened.

This is the situation which has been reached in the 'free' world today, and in Germany something similar had been in evidence in the Weimar Republic, the democracy foisted on Germany by her victors in 1918 and characterized by bitter factional strife, involving not merely debate but even physical conflict. A recent study has given an account of the reaction of a number of German theologians of that day to such pluralism. They could not feel at ease in a climate where, it appeared, any one view could be argued as cogently as its opposite. Typical in this connection was Emanuel Hirsch, who believed that political and historical judgements should be founded ultimately on absolute religious principles. "Human history", he said, "can . . . only be understood by those who see its metaphysical core and its religious connection"; and he found that "reason and freedom" lead ultimately to what he called "the all-encompassing debate about everything", making rationalism an unsettling force.[15] He supported Nazi authoritarian rule because it put an end to this for him disastrous debate; and he was not alone in seeing God's hand in Hitler's rise as an exponent of law, order, stability, and certain truth as against mere opinion. Although this solution to the problem of social instability is unimpressive, the problem itself remains, and is perhaps even more acute today. I fear that pluralism cannot be combined with social stability unless man—religious or atheistic—proves to be considerably more insightful and hence more unselfish than he has shown himself hitherto. The health of a society requires both some general acceptance of certain rules of behaviour and the possibility of questioning existing rules. Conflict between conservatives and innovators is the inevitable result of these two factors, and social stability seems to depend on a fair balance between them. The difficulty is to persuade the conservatives that a certain amount of questioning does not destroy what they are wont to call 'the cement of society', and to persuade the innovators that existing conventions cannot simply be swept away, that reform must proceed in steps, the way from A to Z being through the alphabet. Social and political innovators are apt, like the saints I mentioned above (p. 181), to push their maxims to the absurd for the better exhibition of their own excellence.

Reformers and traditionalists alike do well to bear in mind of what scanty materials all our ideas are composed. Such a book we have read, yet can scarcely produce a word of it. Such a machine we can operate so long as this requires no more than depressing a lever, but we know no more of its mechanism than of the anatomy of the garden snail or the constitution of Japan. Nevertheless—and this is something that I have been much concerned to illustrate in this book—the most powerful of emotions can be linked with the thinnest of ideas. The communist's feelings towards 'bourgeois reactionaries', the conservative's emotions towards 'reds' are often not based on any extensive knowledge and understanding of the entities in question. Rationalists are so often accused of exaggerating the power of reason, but every scientific view of behaviour must surely recognize that all the essentials of the reasoning process are exhibited in other animals as well as in man,[16] and that his reasoning powers are only marginally better than theirs. If, then, we accept that man's knowledge and capacity for understanding the world differs only in degree from that of the chimpanzee, it is ridiculous to suppose him capable of ascertaining absolute truth. What the rationalist says is that, for all reason's limitations, we have nothing else with which to understand the world, and that theologians suppose us capable of absolute truth either by simply alleging that this is so or by positing dubious and vague psychological faculties. Typical in the latter regard is Paul Tillich who posited what he called "ecstatic reason" in order to overcome the crisis of relativism (cf. above, p. 88). According to a recent study, Tillich's ecstatic reason is "existential, a rational decision which crosses the border of mystery through a leap of faith"; and this "concept" has been regarded as one of his "chief intellectual contributions to the twentieth century".[17] It is surely vain to look in such a direction for guidance concerning the problems of modern society.

Chapter Eleven
Atheism and Empiricism

(i) Is Atheism Reasonable?

If someone asks me if I believe in the existence of ectoplasm, I must first ask what is meant by this word. If no intelligible account can be given, it will be reasonable for me to say 'no', as I would if I were asked whether I believe in witchcraft or fairies. It would be difficult to get a clear and consistent definition of either a witch or a fairy, but I am familiar with certain pictures and stories which enable me to form some idea, and I do not believe that it corresponds with anything that really exists. The idea of 'God' is much more vague, so much so that many nowadays avoid any definition, at any rate any intelligible one. It is sometimes said that there need be no conflict between science and religion, for science seeks truth and God is absolute or ultimate truth. This is, however, argument by word-play. Science seeks truth in the sense of true statements or propositions; but God is not true statements. It is easy to make an abstract noun 'truth' from the adjective 'true', but not necessarily helpful.

Many different creatures have been described and received the name God: some are self-contradictory, and others so nebulous that one cannot even begin to inquire whether they have any existence except in the minds of those who have conceived them.[1] There are plenty of animals and plants and other things which I have never seen, but I believe in their existence because pictures and descriptions suffice to give me a sufficiently clear idea of them, and the statements of many people who have seen them concur so closely that I find belief is simpler than supposing these people to have conspired to deceive me or all to have been the victims of an improbable illusion. But if they were to refer to an animal having a particular name, but all gave different and mutually destructive accounts of it and of its habits, and if each description sometimes involved contradictions as well, I should be obliged to withhold my belief in a mere name with which I could associate nothing representable in my mind. This would, in such circumstances, be the only reasonable course, and it would be unjust to ascribe such incredulity to dogmatism.

Local and tribal deities have not been credited with anything so metaphysical as infinite goodness and power. They were less definite but not less finite than other human conceptions. The functions which at various times they have been required to perform are those of saviour, judge, intercessor, executioner, recompenser. The God of the philosophers is a kind of quintessence abstracted from all these and free from all limitations of time and place. The result is inconceivable, but this is generally felt to be an addition to his dignity rather than otherwise.

The God of the philosophers and of the modern religions is a necessary conception if the universe is to be regarded as having a purpose. Sceptics are commonly told that abandonment of religion means destroying all sense of ultimate purpose in life. Purpose is always associated with a mind, and in philosophy God is the mind of the universe. If there were no God, the believer's sense of justice would be outraged. If death ends all, then, he argues, there is no point in life. The revolt of the sense of justice and the conviction that life must have some point are the expressions of a state of anxiety whose resolution requires a situation constructed in the mind. One may, as we saw, (above, p. 130), make a meaningful distinction between practical beliefs, which are subject to experimental control and which are accordingly modified and corrected until they are found to be adequate; and another kind of beliefs which are not controlled in this way, and which may be such as to flatter or comfort, or, in general, to satisfy some emotional requirement, to resolve some state of tension. This kind of belief plays a large part in religion.

In fact one cannot meaningfully ascribe a purpose to life as a whole. Life is filled with purposes of all kinds, objects to be attained, goals to be reached, tasks to be accomplished, yet all these are within life and form but episodes. Life as a whole cannot be said to have a purpose, although many of the actions of which it is made up may have one. A purpose is necessarily restricted. As soon as it is achieved it ceases to exist and must be replaced by another. Purpose, I have said, is to be associated with a mind, and minds are found in animals. What an animal does is only partly attributable to its intelligence. Without a will and a body, a memory and various other powers, an abstracted intelligence would not be capable of very much. And it is only a few animals that can form a purpose, and only in regard to something small and near. Purpose is as much a specific biological character as sexual love or the action of the liver, and it is as absurd to ascribe a purpose to the universe, or to life as a whole, as to ascribe a nervous system to the Milky Way. But there is a natural tendency for men to try to interpret the world at large in terms of their own limited animal inclinations and habits.

Efforts to demonstrate the existence of God are efforts to show that the universe has a purpose, and it seems to be assumed that any such purpose can be relied upon to be good, to include the ultimate satisfaction of our human hopes and desires, or at least of all those which seem to merit consideration. (Most religions and philosophies are concerned only with human aspirations. It is not felt necessary that there should be any 'point' in the lives of spiders and codfish). It has rarely been suggested that the universe has a definitely evil purpose, aiming at our torment and final frustration, though there have been philosophies and religions that predicted such a destiny for the greater part of mankind, not including their own adherents.

It is often said that the only alternative to religious belief is cynicism about ourselves and the world. But I see no reason why a realistic assessment of ourselves and the world should be stamped as cynicism. Those who are indifferent to religion often find satisfaction in their work, which they pursue without fanaticism and which is not infrequently useful. They try to keep in good health and protect their families from disease and accident, but they are not overworried about death, for they are aware that, before they were born, the world went on for a very long time without them, and they would not much wish to have lived in former ages. They think too that the world is likely to go on for an equally long time after they are dead and that they have no reason to expect that it will be much better than it is. Certain rules of life—sensible to follow because found by experience to make for contentment and good health—have nothing to do with religion, but are based on the inquiries which study man and his environment systematically with a view to reaching reliable generalizations that are confirmed in practice. Religious preachers, however, as we have seen in some of the previous chapters, arrive at generalizations without difficulty but often do not try to test them; and some of their generalizations are so framed that no test would be possible.

There has recently been a spate of books purporting to show that scientific developments have lent credence to the hypothesis that God exists. It is noted, for instance, that atoms are no longer supposed to be miniature billiard balls; the "new physics" has "undermined the apparent solidity of matter" and made it dissolve away into "a sort of ghostly mêlée of vibrating energy patterns".[2] This is felt to be a more 'spiritual' conception of matter, more in keeping with religious views. But this kind of refinement of an originally crude theoretical model is exactly what one would expect in the progress of science. One may appropriately distinguish explanation by means of theoretical models, involving analogies (as when heat was taken to be a kind of fluid or an atom as a miniature solar system) and explanation by means of generalization, which concerns only those properties which are really common to the things under investigation. Explanation by means of models often begins by making use of superficial likenesses, whereas real generalization is concerned only with real likenesses. The atom can only superficially be compared to the solar system; but the moon, as a gravitating body in the earth's field, is exactly comparable to the falling apple. The moon has very little similarity to the apple, yet that one character—weight— which they have in common permitted a very fruitful comparison. Explanation by means of models, on the other hand, may jump at almost any plausible analogy, however inexact, and then clip, prune and polish the model until, if possible, only a pure generalization is left. In this way older atomic hypotheses have been progressively refined (cf. below, p. 210f). The fact that "the clockwork universe that Newton constructed, with its solid little atoms bouncing off one another, has now been demolished"[3] is therefore hardly an occasion for religious jubilation. 'Vibrating energy patterns' bring us no nearer to God than do billiard balls. And when another apologist adds that scientists no longer believe in "a clockwork universe slavishly unfolding according to the laws of cause and effect",[4] he seems unaware that the limitations of the idea of cause have long since been stressed by scientists without concessions to religious positions.

Other evidence recently offered is the rapidity of man's evolution from a primate ancestor—best explained, so the Bishop of Birmingham (Hugh Montefiore) thinks, by supposing God's participation in the process. Like many others, he exaggerates the gap between man and other mammals when he says that only man can "cope with concepts". In fact, however, if a dog sees a cat, or even a portion of it, in any position in a wide variety of environments; if he smells a cat, or even if he hears the word 'cat' pronounced in a certain tone by his master, then his reaction is likely to be instantaneous. And he is further capable of distinguishing what one might call this generic cat from the cat who is a personal acquaintance and with whom he amicably shares the fireside. It is inadmissible to hold that he is incapable of concepts in the sense of general ideas; and his behaviour shows that he can 'wield' such concepts. There are dogs who have been ill-treated by children or postmen and who remain hostile to children or to uniformed postmen while showing friendliness to other human beings. Generalization is obviously involved here. The Bishop goes on to say that animals are disadvantaged since it is "almost impossible" to "think in concepts without the use of language".[5] This may be true of the kind of concepts 'wielded' by religious apologists which are often almost entirely verbal—mere words to which strong emotions are linked. But the practical workman can think out and act on a plan without recourse to words. I have discussed this whole issue at length elsewhere.[6] It may of course be true that Darwinian theory does not fully account for the evolution of the human brain from something like that of a chimpanzee; and that, as the Bishop says, "other factors were at work in addition to natural selection through random mutation" (p. 108). But it is unwarranted to infer from this that it is "much more probable that human beings are made in the image of God" (p. 172). And it is simply circular, in an argument for the existence of God, to take as a datum that human beings "have spiritual capacities which enable them to enjoy fellowship with God" (p. 103). For the Bishop, human beings are either "made in the image of God" or they are "the random product of a meaningless universe" (p. 172). A meaningful universe means, for him, one working out a divine purpose: and I have already given my view of the limitations of the idea of purpose.

Montefiore is also impressed by the fact that a human being can "engage in personal relationships" (p. 103); and he thinks that this "cannot be explained scientifically through the complex functioning of his brain" (p. 172). I have just noted that a dog is perfectly capable of a personal relationship to one particular cat, although hostile to the species in general. And many animals have a personal relationship with their mates and their offspring. They will often not accept substitutes if their offspring are taken from them. In chapter 6 (on learning) in his *The Study of Instinct*, (Oxford: 1951) N. Tinbergen records that, if the young of herring gulls are replaced by young of the same age from another nest, the adult bird will accept them only if the transfer is made during their first five days of life. After that, the parent knows her own, even though, as Tinbergen stresses, her chicks and the substitute ones are indistinguishable to a human observer. He adds that approximately the same results have been obtained in experiments with various species of terns (p. 145f). The analogy with human behaviour is striking. The situation which calls forth an instinctive response (parental or, for that matter, erotic) is at first only roughly defined: a young man may, for instance, 'fall for' any one of a considerable number of girls. But once an attachment has been formed, the response is focussed on the particular partner chosen; its continuance depends now on a very exact situation; and to break this 'personal relationship' and accept a new partner becomes a painful process requiring considerable reorientation.

(ii) Absolutist Hankerings

Absolutist hankerings have a long tradition in European thought. Many logicians have believed that logic is directly related to truth and is not dependent on the characteristics of mind which man to a large extent shares with the higher mammals, who also draw inferences. Many metaphysicians think that their intuitions are directly related to the 'eternal verities', and are not to be explained by reference to common animal instincts and human experience and habits. The aesthetician in the same way likes to believe that the principles of beauty are not merely the effect of certain animal propensities which vary with the race and the individual; and the religious person could not for a moment tolerate the view that his beliefs had the same origin as the magical notions of the savage. From absolutist standpoints, 'empirical' knowledge, based on study of the actual world, is apt to look a little inferior. One must of course admit that it may not lead to certainties. But it is far more relevant to religious beliefs than many theologians are disposed to admit. For one thing, many of these beliefs are based on supposedly historical events, for which the evidence is purely empirical. If the Christian religion did not depend on the occurrence of certain events in first century Palestine, there would not have been so much concern among Christians over the books of Strauss and others which put a question mark over so many of these events. Again, one argument which has often been relied on to prove the divine character of Christianity is based on the way it developed. It is alleged that the normal causes which account for the spread of other religions are insufficient to account for that of Christianity. This argument can obviously be confirmed or refuted only by an appeal to the facts of history. Another argument sometimes heard is that from the character of the believer. It is alleged that the courage, constancy and other virtues of the true Christian are not to be accounted for except on the assumption of supernatural aid. This again is an appeal to history, and to test such a view we must compare Christian and non-Christian behaviour. It is also frequently asserted that the believer experiences, as a consequence of his belief, something variously described as emotion, conviction, elation, satisfaction, certitude, which would be quite unaccountable except on the Christian hypothesis. We can all make the test on ourselves and, by forcibly repressing our doubts, bring ourselves to believe what our normal reason finds incredible. If we succeed, we prove only our susceptibility to suggestion, and it would be sensible first to inquire how the experiment has gone with others who have made it, and whether the effects on their character and behaviour are encouraging. Such an inquiry, again, is historical. It means testing notions against ascertainable facts or constructing them laboriously out of patient observation.

A proposition which is inconsistent with experience is untrue, and a lucid and unambiguous proposition of this kind is soon exposed in practice. Hence knowledge based on careful rational inquiry is provisional and subject to revision in the light of new evidence or new interpretations of existing evidence. Furthermore, as one thing can be explained only in terms of another which is supposed to be understood, we have finally either to accept some fundamentals without explanation, or to argue in a circle—explaining A in terms of B, B in terms of C, but C in terms of A. Hence the frequent complaint that reason can reach no bedrock of certainty—a complaint usually coupled with the suggestion that something other than reason can make good this deficiency. I will try to explain why I think it wiser to accept the relativity of all our knowledge.

When I act, it is the real world with which I have to deal, and the effectiveness or otherwise of my actions will depend on whether my ideas correspond sufficiently with the reality. All my ideas are made up out of sensations and memories, and my knowledge of the world can only be my interpretation of these. The way in which I can tell that a sensation has an external cause and is not a delusion or hallucination is to see whether all the other sensations which normally accompany it can be experienced. If, for instance, I smell a rose, I expect also to be able to see and touch it. The fitting of each item of experience into a larger context is the only process, finally, by which we establish the truth of anything (cf. above, p. 139). The sensation (the smell) suggests to me the thing (the rose). But what is the thing? Any description I offer of it in terms of components, qualities, material or other features, is of necessity incomplete. Such a description is, in fact, simply an account of my idea of the thing, and that is quite different from the thing. The qualities I discern in it are the result of my human efforts at abstraction, and the thing is something quite distinct from my thinking processes. However extensive my knowledge of it, this knowledge can always be increased. More care and attention will always add aspects to those previously experienced. I hope, by continuing my investigations, to enlarge and correct my idea, but I do not suppose that my idea can ever correspond even approximately to the real object. In short, the real thing I do not and cannot know, not, as Kant supposed, because it us unknowable, but because the knowledge involved would require more than several lifetimes to acquire even in outline. There is perhaps no detail that I could not become acquainted with by good fortune, but the details are far too numerous ever to be exhausted. In this sense the real thing is something quite distinct from anybody's idea of it. It of course does not follow that anyone's idea of it is as adequate as anyone else's, nor that truth is relative in the sense that my propositions about the thing and your contradictory propositions about it may both be equally true. What does follow is that the 'real' thing exists for me in contradistinction to someone else's idea of it, rather than to my own. When I observe, say the behaviour of a child who tries to pick a rose without appreciating the power of its thorns, I can contrast the real rose with his (inadequate) idea of it. But what I am really doing in such a case is to judge the child's idea, and find it wanting, by comparison with my own. I cannot make the same contrast between my own idea and the reality.[7] Again, when I estimate the chimpanzee's power of analyzing his environment, I take the real world as given. I enquire, for example, how much of the forest where he lives can enter into his conception of the world; and when I compare his achievement in exploiting the forest with that of the human forest-dweller, I measure them both by a common standard, which is, however, only my own conception of the world. Although I believe that there is a real world independent of the ideas which may be formed of it by the chimpanzee or the philosopher, yet the fact remains that I have no access to it different in kind from that of the rabbit or the rat. The objective world in which they appear to live and move is objective only in relation to me, although I can find nothing that is more objective.[8] From this relativity it is hard to see any escape.

(iii) Empiricism and the Nature of Science

We have seen that religious apologists are apt to be severely critical of empiricism. According to Keith Ward, for instance, the view that all knowledge must derive from, or be based on sensory experiences (sense data) is an "odd theory" which "seems to have collapsed in recent years". He allows that we come to know a real world by means of our sensory experiences, but denies that we have to infer its existence from sense-data, and prefers what he calls the "realist" view that "we know it directly"; for only on the assumption that this knowledge is independent of sense data can we explain how we know that things continue to exist when we are not looking at them. And once we allow the "basic belief" that our wives and our office desks go on existing in our absence, " the believer in God can say that belief in God is a basic belief too".[9]

'Existence' is a philosophical term that often serves to befog a relatively simple issue. The dog's behaviour in finding his way to a favourite but distant situation (a place, for instance likely to contain one of his human or canine friends) shows that he continues to believe in its 'existence' even when he has no perception of it. His behaviour also shows that he can identify many a situation from any of the different aspects it presents to his senses. He will, for instance, give the same characteristic response to his master's voice, his visible appearance (from many different points of view), his odour, the sound of his footsteps, and so on. There is no need to assume that any 'direct' knowledge is involved. The dog has learned separately to respond in the same way to all these stimuli, and what helps to unite them in his mind is his common response to them all, and his expectation that any one of them will be linked in his experience with any other. In the same manner, the human being learns to refer such different sensations as the smell, the feel and the sight of a rose to the real rose. Ward admits that "the hypothesis that physical objects exist . . . is useful to help to simplify and make sense of our experiences". But he denies that this hypothesis "is explanatory in the way a scientific theory is—it does not predict exactly what will happen" (p. 64). I have argued the contrary (above, p. 138f), and have said that if I smell a rose, then I expect to be able to see it (above, p. 206). The 'odd theory' that has 'collapsed' is not the view that our knowledge of things is based on our sensations, but the contention that it is possible to describe our knowledge of the world exclusively in terms of sensations, without mentioning things or assuming their existence as the basis of the sensations.

Contrary to what is often supposed, empiricism does not entail regarding ideas as mere copies of sensations (see above, p. 145) nor denying that knowledge depends a great deal on innate capacity (see above, p. 171). Empiricism holds that we see or feel or hear only aspects of a real situation and must construct it in the mind by inference from these (above, p. 96f). When we believe in the North Pole or Queen Anne we are reconstructing a larger space-time portion of our environment from a series of complex perceptions. It is psychologically the same phenomenon when we reconstruct a real dog from the noise of his barking and when we reconstruct the history of England from the reading of books and the observation of monuments or customs. Is the reconstructed dog real? Is our conception of English history true or a myth? In each case we may be more or less convinced, more or less sceptical. In many cases we know how to diminish the sources of error but can never eliminate them altogether.

Ernst Mach touches on these matters in an interesting chapter headed 'hypotheses', where he writes:

> The sportsman finds a feather, and his imagination at once produces the picture of the complete bird, the jay, which has lost it. A current in the sea brings strange plants, the bodies of animals, pieces of carved wood; and before Columbus rises the picture of the still unknown country from which these things have come. Herodotus observes the regular Nile floods and forms the queerest conception about the events with which they are connected.[10]

He adds that the interpolations or extrapolations ('Ergänzungen') are taken from the domain of familiar happenings and are so natural and inevitable that their hypothetical character is not always realized. (When we see marionettes dance, we assume invisible wires. When we see a man driving dangerously and find him incoherent, we assume the influence of alcohol). He does not say, and possibly did not realize, that it is the same process of extrapolation that enables an isolated aspect of a thing (such as the sound of a barking dog) or a single phase of an event to be spontaneously interpreted as the complete thing or the complete event. From a brief glance at the greengrocer's shop front, I observe that he has oranges, bananas, apples, melons and pineapples for sale. But my idea of a banana is much more complex than the visual projection of it that was all that my glance provided.

What Mach does show is that scientific hypotheses are made on the same psychological basis as everyday ones, and that what is involved is merely a more developed stage of a mental process already found among primitive peoples and even among animals. He illustrates what he has in mind by considering the theory that heat is a kind of fluid. We are familiar with the behaviour of fluids, and so, if heat passes through a body as a liquid penetrates any porous object, we may expect certain results. We transfer our expectations from the known case to the new. If there were no resemblance or analogy at all between heat and a fluid, the supposition would be infertile and actions based on it would fail of their purpose. But heat is not a fluid, the resemblance is only partial, so that not all actions based on the supposition are rewarded. When on this basis discrepancies are detected, a rectification of the theoretical model is undertaken, and the 'fluid' has to be endowed with some new property not found in familiar fluids. Successive rectifications may ultimately lead to a conception in which the original notion of fluid is scarcely recognizable. The idea that electricity is a fluid was modified in the same way, and the value of taking fluids as models in these two cases was largely due to an elaborate mathematical technique for dealing with fluids.

There is an unfortunate tendency to regard the theoretical model as indivisible, as something that must be accepted or rejected as a whole. A fluid that lacks some of the familiar properties of fluids is felt to be an impossibility and a contradictory conception, and on this view, if the fluid model cannot be applied integrally, it must be the wrong model. I suspect that some such idea underlies Keith Ward's remarks about the 'collapse' of earlier (particularly Newtonian) views about the nature of reality (cf. above, p. 202).

As the essence of the original hypothesis, the familiar concrete model of naive experience, is gradually transformed into mecha-

nisms remote from common experience, the question is sometimes asked: what is left? What for instance, *is* electricity? What *is*
the atom? The answer is that the *conception* of an atom is the
totality of the phenomena attributed to it. How near this conception is to the reality we cannot say, as scientific investigation has
not yet come to an end.

How important for the progress of science is the testing of
constructive hypotheses has been stressed by way of criticism of
John Stuart Mill, who as a non-Christian and an autodidact with
no university position has received more criticism than respect.
However, what he in fact says shows him well aware of the importance of such hypotheses, both for science and for everyday
thinking. He stresses their "indispensable" role in prompting
observations and experiments which "put us on the road" to
evidence which is confirmatory or otherwise. He adds that the
competent scientist does not go about collecting data indis-
criminately, without having a hypothesis to test:

> Some inducement . . . is necessary for trying one experiment rather
> than another, and although it is abstractedly possible that all the
> experiments which have been tried might have been produced by the
> mere desire to ascertain what would happen in certain circumstances,
> without any previous conjecture as to the result; yet, in point of fact,
> those unobvious, delicate and often cumbrous and tedious processes of
> experiment which have thrown most light upon the general constitu-
> tion of nature would hardly ever have been undertaken . . . unless it had
> seemed to depend on them whether some general doctrine or theory
> which had been suggested but not yet proved should be admitted or
> not.

He emphasizes the importance of having a working hypothesis
when he adds: "we begin by making any supposition, even a false
one, to see what consequences will follow from it; and by
observing how these differ from the real phenomena, we learn
what corrections to make in our assumptions". And he notes on
the next page that it is not only scientists who go about things in
this way:

> Let anyone watch the manner in which he himself unravels a compli-
> cated mass of evidence: let him observe how, for instance, he elicits the
> true history of any occurrence from the involved statements of . . .
> witnesses; he will find that he does not take all the items of evidence

into his mind at once, and attempt to weave them together; he extemporizes, from a few of the particulars, a first rude theory of the mode in which the facts took place, and then looks at the other statements one by one, to try whether they can be reconciled with that provisional theory, or what alterations or additions it requires to make it square with them.[11]

W. S. Jevons has said, criticizing Mill, that Huxley and Tyndall advocated the use of hypotheses in science[12]—as if Mill had been against it! More recently, Professor Peter Medawar has declared that "Mill feared the imaginative element in hypotheses", which in fact is "one of science's chief glories."[13] Mill had said, apropos of the undulatory theory of light, that, if such a hypothesis leads to the correct prediction of hitherto unobserved facts, it is not necessarily correct, even though "such predictions and their fulfilment are well calculated to impress the uninformed". Medawar takes this as evidence of a basic mistrust of hypotheses. But the point Mill is actually making is that the fulfilled predictions show not that light consists of waves, but that its behaviour *is in some ways* similar to that of waves. "It does not follow, because some of the laws agree with those of undulations, that there are any actual undulations. . . . Even the undulatory hypothesis does not account for all the phenomena of light."[14]

What Mill's critics accuse him of is: identifying science with induction, which he defines as "that operation of the mind by which we infer that what we know to be true in a particular case or cases will be true in all cases which resemble the former in certain assignable respects". It is "the process by which we conclude that what is true of certain individuals of a class is true of the whole class, or that what is true at certain times will be true in similar circumstances at all times".[15] He insists that the proposition based on an induction includes more than the evidence on which it is based. When I observe, as a result of a number of dissections, that the brains of certain hedgehogs have certain features, I infer that these are present in all hedgehog brains. Mill says it would be no case of induction if I merely stated this of the particular hedgehogs examined. He thus distinguishes between description and induction and accuses Whewell of confusing the two. He and Whewell were arguing about what was involved in Kepler's discovery of the orbits of the planets. Mill held that Kepler merely ascertained that the orbit of, for instance, Mars, was an ellipse; that he determined and described the fact and in doing so added nothing to the data which he had established (p. 344). Whewell, however, said that the ellipse was not given in the facts; that these were merely a set of observed points which might have been joined by all kinds of curves; that Kepler was the first to recognize that the only curve which would accommodate them all was an ellipse; and that he therefore guessed that an ellipse would also accommodate any further points which anybody should subsequently establish.[16]

Kepler's discovery of the true orbit was certainly hypothesis, and not mere description, as Mill maintained. Indeed it was the last of a succession of hypotheses which Kepler had tried out as— in Mill's own words—"a succession of guesses". Mill adds that "we know from Kepler himself that before hitting upon the conception of an ellipse, he tried nineteen other imaginary paths which, finding them inconsistent with the observations, he was obliged to reject".[17] Each successive hypothesis aimed at prompting subsequent observations which either confirmed or discredited it. Even today, presumably, there are positions of the planets that have never been observed; but so many observations have been made in conformity with the elliptical hypothesis that further observations are predicted with confidence.

It was earlier thought that the planets moved in circles, with the earth as centre. The distortion from purely circular motion represented by an ellipse was duly explained by supposing that they are influenced by the pull of the sun as well as that of the earth. That Mill is not absolutely clear as to the difference between hypothesis and induction is betrayed when he says:

> The assertion that the planets move in ellipses was but a mode of representing observed facts . . . , while the assertion that they are drawn, or tend, towards the sun, was the statement of a new fact, inferred by induction.[18]

The hypothesis of attraction is not an induction. By induction we infer, from a limited number of observations, a general law. But an explanation of the law by means of some hypothesis is not part of the induction. Mill seems to assume that an induction in itself necessarily involves some hypothesis.

If Mill and Whewell had been on friendly terms, they could easily have resolved their differences on this matter. But Whewell was a churchman and Mill a rationalist, and perhaps Mill felt towards the cleric an instinctive opposition, prompted possibly by some religious pronouncement such as is certainly to be found in Whewell's great *History of the Inductive Sciences*, or by such real and substantial differences between them as on the subject of "necessary truth". On the other hand Whewell, as Master of Trinity College and author of the aforementioned *History*, could not allow himself to be lectured by a layman.

One can only wish that controversy were habitually conducted with the candour that characterizes practically everything Mill wrote. On an issue where he really did disagree fundamentally with Whewell, he found it fortunate that the opposite side had found so able a champion: for:

> whoever is anxious that a discussion should go to the bottom of the subject must rejoice to see the opposite side of the question worthily represented.[19]

Finally, it is of interest to note that, while the ideas of vibration and wave propagation were essential to the development of the science of light, and the idea of a fluid to that of the science of electricity, these ideas into which the data of experiment were fitted were all borrowed from previous experience in other fields. Every hypothesis, before it can be applied to a new set of facts, must be borrowed from some domain in which it is already recognized. As Jevons has said:

> No hypothesis can be so much as framed in the mind unless it be more or less conformable to experience. As the material of our ideas is derived from sensation, we cannot figure to ourselves any agent but as endowed with some of the properties of matter. All that the mind can do in the creation of new existencies is to alter combinations or the intensity of sensuous properties.[20]

He explains how the facts of experiences are entwined, exaggerated, magnified or modified in the imagination; but there must be some fact of experience to begin with.

To trace the process back to the beginning means to trace the development of the human mind back to pre-human conditions.

The dog, from the observation of a small black patch almost hidden in the bushes, forms the hypothesis that he is in the presence of a cat, and further exploration confirms or falsifies this theory. That the beginnings of the reasoning process, based on experience, can be witnessed in creatures other than man was clear enough to Mill. "Animals", he said, "profit by experience and avoid what they have found to cause them pain in the same manner, though not always with the same skill, as a human creature. Not only the burnt child but the burnt dog dreads the fire".[21]

Conclusion: How Religion Survives Criticism

(i) The Framework of Our Beliefs

All the higher animals show curiosity. It is a valuable impulse which prompts them to learn more about their environment. Man, who has a greater capacity for learning, is therefore more curious than other animals; but, paradoxically, his greater capacity makes him more liable to error, for this capacity depends on memory. Memory enables an animal to combine past experiences with present ones and so to form a mental picture of regions which would be much too large to be surveyed at one time; and it allows him to form ideas of processes which can be observed only over a prolonged period. In man this power of the imagination has developed to the point where he can represent to himself, at least after a fashion, vast regions which he has never known and events which occurred before he existed or will occur after he has vanished. This representation of the immense and the remote becomes more and more inadequate as the expanse of time or space which it embraces grows greater; for, whereas our idea of the immediate environment is continually checked and corrected by new experience, no direct experience can correct our ideas of things so remote.

This correction, however, is made to some extent possible by *indirect* experience, which has enabled men to make use of one another's experience. From books and the reports of travellers we can often form useful ideas of distant places and past events. Such knowledge, derived from the experience of others, depends, of course, on the effectiveness of language, and this depends to a large extent on the systematization of methods of observation and description to ensure that reports are fairly comparable and descriptive terms uniform. Science may be regarded as the organization of the methods of indirect experience. The fundamental methods of science are only specialized forms of common types of behaviour found in all men and in some other animals, but made more productive by co-operation and language.

Historical facts such as the events which are alleged in the Bible to have occurred are, then, impossible to verify in any direct way. Whether my friend has been injured or not I can find out by visiting him and observing his condition, but events of the remote past are only to be inferred—from records, reports, traditions, and occasionally from obvious physical consequences. In all these cases the inferences we make depend upon a framework of knowledge which we regard as established and into which these individual items must be fitted, as we saw in chapter 8 above. Since, then, there is no exegesis without presuppositions, it is sometimes argued that conservative religious presuppositions are at least as good as any others.

The fitting of each item of belief into a larger context or framework is in fact important apropos of all our beliefs, including the ones which concern practical and everyday affairs. If the choice of framework were arbitrary, it is difficult to see how the species could have survived. Fantastic beliefs remaining uncorrected on matters of any practical importance would have led to the elimination of the believers. In actual fact, the framework with which religious conservatives and their less religious compatriots operate includes so much in common that an explanation is needed as to why it does not extend to religious beliefs. The common elements are there because they represent beliefs which are not independent of experience, but which result from it. We all know what to expect of things we deal with constantly. Other things are to some extent beyond our ken, but we may have ideas about them nevertheless, and here the likelihood of illusion and error is considerable. People with no knowledge of chemistry may be prepared to keep what is called an open mind as to whether ether is a good fire extinguisher. A chemist has a framework of knowledge, constructed from experience, which will lead him to have a decided view on the matter. The part of a man's framework which may have been constructed without the checks of experience is not for that reason the more reliable.

Let me press this point concerning the correction of our ideas by experience. When our ideas about our immediate environment are very incomplete or erroneous, our behaviour is likely to be ill-adapted to our needs, so that we expose ourselves to some immediate unpleasantness. But in this way attention is called to our mistake, and we may be led to rectify it. If, for instance, we act on the belief that ether is a good fire extinguisher, we shall be in for a rude shock, and if we survive the experience, the belief will not survive with us. On the other hand, any ideas we may have formed about the nature of the universe, or about the distant future or past, are unlikely to lead to any *noticeably* inappropriate reactions on our part. Thus we may well persist in erroneous beliefs of these kinds all our lives without experiencing the smallest surprise or disappointment.

This difference is important. It explains why even the most primitive peoples sometimes appear to have made considerable progress in the practical arts while continuing to hold quite groundless beliefs in matters which do not lend themselves to experimental control. The role of language is here significant. Practical devices, tools, weapons and methods can be transmitted without loss, since they do not require the assistance of verbal explanation. But beliefs which admitted of no practical demonstration and could be checked by no intelligible test could be entrusted only to words or to other equivocal ciphers and symbols which each generation had to interpret afresh according to its lights.

The difference between these two kinds of beliefs also explains why in our civilized societies people who are highly educated in fields where all theories are subjected to experimental tests can at the same time—to use their own phrase—'believe in the Bible'. They have never bothered with critical study of it, for erroneous views on it do not expose them to any obvious unpleasantness. To explain the difficulties which lie in the way of accepting any Biblical book at its face value means descending into details, and this, they are convinced, is mere trivial pedantry. The simplest way to avoid confronting difficulties is to keep to generalities. Many people are prepared to believe—have been brought up to believe—that 'in some way' or 'in some sense' the Bible is God's revelation. And God himself in such thinking may be no more than a sort of something somewhere. It is a long way from this attitude to full-blooded Fundamentalism. But such an attitude does provide the preacher and the conservative theologian with the essential basis on which he can build.

A good example of the technique of sticking to generalities is a recent book by Harry R. Boer, a theologian and missionary teacher for many years.[1] He admits contradictions in what is alleged of Jesus in the gospels—in, for instance, the location of his resurrection appearances and the persons to whom they were vouchsafed. I would add that even the nature of these appearances is not the same in the various accounts. (Did Jesus return for a time to normal life with his disciples, or appear only from on high with a body of heavenly radiance?). Yet, says Boer, "that Jesus truly rose from the dead is the common and abiding teaching" (p. 83). Again, the focus of his ministry may have been in Judea, as the fourth gospel holds, or in Galilee, as the other three maintain: yet the documents agree that there was a ministry. Having discerned such "common and abiding teachings" in the records (he repeats the phrase as in a litany), Boer confidently accepts them as informing us about the doings of "the Second Person of the eternal Trinity" (p. 85).

The religious conservative who argues that, because there must be presuppositions in exegesis, we are free to lean towards those that please us best, is insinuating that his presuppositions, his framework are as much justified by experience as any others. But this is not so. Walking on water, turning it into wine, emerging from the tomb and consuming fish with one's friends are not what we normally come across. If one is faced with implausible stories in ancient documents of unknown authorship, written up to two generations later than the alleged occurrences described, and without external support, is it then sensible to believe that these stories are true—particularly when (as is the case with the gospel accounts of Jesus's virgin birth and resurrection appearances) there are crass contradictions between the narratives which make them mutually exclusive? That such divergent accounts could be written by authors who had already come to believe (for reasons which need to be investigated) that Jesus was virgin-born and rose from the dead is perfectly plausible; that their narratives provide any *basis* for such belief is not. The events alleged in these stories did not form the basis of the faith, but the stories resulted from faith. There are canons of evidence generally accepted by historians, and such gospel narratives fall foul of them; that is why even many Christian scholars have come to regard them as legends. One suspects that the Professors of Science who today loudly proclaim their acceptance of the miracles recorded in these and other gospel stories—*The Times* of 13 July 1984 published a letter from fourteen such signatories—are less well acquainted with the inadequacy of the documentary evidence than are many of their theological colleagues.

The growth of science has resulted in the specialization of methods in different fields, and the accumulation of knowledge has been such that no one can any longer assimilate more than a small fraction of it; and, as knowledge is recorded in a form which can be understood only by those suitably equipped, each individual, in fields where he lacks the special knowledge which gives him access to the recorded stock of information, is still dependent on more primitive modes of forming his ideas. Thus in a scientific age crude ideas are commonly found in the same mind which, in some particular domain, is equipped with highly adequate ones; and we find men reasoning like scientists in one context and like ignoramuses in another. One really cannot investigate the grounds of all one's beliefs, and one cannot refrain from belief. The ethics of the question seem to be: test rigidly those beliefs which determine one's behaviour in important matters, in matters where there are significant consequences. But when it takes a lifetime to acquire adequate knowledge even in one chosen field, this injunction becomes all too burdensome. Where knowledge comes to an end, the mythmaker finds his opportunity. He may be primarily concerned to make a good story, or he may seek to edify and point a moral. Or he may try to explain and justify certain articles of a prevailing creed, certain ritual practices or certain laws. It is not impossible that he may be concerned to ascertain the true account of things and that, in comparing different stories, he adopts that which seems to him more natural and more credible. It may be that all these motives combine to produce the result that survives.

(ii) Fundamentalism Past and Present

That many people are content to believe what they are told is to be expected also from man's social nature. The solitary animal faces the universe alone. His knowledge of the environment is acquired by personal experience through direct contact, and that part of the environment of which he has no direct experience remains unknown to him and without influence on his behaviour. But the member of a herd or society has additional resources. By attention to the reactions of other members of the herd, he is able to react indirectly to events which are not accessible to him through his own senses. In this way his attention becomes focussed more on the action of his fellows and less on the remainder of the environment. Thus, in the case of human societies, whenever an immediate response to the non-human elements in the situation is not required, there is a tendency to respond chiefly to the human elements. Instead of forming his own judgement, the individual tries to determine what the prevailing opinion is, and the habit thus developed may easily overwhelm tendencies to independence.

Such conformity in the majority provides the small minority in whom tendencies to independence are strongly developed with a motive for dogmatizing. Those who seek power first try to impose certain beliefs and acquire in doing so the prestige associated with special knowledge. Fundamentalist groups illustrate the willingness of millions to trust in the authority of individual leaders. Barr has noted that the authority of the great evangelists in Fundamentalism is far greater than that of bishops or other leaders in the institutional church, or of scholars or theologians in non-fundamentalist Christianity.[2] In the ancient world, with no railways, no press, no regular post, no radio or television, the scope of charismatic preachers was much more limited. Their present-day success in winning followers on a huge scale naturally increases their own confidence, often to the point where they suppose themselves to be really inspired. When a man believes that he is revealing some deep truth imparted to him by a superior power, he may not even expect to understand what he is saying. Or if he does his critical judgement may be dulled in the agitation of the afflatus. The visible symptoms of inspiration will impress not only the preacher but also his hearers. This conviction of special inspiration does not so readily arise in the minds of men who owe their superior powers to knowledge legitimately acquired; for they know the source and limitations of their capacity, and so are not so ready to assume the authoritative tone. Furthermore, the active missionizing required of the zealous preacher does not readily comport with a life spent in study and inquiry. Intellectual processes mediate between instincts, which supply the driving force, and actual behaviour. They guide the animal into the type of behaviour which seems best suited to satisfy the instinct. But energy is consumed in these intellectual processes, and if they are complex and protracted, the resulting behaviour loses much of the energy originally available. Hence we commonly find greater energy in action from men whose intellectual processes are brief and limited.

The history of the sciences shows that, in the early days of investigation of a particular set of occurrences, it is relatively easy for a pioneer to get his own explanatory theory concerning them into a textbook; but that to dislodge that theory and have it replaced by another in standard works of reference is much more difficult. The earlier theory is regarded as established and can be made to yield only to a thoroughly soundly-argued alternative.

We see much the same in the history of Bible interpretation, with the added complication that established interests are capable of surviving even the best-argued theories. Barr has noted that, by the time critical study of the Bible began, "an understanding of the Bible in which this critical approach had no place had a millennium and a half of established authority to go on".[3] And so we find that a recent apologist does not scruple to defend the traditional view that David wrote Psalm 110 by noting that "possession is nine tenths of the law".[4]

Biblical criticism should not be taken necessarily to imply hostility towards religion; it is not an attempt to prove the Bible wrong, any more than literary criticism is a debunking of literature. A critical theologian—one who was himself involved in a serious controversy over Biblical inspiration and inerrancy—has justly said that "criticism is simply the careful examination of the facts to discover what they really teach".[5] Extremely valuable criticism of the Bible has been conducted by many scholars who, so far from being anxious to discredit it, have been professed Christians.

I have tried to show in my opening chapter that the basic Fundamentalist position that the Bible is totally inerrant is best countered with detailed arguments which such scholars have assembled. Fundamentalists are often educated persons—they include many from the professional classes—but they are largely ignorant about what has been established concerning how the various books of the Bible came to be composed. They have simply turned their backs on the results of critical research. But this return to the old-time faith nevertheless puts them in a position which is really quite different from that of the old-timer, whose faith was formed in a world where Biblical criticism had not yet come into existence. The theologian Professor A. Richardson indicates the difference with the help of analogy with developing views on astronomy:

> The contemporary doctrine of plenary inspiration is not really the same view as that which prevailed up to the end of the eighteenth century. Until then there was no serious alternative, short of complete scepticism, to the traditional view of revelation, just as before Copernicus it was not a rational possibility for men to adopt any alternative cosmology to the Ptolemaic. But the position of a man who insists after the Copernican revolution that the sun goes round the earth is not really the same position as that of the pre-Copernican astronomers. He has in fact taken up an attitude to evidence which the pre-Copernicans had not been able to consider, and which would in all reasonable probability have caused them to modify their Ptolemaic views, if they had had access to it. His attitude to the authority of Ptolemy is quite different from theirs; for them Ptolemy was the only known standard of truth, and accepting Ptolemy did not involve rejecting Copernicus. In the same way the claim, so frequently made, that the conservative evangelicals are maintaining the historic or traditional position is only formally true; the traditional position did not in fact reject evidence which in the nature of the case its pre-nineteenth-century adherents could not have considered.[6]

In the nineteenth century there was much more widespread awareness of Biblical criticism than there is today because the exponents of the then novel critical scholarship could not avoid frequent exchanges with conservative opponents which attracted very wide interest. Today critical research is no longer primarily concerned with such questions as: what are the sources and dates of the books of the Bible? how did disparate material come to be unified in a given book and ascribed to an author who did not in fact write it? Such matters are now regarded in critical circles as settled, and the relevant traditional conservative views are ignored because—I again quote Professor Barr—"they are no longer considered to be a substantial or significant position" (p. 132). He says too that, although the amount of "harmonization" that is necessary to sustain the conservative belief in an inerrant Bible is very great, "it is probable that very few fundamentalists, apart from scholarly apologists, are aware of the amount involved. This is just as well for the fundamentalist movement, for there is no element in the entire fundamentalist approach to the Bible that is more likely to draw upon itself ridicule and derision from without and a deep sense of absurdity from even within the ranks of the faithful" (p. 61). In another work he notes that Fundamentalism is today a major source of recruitment to Christianity: "For good or ill, it is a fact that many of those who enter the active life of Christian faith enter it through the gateway of Fundamentalism".[7] This, as we saw from the comment of Professor Hick (above, p. 19), is a further reason why many liberal theologians are today reluctant directly to attack it.

(iii) Circumstances Favouring Religious Conformity

Phenomena in some ways like Fundamentalism—for instance Puritanism in sixteenth-century England or Pietism in seventeenth-century Germany—have appeared, spread, reached a zenith and then declined. That these mental maladies seem to sweep like a plague across a country points to the influence of imitation, suggestion. The minds which are thus affected are not essentially different from minds in other epochs; and their transient obsessions are not always religious. Such expressions as 'Storm and Stress', 'Wertherism', 'Enlightenment', and 'Romanticism' suggest that all kinds of attitudes and philosophies may for a time become fashionable. In such phenomena we have to look for the material occasion, the leading spirits and the susceptible minds, and also the perennial conditions which determine the obedience of the masses. The previous pages of this 'Conclusion' have attempted some account of this latter factor. Let us turn now to the material occasions which favour religious conformity.

The simple mechanism of association of ideas is often important here. Free-thinking flourished in eighteenth-century England (in the form of the Deist movement) and in France (among the Encyclopaedists and others) until the development of the French Revolution from 1790 suggested that disbelief in the old orthodoxy was apt to lead to mob-rule and regicide. The result was that these two countries became in many respects more religious in the first half of the nineteenth century than they had been in the previous fifty years. By 1850, however, free-thinking had recovered much of its influence, as we can see from Matthew Arnold's *Culture and Anarchy* (1869), where, as T. S. Eliot put it, he tried to "set up culture in the place of Religion".[8] Arnold supposed that religion was doomed, and he hoped to save something from the wreck. He believed, as many before and since, that without religion there could be no morality and no social stability, but he could not believe that the dogmas of the church would survive the discoveries of the nineteenth century. He was, it seems, indignant with Strauss and with Colenso (who had been as critical of the Old Testament as Strauss was of the New), but perhaps chiefly for letting the cat out of the bag; and he tried to substitute his 'Culture' for religion before the latter had been completely discredited. He was, however, mistaken, for religion took on a new lease of life in the twentieth century, when—as we may see from Eliot's essay from which I have already quoted—Arnold's revolt came to be treated with derision by the faithful.

One important factor in religion's recovery has been the reaction against Communism—again an illustration of the efficacy of association of ideas. The odium attaching to Communism has been transferred to all criticism of religious belief, since the Communists have constituted themselves the official directors of the anti-religious movement; and disinterested inquirers are mortified to find themselves in the same camp as Marxist zealots who can be as fanatical as the proponents of any other revelation. According to Barr, actual Communism is "an entity almost totally unknown by experience to fundamentalists but bulking largely in their mythology"; and even "mild socialist tendencies" and "the occasional radical opinions of quite conservative Americans" are, he implies, deprecated as concessions to Communism.[9] The same mentality will deplore any deviation from full-blooded Biblical Christianity as a like concession. A zoologist, Anthony Barnett, has noted how convenient it is to "have some class of people, marked off fairly sharply from one's own group, towards whom one can direct . . . aggressiveness without offending the neighbours".[10] In England the Catholics—Papists as they were called— were long utilized as the channel into which to direct the resentment of the people. In France on certain celebrated occasions it was Huguenots or other Protestant heretics. Given a little animosity, it is easy to convert smouldering embers into a blaze of hatred. The Jews seem to have been provided by a considerate Providence as an ideal subject for this purpose, for in nearly every country of Europe they were long treated as a kind of general scapegoat and held responsible for every great disaster. Hitler, who understood something of political strategy, said that the skill of a political leader is shown in his ability to concentrate a nation's hate on one enemy, that its attention must not be divided by presenting it with a plurality of enemies.[11] Accordingly, he himself identified all his enemies—Marxism, social democracy and international capitalism—with the Jews. Today Communism, or anything that can be associated with it (however arbitrarily) has, in democratic societies, taken over their role. We hear much about defending 'Christian values' against Communism, when in fact Communism can be criticized much more effectively on rational than on such religious grounds. The struggle against Communist ideology is needlessly handicapped by association of democratic ideals with superstition.

Another factor which has benefited religious beliefs is that there is today something of a reaction against science. Applications of scientific discoveries have led to degradation of environments and, even more prominently, to terrifying developments in armaments (cf. above, p. 21). People are very suggestible when frightened, and Western Europeans and Americans, taught from childhood to regard the Bible with respect or even with reverence rather than to read it critically, are ready to believe that atomic physics has at last confirmed the prophecy of (pseudo) Isaiah ("the foundations of the earth shake", etc. cf. above, pp. 11f, 87). The reaction against science has led to attempts to reinstate ancient myths concerning the origin of the universe and of life. The tactics involved include taking advantage of all the differences of view among scientists and suggesting that criticisms of detail are criticisms of general principle, and that statements of unsolved difficulties are confessions extracted from reluctant witnesses. This and that important problem, we are told, remains unsolved, and the methods hitherto employed are therefore useless. But these methods are simply the scientific method. Therefore there must be something wrong with the scientific method, and so we must turn away from science and look for salvation elsewhere. This familiar argument applies equally, of course, to any alternative method. The problems which have not been solved by 'science' have not so far been solved by any other system. If there is some new way, hitherto untried, instead of merely boosting it, it would be better to put it to the test. If there is some restricted method adhered to exclusively by men calling themselves scientific, then nothing could more effectually destroy such an artificial monopoly than the practical demonstration that other methods can achieve better results. But until the human animal changes his character and constitution, he is likely to remain dependent on the same intellectual processes as he has had to rely on hitherto for the finer adjustment of his behaviour to his various needs.

Yet another factor in religion's recovery has been what Professor Penton has called "disillusionment with chaotic political, social and economic conditions throughout much of the world".[12] Jehovah's Witnesses, for instance, are convinced that things have become so much worse since 1914—a date to which they attach great importance—that the end of the world, said in some gospel passages to follow such worsening, cannot now be long delayed. But in fact the record has by no means been one of universal unmitigated deterioration since 1914. The European war which then began was indeed more swiftly destructive of life than its predecessors, but not more brutal, nor more pernicious in its effects than, say, the Thirty Years' War (1618-48) which practically annihilated Germany and prostrated her for two whole generations after its conclusion. Its historian has noted that "the losses of the civil population were almost incredible", and that "outrages of unspeakable atrocity were committed everywhere".[13] Wars apart, the industrial horrors of the eighteenth and nineteenth centuries, and much of the filth, squalor and poverty of life both in town and in country of those times, have been abolished in a substantial fraction of the world. Here it is ignorance not of the Bible but of history that boosts the religious case. As Medawar has observed (cf. above, p. 3), it is precisely because today so many people are better fed and less exhausted by their work than ever before that they have energy and leisure to depress themselves by musing on what they call 'the Human Predicament'.

I have mentioned the efficacy of fear and disillusionment, but, more generally, whenever the subject of belief arouses strong emotions of any kind, we are apt not to judge very well. We are all more inclined to believe what we should *like* to believe and sometimes what we *fear* to believe (cf. above, p. 132). On the other hand, if we have no interest in the matter at all, we shall judge carelessly. The best conditions for a right judgement seem to be a situation where our interest does not lie on one side or the other, but merely in ascertaining what the facts are; where we do not care what the truth is, but are very anxious to know it. The strongest opposition to irreligion naturally comes from those whose prestige and even livelihood would be threatened by a widespread loss of faith, and such persons are still very numerous. That their arguments are often illogical is no discredit to their intelligence, as quite intelligent people will reason illogically in defence of a cherished belief. The matter is made still worse by the natural tendency in every writer who has committed himself in public to a particular point of view to defend it even against valid criticism, because of another tendency in critics to triumph over every point gained. I may know that I have made a mistake and I might be willing to admit it, if I did not also know that such an admission would be the occasion for gloating. So I am tempted to defend myself by resorting to some quibble. This partiality to one's own opinions is still more pronounced in those who claim to be authorities. An authority is one whose opinion is more valuable than that of other people. If he is forced to admit that he is wrong, this amounts almost to humiliation and suggests that he is not an authority at all but is merely masquerading as one. In all these ways, emotion can interfere with sound judgement.

A really far-reaching movement often owes its success to its appeal to a number of basic human tendencies, and not just to one. Moral indignation towards clergy judged by the standard of their own teaching has often, since the establishment of Christianity in the Roman Empire, appealed to social instincts, but was seldom sufficient to effect an upheaval unless allied with appeal to the self-regarding instincts represented by economic interests (as in the cases of the Cathari and the Waldenses) or political ones, as at the Reformation. A potent factor that has often reinforced religious ideas and sentiments is patriotism. Protestantism was helped in Elizabethan England by Catholic Spain's emergence as the national enemy, just as Fundamentalism in America today profits from patriotic revulsion against Russian atheism. It has repeatedly been noted how in Scotland, Northern Ireland, and Wales a very conservative evangelicism has tended to become a focus of national feeling. In the case of Wales, religious revivals have been remarkable for their links not only with Welsh longing for political independence but also with the ancient musical culture of Wales which provides fervent hymn-singing in the chapels.[14] Two or three factors reinforcing each other are far more potent than one in isolation. As for patriotism, while I accept that any community must be prepared to defend itself against enemies, I also think that our educators need to do more to warn against patriotism's negative aspects: for it can all too easily become a way of satisfying and of nourishing one's own importance. Feeling ourselves part of a majestic whole, we have the satisfaction of admiring ourselves.

(iv) Thin Ideas and Strong Emotions

In a pluralistic society such as exists in Britain today, absolutist claims for Christianity are less common than they were a century ago, and many Christians realize that a *modus vivendi* with fellow citizens of other faiths would be hampered by insistence on the kind of exclusiveness claimed in such passages as John 14:6 ("I am the way and the truth and the life: no one cometh unto the Father but by me") or Acts 4:12 ("In none other is there salvation"). One consequence is a greater readiness—in the words of a Church of Scotland Minister—to "see the force of many critical arguments" concerning what is in the Bible, and even to deplore, as this same Minister does, the tactic of clergymen who, while professing doubts in private, are afraid to confront their congregations with such "dangerous" thought.[15] The great majority even of educated Christians remain ignorant of these critical arguments, and it is not easy to explain the situation to them. They are apt to suppose that they can disbelieve a great many things stated in the Bible, without in any way discrediting what they wish to retain.

Some scholars, we saw, have tried to surmount the difficulties by saying that much in the gospel story, although literally untrue, is a symbolical representation of profound truths. It is fashionable today to stress the importance of symbols and symbolism in connection with all forms of literature. But, first, 'profound' ideas are much less valuable than clear ones—my own experience is that profundity and subtlety are qualities in a person or book to be treated with the greatest suspicion—and, second, if symbols are to be of any use they must symbolize something; and if a writer does not indicate what his symbols represent, he might as well write in an unknown language. If he pretends that what he expresses symbolically cannot be expressed in any other way, then he is simply not to be believed.

The quest for symbols in the Bible is often closely related to pseudo-argument in the form of the use of familiar words of very vague meaning (see chapters 4, 5, and 6 above). It is inevitable that very many common words should have a number of meanings. To use a different word for every different idea or thing would place an intolerable burden on the memory. In normal intercourse, the meaning of such ambiguous words is explained by the context or by the situation in which they are used. In a context which consists almost entirely of equally ambiguous words, there is no possibility of determining the meaning. Yet the familiarity of the separate words makes the unwary reader suppose that there must be some meaning behind the whole proposition in which they occur. Sometimes, we saw, the emotional colouring of the words is more important than any meaning that might be attached to them. Although in such cases emotions are linked to words rather than ideas, it is nevertheless supposed not only that the words represent ideas, but also that the ideas denote things which really exist; and the impossibility of representing these things by any real ideas suggests their 'supernatural' or 'transcendent' character.

A really general idea of things which really exist is a composite in which none of the differences of the individuals are wholly lost. Thus an adequate idea of a mammal will include ideas of such divergent types as elephants, bats, and whales. But most general ideas are attained only with considerable loss (cf. above, p. 71) Ultimately the process of generalization leads to scarecrow ideas with almost no intelligible content, which can function only in virtue of some symbol, some vicarious element to which the appropriate emotions are linked.

How thin the ideas can be to which powerful emotions are linked can be seen with beliefs involving fear and hatred. Such beliefs are first generated in relation to specific concrete situations or objects, but are readily transferred to related or associated objects. Dr. Johnson disliked Scotsmen, Heine hated the English, Hitler the Jews. The Communist hates the Bourgeois. Sometimes it is possible to trace such comprehensive antipathies to a simple origin—to offence given by particular individuals. In some cases there is a more direct natural basis for the repugnance, as with members of different races. Differences of smell and facial feature provide at least a distinguishing mark and a direct physical stimulus. Often, however, the diagnostic character of the enemy is more obscure. His dress and outward habits may betray him, but generally it is not until he has committed his beliefs to speech or writing that he can be recognized as belonging to the hated sect. But whatever the means of recognition, the object of repugnance or fear is something constructed in the mind, and all the emotion associated with this is immediately liberated as soon as an individual person, whether rightly or wrongly, becomes identified with the conception. What I am here concerned to stress is that this conception may be the sketchiest of notions, may involve little more than a name. What is characteristic is the emotional attitude towards everything that is identified with it. Party hatreds can be explained in this way; for the hatred is quite real, yet is generated by no direct and natural stimulus. It ought by now to be obvious that beliefs which are emotionally based can have dreadful consequences. Hitler believed that the salvation of Germany depended on the elimination of the Jewish race. He was an extremely ignorant man and knew no more about the effect of racial character than about nuclear physics, and he never tried to increase his knowledge. He believed in his inspiration and reasoned emotionally and instinctively. Unfortunately he was able to put himself in such a position of power that he could act on his beliefs.

(V) Finale

Although instincts determine the principal motives they do not alone determine behaviour; for behaviour, especially human behaviour, is characterized by the adaptation of means to ends, and such adaptation depends on knowledge and belief. True and erroneous beliefs may be equally effective, and there is no psychological difference in their mode of formation. But since some beliefs are determined more by desire than by experience, it is important to understand how desires and fears are related to beliefs. Even scientific beliefs are not altogether uninfluenced by desires and fears, which may be merely related to reputation. One does not wish to be looked down upon for holding an erroneous belief, and so one takes every precaution to avoid error. But since the error becomes disagreeable only when it is exposed and recognized by other people, this motive for accurate investigation and sound generalization ceases to be effective when the belief is held by all one's influential associates. In that case one may shrink from any inquiry likely to lead to a different view.

Beliefs, then, are due only in part to deduction from experience. In part they are due to deference to the authority of other people. The more extensive the knowledge available in a community, the less is it possible for each individual to acquire it all for himself by his own efforts and explorations. In modern society we learn nearly everything from our tutors and are therefore dependent on our judgement of their reliability. We are naturally more credulous than our ancestors of the eighteenth and nineteenth centuries. The power to propagate ideas has increased enormously since then, but there has been no corresponding increase in power to estimate the value of ideas.

In this book I have discussed various issues connected with religion and philosophy, and have tried to show that these two subjects, as they have been and still are cultivated, contain a large element of hocus-pocus, by which I mean the use of language not in the sincere attempt to express ideas, however crude and inadequate these may be, but with the purpose of persuading the reader or hearer of the philosopher's or the religious apologist's depth. Such hocus-pocus is much in evidence at the universities, and the same is true of university literary studies, as I know all too well from my own university experience. Some of the methods of teaching employed result in great facility in handling words, but less often conduce to clear writing or consistent thinking. And the traditional division of knowledge into 'Arts' and 'Sciences' is sometimes understood as implying that rational methods of inquiry are strictly appropriate only in such subjects as chemistry and physics. Subjects which affect personal habits and status more or less closely tend to be discussed only on the understanding that inconvenient conclusions are avoided. There is strong pressure to keep them in a separate category and to make sure that it is in the interest of the special class of scholars trained to deal with them to maintain the system.

Notes

Chapter One: The Fundamentalist Mentality

i. Jehovah's Witnesses

N.B. The Hebrew name for God is properly 'Yahweh', not 'Jehovah', but reverence prevented the Jews from uttering it. In reading the scriptures they substituted 'Adonai' ('Lord'), the vowel points of which were added to the consonants of the Hebrew text to indicate the substitution. The form 'Jehovah' is a misreading which combines the consonants of 'Yahweh' with the vowels of 'Adonai'.

1. My reference numbers 1–4 designate the following publications: 1 and 2 = *Awake!*, 8 August, 1985, and 8 January, 1986. 3 and 4 = *The Watchtower*, 1 August, 1985, and 1 January, 1986.

2. P. B. Medawar, review of Teilhard de Chardin's *The Phenomenon of Man*, in *The Art of the Soluble*, London:Methuen, 1967, pp. 79–81; reprinted in Medawar's *Pluto's Republic*, Oxford University Press, 1984, pp. 249–51.

3. On this, see A. Rogerson's informative book *Millions Now Living Will Never Die. A Study of Jehovah's Witnesses*, London: Constable, 1969, p. 97.

4. I recommend H. H. Rowley's *The Growth of the Old Testament*, London: Hutchinson University Library, 3rd edn., 1967; or the article 'Pentateuch' in *Dictionary of the Bible*, 2nd edn., revised by F. C. Grant and H. H. Rowley, Edinburgh: T. and T. Clark, 1963.

5. W. H. Bennett, *Exodus*, pp. 175–6, in *The Century Bible*, General Editor W. F. Adeney, Edinburgh: T.C. and E.C. Jack, no date.

6. For details, see the articles 'Life' and 'Resurrection' in *Dictionary of the Bible*, as cited in note 4 above.

7. This argument is put explicitly by J. F. Rutherford in his *The Harp of God*, Brooklyn: (presumably) Watchtower Bible and Tract Society 1921, chapter 6, pp. 122, 125. Rutherford was the Witnesses' leader in America at the time of writing.

8. The Catholic Church has long realized that, even if a human father had no part in generating Jesus, sin could have been transmitted to him through his mother. Thus the Church has found it necessary to supplement the doctrine of the virgin birth from Mary with that of the 'immaculate conception' of Mary from her mother—not in the sense that she had no human father, but that, as soon as she was conceived in her mother's womb, the Holy Ghost cleansed her of the original sin inherited from her parents. Pius IXth's Bull of 1854 maintains that this doctrine is "revealed by God and therefore to be firmly and steadfastly believed by all the faithful." It had been flatly denied by Thomas Aquinas, who declared that it was to the greater glory of the Virgin that she should not have been exempt from original sin (*Summa Theologiae*, tertia pars, quaestio 27—de

Sanctificatione Beatae Virginis). A little earlier (in the twelfth century) St. Bernard had condemned the doctrine of the immaculate conception as a presumptuous novelty. The nature of the forces which made it into orthodoxy are revealed by J. P. Junglas, *Die Lehre der Kirche*, 4th edn., Bonn, 1946, who tells (chapter 1, section III, 4) of "holy men" who "could not bear to hear that Mary was under the influence of the Devil, even for a single moment".

9. For details see my *The Jesus of the Early Christians*, London: Pemberton, 1971, chapter 1.

10. Cf. above, pp. 41f and 69.

ii. Biblical Prophecies About the End of the World

11. Shirley Jackson Case, *The Millennial Hope. A Phase of War-Time Thinking*, Chicago: University of Chicago Press, 1918, p. 205.

12. Marley Cole, *Jehovah's Witnesses*, London: Allen and Unwin, 1956, pp. 66–7.

13. Details in my *The Historical Evidence for Jesus*, Buffalo: Prometheus, 1982, chapter 4.

14. Bruce M. Metzger, 'The Jehovah's Witnesses and Jesus Christ', *Theology Today*, 10 (1953), p. 69. My only criticism of Metzger's very informative article concerns his statement, made in reproof of the Witnesses' refusal to accept the doctrine of the Trinity, that the New Testament contains "abundant proof" of this doctrine (p. 73). There are, of course, many passages asserting some relation between Father, Son, and Holy Ghost. But the essence of the doctrine of the Trinity is that these three are *one*, and that is asserted only in certain versions of 1 John 5:7–8, in words which are admitted even by many Catholic authorities to be interpolated. In the Authorized Version, this passage is given as: "For there are three that bear record (*in heaven, the Father, the Word and the Holy Ghost: and these three are one. And there are three that bear witness in earth*), the spirit, and the water and the blood; and these three agree in one". As Metzger is very well aware, the words in brackets have no equivalent in the oldest Greek mss, and are omitted in the Revised Version. Cardinal Newman admitted that the doctrine of the Trinity is absent even from the writings of the early Fathers (*Essay on the Development of the Christian Doctrine*, new edn., London, 1878, pp. 14ff). He salvaged it by "interpreting the early Fathers by the later" (p. 15).

15. Henry Preserved Smith, *Essays in Biblical Interpretation*, London: Allen and Unwin (and Boston: Marshall Jones), 1921, p. 180.

16. M. J. Penton, *Apocalypse Delayed, The Story of Jehovah's Witnesses*, Toronto: University of Toronto Press, 1985, p. 3.

17. Matthew 2:15 alleges that the return of the infant Jesus and his family from Egypt fulfils the 'prophecy' of Hosea 11:1, "out of Egypt did I call my son". But 'son' here means the nation, Israel, and Hosea is referring here to the exodus of Israel from Egypt under Moses. At 2:23 Matthew records that the holy family settled in Nazareth to fulfil a prophecy that Jesus "should be called a Nazarene". There is no such prophecy in the Old Testament, but it is nevertheless pretty clear what Matthew had in mind. As Howard C. Kee has noted, he took "the consonants of the Hebrew text of Isaiah 11:1, in which the Messiah is called a

'shoot' (= n-tz-r, in Hebrew) and, by providing it with different vowels (which can be done readily in Semitic languages), he has produced a prophecy about Jesus's coming from the obscure hamlet of Nazareth" (*Miracle in the Early Christian World*, New Haven and London: Yale University Press, 1983, p. 186 n.). Nazareth is not mentioned by Josephus, the Mishnah or the Talmud, but is named in an inscription from the third or fourth century of our era discovered at Caesarea in 1961 (see M. Avi-Yonah, 'A List of Priestly Courses from Caesarea', *Israel Exploration Journal*, 12 (1962), pp. 137–9). Excavations show that the place was occupied at the beginning of the Christian era. (See Clemens Kopp, *The Holy Places of the Gospels*, English translation, Edinburgh and London: Nelson, 1963, p. 61).

18. H. P. Smith, *op. cit.* in note 15 above, pp. 176–7.

19. H. H. Rowley, *op. cit.* in note 4 above, p. 89. R. E. Clements's recent commentary on *Isaiah 1–39* (in the New Century Bible Commentary Series, London: Oliphants/Nelson, 1980) dates the apocalyptic material of Isaiah 24–27 about 300 years later than the time of the historical Isaiah, and notes that all 39 chapters, as we now have them, grew over a long period of time from a desire to interpret the message of the prophet in the light of later events (p. 3). The same is true of other prophetic books in the canon. R. P. Carroll has noted that, while it is difficult enough to extract reliable biographical information about Jesus from the gospels, it is even harder to construct biographies of the prophets from Biblical books which bear their names, as these, like the gospels, represent a redaction of many layers of material of different provenance and date. In Carroll's view, the book of Jeremiah, for example, has "buried" the historical prophet "beneath a massive amount of later presentation, interpretation and functional development" (*From Chaos to Covenant*, London: S.C.M., 1981; also Carroll's commentary on Jeremiah, in the series 'The Old Testament Library', London, 1986). That Jesus has been similarly 'buried' has been widely admitted by Christian scholars, as I show in chapter 3 of this book (e.g. p. 68 above).

20. This is generally admitted. See, for instance, *The Oxford Dictionary of the Christian Church*, ed. F. L. Cross (Oxford University Press, 1958 or later reprint), article 'Isaiah, Book of'. Details in my *The Jesus of the Early Christians*, as cited in note 9 above, pp. 28–30.

21. Adolf Kamphausen, article 'Daniel, Book of', paragraph 8 in *Encyclopaedia Biblica*, ed. T. K. Cheyne and J. S. Black, London: A. and C. Black, 1909.

22. Karl Popper, *Unended Quest*, London: Fontana/Collins, 1976, chapter 8, p. 38. Cf. Popper's *Conjectures and Refutations. The Growth of Scientific Knowledge* 4th edn., London: Routledge, 1972, pp. 34–7.

iii. Biblical Inerrancy and Authoritarian Sects

23. *Reasoning From the Scriptures*, Brooklyn: Watchtower Bible and Tract Society, 1985, pp. 328, 439.

24. *Ibid.*, p. 205.

25. Francis Watson, *Paul, Judaism and the Gentiles. A Sociological Approach*, Cambridge: Cambridge University Press, 1986, e.g. p. 40.

26. Graham Shaw (who was until recently Chaplain of Exeter College Oxford) has noted Paul's cursing of his Christian opponents as "the first recorded anathema in Christian history", not to be trivialized as the work of the dogmatic Church of a later century, but firmly embedded in one of the earliest documents of the first (*The Cost of Authority, Manipulation and Freedom in the New Testament*, London: S.C.M., 1983, p. 44). Both Shaw's book and Watson's are healthy correctives to the tendency to idealize Paul.

27. W. A. Meeks, *The First Urban Christians. The Social World of the Apostle Paul*, New Haven and London: Yale University Press, 1983, pp. 145–6.

28. William James, *The Varieties of Religious Experience*, (Gifford Lectures on Natural Religion delivered at Edinburgh, 1901–1902 and first published in 1902), lecture 2.

iv. Conservative Christianity Generally

29. John Hick, in *Jesus in Myth and History*, ed. R. J. Hoffmann, Buffalo: Prometheus, 1986, p. 211.

30. R. S. Wallace, *The Message of Daniel*, Leicester, 1979, p. 19.

31. See Nietzsche's *Menschliches Allzumenschliches*, vol. 2, aphorism no. 295; and Hitler's *Mein Kampf*, vol. 1, chapter 6. Nietzsche was obligatory reading for Nazis because he opposed egalitarianism and claimed special privileges for the superman. But he was not consistently pro-German (he even thought of forming an anti-German league), said next to nothing about Jews, and did not proclaim the inequality of races. For details see J. R. Baker, *Race*, Oxford: Oxford University Press, 1974, pp. 44–6, 55–9.

32. For instance, Keene's second booklet declares (p. 6) that "according to the Gospels" Peter "was chosen to be the rock upon which the Christian Church was built". Any competent New Testament commentary will give the information that this doctrine appears not 'in the gospels', but only at Matthew 16:18; that—I quote F. W. Beare's excellent commentary on this gospel (Oxford: Blackwell, 1981)—"nowhere else in the Gospels does Jesus speak of founding a church. The very word 'εκκλησια, 'church', does not occur anywhere else in the gospels, except for Matthew 18:17, which is itself suspect and actually uses the word in a different sense". Beare goes on to note New Testament evidence that conflicts with the idea that Peter enjoyed any such primacy as Matthew makes Jesus assign to him; and he concludes that the relevant saying was never said by Jesus, but "originated in some debate within the Palestinian community" (pp. 353–4).

33. For a full discussion, see C. L. Mitton's commentary on Ephesians in the New Century Bible series (London: Oliphants/Nelson, 1976).

Chapter Two: The Rise of Radical Biblical Scholarship

i. De Wette

For details of the work of de Wette referred to, see p. 26 above.

1. Moses is not mentioned in any ancient source outside the Bible. The Egyptian captivity of the Israelites in which, according to the Bible, he was active, involved them (so we read at Exodus 1:11) in building the cities of Pithom and Raamses in the eastern delta. If this information is reliable, it takes us to the period of the Pharoah Rameses II (1290–1223 B.C.), for an administrative letter of this time refers to the provision of corn for foreign captives who were drawing stones for the great gateway of one of the buildings of the city of Raamses: see David Daiches, *The Quest for the Historical Moses* (Robert Waley Cohen Memorial Lecture, 1974), London: Council of Christians and Jews, 1975, p. 7; and Martin Noth, *The History of Israel*, (2nd edn. of the English translation of Noth's *Geschichte Israels*), London: A. and C. Black, 1960 (or later reprint), p. 120. Daiches adds (p. 9) that "most, but not all scholars agree that Rameses II must have been the Pharaoh of the exodus, and that the date of the exodus must have been about 1270 B.C.". Cf. also J. Maxwell Miller, *The Old Testament and the Historian*, London: S.P.C.K., 1976, pp. 78–9. However, the *History of Ancient Israel and Judah* by J. Maxwell Miller and John H. Hayes (London: S.C.M., 1986) finds that the mention of the two Egyptian cities at Exodus 1:11 "falls short of establishing a clearly fixed point between biblical and Egyptian history or, for that matter, even of serving as actual proof of the historicity of the biblical account. One would expect Israelite storytellers to be familiar with and to use authentic Mesopotamian and Egyptian names and customs in their narratives in any case" (pp. 67–8). These two authors insist that there is no "reference to an Israelite sojourn in Egypt, the exodus or the conquest of Palestine in any ancient source contemporary with the time when these events are said to have occurred" (p. 64).

2. Otto Kaiser gives a lucid summary of the history of research into the Pentateuch in his *Introduction to the Old Testament*, English translation Oxford: Blackwell, 1975 (or later reprint), pp. 33–45, and notes that the beginner surveying Pentateuchal criticism may well feel forced to exclaim: "The Pentateuch is not Mosaic but a mosaic!" (p. 44).

3. John Rogerson, *Old Testament Criticism in the Nineteenth Century. England and Germany*, London: S.P.C.K., 1984, pp. 28–9.

4. Concerning the origin of the passover, de Wette surmises that it was originally a private and family custom, not one which originated from any legal enactment (p. 296). This implies that the story in Exodus 12 of its origin is a circumstantial myth to explain an existing rite. Later (II, p. 196) he actually says, when discussing Exodus, that it belongs in its plan "to deduce the origin of the holy laws from historical facts".

5. A recent student of Chronicles confirms that the *drknym* of 1 Chronicles 29:7 are still generally understood to be Persian darics, a coin first minted by Darius I (H. G. M. Williamson, *Israel in the Books of Chronicles*, Cambridge: Cambridge University Press, 1977, p. 84).

6. 1 Chronicles 3 lists the descendants of David and gives six generations of descendants after Zerubbabel (the leader of one of the bands that returned from the Babylonian exile early in the sixth century, between 538 and 520 B.C.). There is some variation as between different manuscripts at this point (as so often when lists of names are involved), but as Williamson has noted (*loc. cit.* in note 5 above), the Massoretic text "is generally thought to give six generations after Zerubbabel, providing a *terminus post quem* of c. 400 B.C.". As evidence against dating Chronicles in the period of the Greek empire, Williamson points to the total lack of any traces of Hellenistic influence (linguistic or ideological) on the

work—an argument from silence which "carries some weight in view of the very considerable impact (both positively and by reaction) of Hellenism on Jewish religion and literature" (p. 83). Jacob M. Myers also argues, in his commentary on 1 Chronicles in the Anchor Bible Series (New York: Doubleday, 1965, p. lxxxix), that "all indications point . . . to a date around 400 B.C. for the composition of the Chronicler's work".

7. That Chronicles drew directly from earlier books in the Old Testament is what scholars today still believe. Myers (op. cit. in note 6 above, p. lxii) affirms that the Chronicler had at his disposal the final or 'Priestly' redaction of Genesis, Exodus, Leviticus and Numbers, and also "the great history of the Deuteronomist, which included the books of Deuteronomy, Joshua, Judges, Samuel and Kings". On this 'great history', see Martin Noth's The Deuteronomistic History, Sheffield: J.S.O.T. Press, 1981 (the English translation of Noth's Überlieferungsgeschichtliche Studien, 3rd edn., 1967).

8. Noth dates Deuteronomy (and the other books of the Deuteronomistic historian (cf. note 7 above) at about 550 B.C. (op. cit. in note 7 above, p. 12). He says that there is no trace of Deuteronomistic editing in the first four books of the Old Testament (p. 15); and the final or 'Priestly' editing of this material is now regarded as the latest element in the Pentateuch, dating from the Babylonian exile (586–538 B.C.) or later, but not later than 400 B.C. (the approximate date of Chronicles, which uses the whole Pentateuch as a source).

9. G. Grote, History of Greece (1846–56); 10 volume edn., London: John Murray, 1903, vol. 1, p. 382.

10. Since de Wette wrote, clay tablets inscribed with cuneiform writing have been found in one of the palaces of the Assyrian kings and deciphered to give a story much older than that of the Deluge in Genesis, but closely resembling it. For details, see R. D. Barnett, Illustrations of Old Testament History, 2nd edn., London: British Museum Publications, 1977, ch. 1, and E. Sollberger, The Babylonian Legend of the Flood, 3rd edn. London: British Museum Publications, 1971.

11. Quoted by Rogerson, as cited in note 3 above, p. 233n.

12. Ibid., p. 234.

13. Cf. de Wette's comments (II, pp. 94–5) on the unpleasant story of Genesis 19:30–38, namely that it is designed to show that Moab and Ammon are kindred nations to the Israelites but markedly inferior to them.

14. Strauss pointed out that, although Matthew (unlike Luke, who supplies a totally different genealogy of Jesus) makes the pedigree run from David through Solomon and the line of kings, he yet omits four of these from the list given in the Old Testament. Since Matthew is avowedly anxious to present the ancestors of Jesus in three groups of 14 names, Strauss inferred that these omissions enable him to bring out his second group of 14, and also to conclude each group with a personage associated with an important historical event.

15. D. F. Strauss, Streitschriften, 1 Hft., Tübingen, 1838, pp. 3–6.

ii. Strauss

16. A. Schweitzer, The Quest of the Historical Jesus, English translation by W. Montgomery, 3rd edn., London: A. and C. Black, 1954, p. 78.

17. Horton Harris, *D.F. Strauss and His Theology*, Cambridge University Press, 1973, pp. 41, 281–2 (hereinafter cited as Harris).

18. Quoted by Harris, p. 60.

19. *Das Leben Jesu für das deutsche Volk bearbeitet* (Strauss's second *Life of Jesus*, 1864), authorized English translation entitled *New Life of Jesus*, 2nd edn., London: Williams and Norgate, 1879 (hereinafter cited as NL), vol. 1, p. 412.

20. Strauss, *Das Leben Jesu kritisch bearbeitet*, 4th edn., 2 vols., Tübingen, 1840, paragraph 13 (vol. 1, pp. 63ff). The first edition, published at Tübingen in two volumes in 1835, has recently (1969) been reprinted at Darmstadt. But the fourth edition gives a fuller account of these and other matters. The paragraph numbering is not identical in these two editions.

21. See Rev. Dr. V. Taylor's *The Gospel According to St. Mark*, 2nd edn., London: Macmillan, 1966, p. 67.

22. Strauss, *op. cit.* (4th edn.), in note 20 above, paragraph 102 (vol. 2, pp. 188–9).

23. W. G. Kümmel, *Introduction to the New Testament*, English translation of the 17th revised German edn., London: S.C.M., 1975, p. 121.

24. F. W. Beare, *The Earliest Records of Jesus*, Oxford: Blackwell, 1964, p. 13.

25. C. Burger (*Jesus als Davidssohn*, Göttingen: Vandenhoeck and Ruprecht, 1970) has shown that the location of the Messiah's birth at Bethlehem was not in fact universal in pre-Christian Jewish tradition. But it was not uncommon, and that suffices for Strauss's argument.

26. Strauss, *Der alte und der neue Glaube* (The Old Faith and the New), Leipzig, 1872 (cited hereinafter as *Glaube*), p. 51.

27. I have discussed the gospel birth and infancy narratives in detail in chapter 1 of my *The Jesus of the Early Christians*, London: Pemberton, 1971, where I acknowledge my considerable debt to Strauss.

28. Sir Edwyn Hoskyns and Noel Davey, *The Riddle of the New Testament*, London: Faber and Faber, 1931, chapter 4, p. 80 (1958 edn., p. 60).

29. F. C. Grant, *The Gospels, Their Origin and Growth*, New York: Harper, 1957, and London: Faber and Faber, 1959, p. 35.

30. Barnabas Lindars, *New Testament Apologetic*, London: S.C.M., 1961.

31. Robert Morgan, 'Nothing more negative', in *The Trial of Jesus*, ed. E. Bammel, London: S.C.M., 1970, p. 136.

32. Strauss, *op. cit.* in note 20 above (4th edn.), paragraph 16 (vol. 1, p. 104).

33. It has, however, been repeatedly pointed out (both before and after Strauss's life-time) that when Tacitus wrote (about A.D. 120) that "Christians derive their name and origin from Christ who was executed by sentence of the procurator Pontius Pilate in the reign of Tiberius" (*Annals*, 15:44), he was simply uncritically repeating what the Christians of his day were alleging about Jesus. For a detailed discussion see my *The Historical Evidence for Jesus*, Buffalo: Prometheus, 1982, pp. 16–17. So conservative a theologian as R. T. France finds my discussion of this issue "entirely convincing" (*The Evidence for Jesus*, London: Hodder and Stoughton, 1986, p. 23).

34. 'David Strauss der Bekenner und der Schriftsteller' (1873), the first of Nietzsche's *Unzeitgemäße Betrachtungen* (Thoughts out of Season) in *Werke*, ed. A. Baeumler, Leipzig, 1913, vol. 1, p. 78. In the early part of this essay, Nietzsche uses the terms "German culture" and "style" in such a way as to show that they have a pronounced moral flavour, but not as the names of definable notions. He calls Strauss a "cultural philistine", described in section 2 of his essay as "an obstacle to all strong and creative men, the labyrinth of all doubters

and strayers from the path, the morass of all that are tired, the fetter upon the feet of all those that run in quest of high aims, the poisonous fog of all fresh seeds, the withering sand desert of the German spirit which seeks and yearns for a new life". Out of such rhetoric we have to extract our definition if we can. Nietzsche relies on this emphatic manner to browbeat his reader. One does not want to be classed among the philistines, and any admission of inability to understand this writing might lay one open to the charge. The principal offence of Strauss seems to be that, being a philistine, he had the audacity, in the work under review (his *Der alte und der neue Glaube*), to found a new religion. Nietzsche's scorn may well have been prompted by the fact that he contemplated the same course and did not tolerate rivals.

35. F. C. Baur, *The Church History of the First Three Centuries*, English translation of the 3rd edn. of Baur's work of 1853 by A. Menzies, London, vol. 1, 1878, pp. 76ff.

36. Strauss, *Der Christus des Glaubens und der Jesus der Geschichte. Eine Kritik des Schleiermacher'schen Lebens Jesu*, in *Gesammelte Schriften*, ed. E. Zeller, vol. 5, Bonn, 1877, p. 36n.

37. E. Haenchen, *Die Bibel und Wir*, Tübingen: J.C.B. Mohr, 1968, p. 126.

38. E. Haenchen, *Gott und Mensch*, Tübingen: J.C.B. Mohr, 1965, p. 84.

39. I have discussed this matter further in my *Did Jesus Exist?*, 2nd edn., London: Pemberton, 1986, chapter 5, and also in my *The Historical Evidence for Jesus*, as cited in note 33 above, pp. 149–150. Haenchen's commentary on the Acts of the Apostles is available in an English translation (Oxford: Blackwell, 1971).

40. H. Braun, *Gesammelte Studien zum Neuen Testament und seiner Umwelt*, 3rd edn., Tübingen: J.C.B. Mohr, 1971, p. 288.

41. See M. D. Conway's pamphlet, *Strauss*, London, 1874, pp. 18–19.

42. H. J. Hillerbrand, *A Fellowship of Discontent*, New York: Harper and Row, 1967, pp. 129, 158.

43. K. Barth, *Die Protestantische Theologie im neunzehnten Jahrhundert*, Zürich Evangelischer Verlag, 1947, p. 515; English translation *Protestant Theology in the Nineteenth Century*, London: S.C.M., 1972, p. 568.

44. Strauss, *Die Halben und die Ganzen*, in *Gesammelte Schriften*, as cited in note 36 above, vol. 5, p. 189.

45. Schweitzer, *op. cit.* in note 16 above, p. 233.

46. H. Zahrnt, *The Historical Jesus*, English translation by J. S. Bowden, London: Collins, 1963, pp. 102–3.

iii. Wilhelm Tell

47. On Freudenberger, Iselin and Voltaire see F. Heinemann, *Tell-Bibliographie*, Bern, 1907, pp. 26–30. On Gibbon see E. Bonjour, H. S. Offler and G. R. Potter, *A Short History of Switzerland*, Oxford: Clarendon, 1952, pp. 203–4.

48. O. Lorenz, *Leopold III und die Schweizer Bünde*, Wien, 1860, p. 31; Waitz, review of Kopp's *Geschichtsblätter* (cf. note 49 below) in *Göttingische Gelehrte Anzeigen*, 1857, vol. 1, p. 717. Cf. A. Huber, *Die Waldstätte*, Innsbruck, 1861, p. 12. Huber also gives (pp. 89 ff) an excellent survey of the evidence (or lack of it) in

the chronicles. The stages in the construction of the Tell legend are outlined by W. Vischer, *Die Sage von der Befreiung der Waldstätte*, Leipzig, 1867.

49. J. E. Kopp, 'Zur Tell-Sage', *Geschichtsblätter aus der Schweiz*, vol. 2, Luzern, 1856, p. 330.

50. On Justinger see *ibid.*, pp. 350–1.

51. See Kopp's letter of 11 January, 1833, quoted by A. Lütolf, *J.E. Kopp*, Luzern, 1868, p. 101; and J. Dierauer, *Geschichte der schweizerischen Eidgenossenschaft*, Gotha, 1887, vol. 1, p. 145.

52. See Kopp's 'Zur Tell-Sage', in *Geschichtsblätter aus der Schweiz*, vol. 1, Luzern, 1854, pp. 314–15. On other forgeries and interpolations discovered by Kopp, see Waitz, *loc. cit.* in note 48 above, pp. 740–1.

53. If this appears platitudinous, I would point out that K. C. King had cause to protest against historians who take the twelfth-century evidence of the *Nibelungenlied* as sufficient proof of Burgundian conditions of the fifth century. See his 'On the Naming of Places in Heroic Literature', *Oxford German Studies*, 2 (1967), pp. 16–17.

54. J. M. Robertson, *Christianity and Mythology*, 2nd edn., London: Watts, 1910, pp. 126–7.

Chapter Three: The Liberal Defence

N.B. Once full details of a book have been given, further references to it are simply page numbers in the text of my chapter—except where more than one book by a given author is mentioned in these notes.

1. J. H. Newman, *Apologia Pro Vita Sua* (1864), with an introduction by W. Wood, Oxford University Press, 1913, pp. 353–4.

2. J. L. May, *The Oxford Movement*, London: John Lane, 1933, p. 91.

3. A. R. Vidler, 'Historical Objections', in *Objections to Christian Belief*, London: Constable, 1963, p. 77. Notwithstanding its title, this book is a defence of Christianity, not an attack on it.

4. J. Hick, *The Myth of God Incarnate*, London: S.C.M., 1977, p. ix.

5. J. S. Bezzant, 'Intellectual Objections', in *op. cit.* in note 3 above, p. 82.

6. W. D. Davies, *The Setting of the Sermon on the Mount*, Cambridge: Cambridge University Press, 1963, p. 416.

7. F. W. Beare, *The Gospel According to Matthew*, Oxford: Blackwell, 1981, pp. viii, 29.

8. D. Cupitt and P. Armstrong, *Who Was Jesus?*, London: BBC Publications, 1977, pp. 32–3.

9. Morna Hooker (Lady Margaret Professor of Divinity at Cambridge), quoted by Keith Ward, *The Turn of the Tide. Christian Belief in Britain Today*, BBC Publications, 1986, p. 96.

10. Stewart R. Sutherland, *God, Jesus and Belief*, Oxford: Blackwell, 1984, pp. 137, 174.

11. C. H. Dodd, *The Founder of Christianity*, London: Collins, 1971, p. 31.

12. James P. Mackey, *Jesus. The Man and the Myth*, London: S.C.M., 1979, p. 122.

13. R. E. Brown, *The Birth of the Messiah*, London: G. Chapman, 1977, pp. 7, 497; cf. Keith Ward's recent statement (in *op. cit.* in note 9 above, p. 122) that "a great many theologians, . . . including many Roman Catholic theologians", would say that "the virgin birth never really happened" and was only "a symbol which was later put into historical form".

14. John Hick, *Death and Eternal Life*, London: Macmillan, 1985, pp. 171, 175–7.

15. David E. Jenkins, *Living With Questions. Investigations into the Theory and Practice of Belief in God*, London: S.C.M., 1969, p. 137.

16. David Jenkins, transcript of his 'Credo' interview broadcast on London Weekend Television on 29 April 1984; quoted from Conor Cruise O'Brien's article in *The Observer*, 5 August, 1984.

17. Murray J. Harris, *Easter in Durham*, Exeter: Paternoster Press, 1985, pp. 31–2.

18. For a detailed discussion of symbolism in thinking, see F. R. H. (Ronald) Englefield, *The Mind at Work and Play*, Buffalo: Prometheus, 1985, chapter 6.

19. Ernst Cassirer, *The Problem of Knowledge*, chapter 18 ('The History of Religion'), New Haven and London: Yale University Press, 1950, p. 295.

20. David E. Jenkins, *The Contradiction of Christianity*, London: S.C.M., 1976, p. 148.

21. *Ibid*, pp. 87, 121; cf. Jenkins's *The Glory of Man*, London: S.C.M., 1967, p. 22.

22. David E. Jenkins, *op. cit.* in note 15 above, pp. 147–8.

23. *The Glory of Man*, as cited in note 21 above, pp. 34, 45.

24. R. Bultmann 'New Testament Mythology', in *Kerygma and Myth*, ed. H. W. Bartsch, London: S.P.C.K., 1953, vol. 1, pp. 19, 39–42.

25. J. Hick, *op. cit.* in note 4 above, p. 179.

26. R. Bultmann, *Jesus Christ and Mythology*, London: S.C.M., 1960, p. 20.

27. J. Hick, *Death and Eternal Life*, as cited in note 14 above, pp. 199, 201, 245–6.

28. William Ledwich, *The Durham Affair*, Welshpool: Stylite, 1985, pp. 7, 14.

29. Newman himself defined faith as "the absolute acceptance of the divine word with an internal assent, in opposition to the informations, if such, of sight and reason". And "the exercise of reason instead of faith in matters of faith" is what he called "rationalism" and explicitly rejected. See his *Essay on the Development of the Christian Doctrine*, new edn., London, 1878, pp. 191, 325.

30. Paul Badham, *Christian Beliefs about Life after Death*, London: S.P.C.K., 1978, pp. 33, 35, 37, 47, 56. Concerning the Commission on Doctrine, Badham refers to *Doctrine in the Church of England*, London, 1962, p. 89.

Chapter Four: Theology of Reassurance: Tillich

I refer to Tillich's works with the following abbreviations:

Sh = *The Shaking of the Foundations* (a collection of Sermons), London: S.C.M., 1949.
ST = *Systematic Theology*, London: Nisbet, 3 vols., 1953, 1957, 1964.

These works are not translations but were published originally in English.

1. J. A. T. Robinson, *Honest to God*, London: S.C.M., 1963, p. 44.

2. W. and M. Pauck, *Paul Tillich. His Life and Thought*. Vol. 1, *Life*, London: Collins, 1977, p. 232.

3. Robinson, *op. cit.*, pp. 22, 54–56.

4. J. Heywood Thomas, *Paul Tillich. An Appraisal*, London: S.C.M., 1963, p. 55.

5. John Locke, *An Essay Concerning Human Understanding* (1690), Book 3, chapter 6, paragraphs 2–9.

6. A. Thatcher, *The Ontology of Paul Tillich*, Oxford University Press, 1978, p. 10.

7. Thomas, *op. cit.* in note 4 above, p. 71.

8. Metaphysical objections to this view have been dealt with by R. Englefield, *The Mind at Work and Play*, Buffalo: Prometheus, 1985, particularly chapter 17; cf. above, pp. 206 ff.

9. W. Kaufmann, *The Faith of a Heretic*, Garden City, N.Y.: Doubleday, 1961, p. 90.

10. Robinson, *op. cit.* in note 1 above, p. 57.

11. W. N. Mahan, *Tillich's System*, San Antonio: Trinity University Press, 1974, p. 111.

12. Englefield makes this point in his article on John Robinson (*New Humanist*, Winter, 1982). This chapter is indebted to his article for other points too, and also to his recently published book (mentioned in note 8 above).

13. W. Sargant, *Battle for the Mind. A Physiology of Conversion and Brain-Washing*, London: Heinemann, 1957, p. 78.

14. *Ibid.*, p. 138.

15. Quoted by M. Argyle and B. Beit-Hallahmi in their *The Social Psychology of Religion*, London and Boston: Routledge, 1975, p. 44.

16. Quoted by Sargant, *op. cit.*, in note 13 above, p. 131.

Chapter Five: Disparagement of 'Scientific Truth': Collingwood

1. Quoted from Santayana's *Interpretations of Poetry and Religion*, London: Black, 1900, p. 91, by F. R. H. (Ronald) Englefield, *The Mind at Work and Play*, Buffalo: Prometheus, 1985, p. 169.

2. W. J. van der Dussen, *History as a Science. The Philosophy of R. G. Collingwood*, The Hague and London: Nijhoff, 1981, pp. 13–14.

3. W. M. Johnston, *The Formative Years of R. G. Collingwood*, The Hague: Nijhoff, 1967, pp. 114, 120.

4. W. Windelband, *Geschichte und Naturwissenschaft*, Strassburg edn. of 1904, p. 21.

5. E. Mach, *Erkenntnis und Irrtum*, 5th edn., Leipzig: J. A. Barth, 1926, pp. 126–8.

6. Englefield, *op. cit.* in note 1 above.

7. John Locke, *An Essay Concerning Human Understanding* (1690), Book 4, chapter 7, paragraph 9 (italics mine).

8. Thomas Reid, *Essays on the Intellectual Powers of Man* (1785) Book 5, chapter 2 (1827 edn., p. 228; italics mine).

9. David Hume, *A Treatise of Human Nature* (1739), Book 1, part 1, chapter 7.

10. W. James, *The Principles of Psychology* (1890), chapter 9.

11. T. Ribot, *L'Evolution des idées générales*, Paris, 1897, p. 149.

12. Englefield, *op. cit.* in note 1 above, p. 170.

13. Windelband says: "Every causal explanation of any historical event presupposes general ideas of the general course of things; and historical demonstrations, reduced to their purely logical form, always have as a major premiss natural laws of events, particularly of psychological events" (*op. cit.* in note 4 above, p. 23).

14. See my *Herder and After*, The Hague: Mouton, 1959, pp. 223 ff and 269 ff.

15. Johnston, who thinks that *Speculum Mentis* "in some ways achieves an excellence which its author never surpassed", nevertheless admits that "it seems probable" that the work "is intended to justify Collingwood's pursuit of two academic professions, historian and philosopher" (*op. cit.* in note 3 above, pp. 94, 144).

16. W. H. Walsh, 'Collingwood and Metaphysical Neutralism', in *Critical Essays on the Philosophy of R. G. Collingwood*, ed. M. Krausz, Oxford, 1972, p. 143.

17. Alan Donagan, 'Collingwood and Philosophical Method', *ibid.*, p. 12.

Chapter Six: Christianity Without Religion: Bonhoeffer

1. E.g. by J. D. Godsey, *The Theology of Dietrich Bonhoeffer*, London: S.C.M., 1960, p. 248.

2. Bonhoeffer, *Widerstand und Ergebung. Briefe und Aufzeichnungen aus der Haft*, ed. E. Bethge, 7th edn., Munich: Kaiser Verlag, 1956, p. 268. Further references to this volume will be page references in my text. It includes the essay 'Nach Zehn Jahren'.

3. *World come of Age. A Symposium on Dietrich Bonhoeffer*, ed. Ronald G. Smith, London: Collins, 1967, p. 9.

4. E. Bethge, *Dietrich Bonhoeffer*, Munich: Kaiser Verlag, 1967, pp. 889–90.

5. For example W. Hamilton, '"The Letters are a particular Thorn": Some Themes in Bonhoeffer's Prison Writings', in Smith, *op. cit.* note 3 above, pp. 140, 142.

6. B. Klappert, 'Weg und Wende Bonhoeffers in der Israelfrage', in *Ethik im Ernstfall*, ed. W. Huber and Ilse Tödt, Munich: Kaiser Verlag, 1982, p. 86.

7. E. Feil, *Die Theologie Bonhoeffers*, Munich: Kaiser Verlag, 1971, p. 381.

8. Hamilton, *op. cit.* in note 5 above, p. 145.

9. D. H. Hopper. *A Dissent on Bonhoeffer*, Philadelphia: Westminster Press, 1975, p. 141.

10. R. G. Smith in *op. cit.* in note 3 above, p. 18.

11. Hamilton's essay (see note 5 above), p. 154.

12. J. A. Phillips, *The Form of Christ in the World. A Study of Bonhoeffer's Christology*, London: Collins, 1967, p. 192.

13. A. MacIntyre, 'God and the Theologians', in *The Honest to God Debate*,

ed. D. L. Edwards, London: S.C.M., 1963, pp. 221–2.

14. J. A. T. Robinson, *Honest to God*, London: S.C.M., 1963, p. 76.

15. A 'Predigtmeditation', printed in Bonhoeffer's *Gesammelte Schriften*, ed. E. Bethge, vol. 4, Munich: Kaiser Verlag, 1975 pp. 498–9. (N.B. This edition of his writings does not include the prison letters.)

16. J. W. Woelfel, *Bonhoeffer's Theology*, Nashville: Abingdon Press, 1970, p. 296.

17. See Bonhoeffer's letter of 25 July 1942 (written before his imprisonment), printed by G. Krause, 'Bonhoeffer und Bultmann', in the Bultmann Festschrift *Zeit und Geschichte*, ed. E. Dinkler, Tübingen: J.C.B. Mohr, 1964, p. 457n.

18. See Robinson's article in *The Observer* (London), 17 March 1963, discussing his *Honest to God*.

19. G. Denzler and V. Fabricius, *Die Kirchen im Dritten Reich*, Frankfurt a.M.: Fischer, 1984, vol. 1, p. 179.

20. E. Bethge, in *Bonhoeffer: Exile and Martyr*, ed. J. W. de Gruchy, New York: Seabury, 1975, pp. 11–13.

Chapter Seven: Humanist Religion: Julian Huxley

1. I cannot here attempt any discussion of the nature of magic. For a recent account, and for criticism of J. G. Frazer's well-known view, see F. R. H. (Ronald) Englefield, *The Mind at Work and Play*, Buffalo: Prometheus, 1985, chapter 15.

2. C. H. D. Clark, *The Scientist and the Supernatural*, London: Epworth Press, 1966, p. 16.

3. E. Westermarck, *The Origin and Development of the Moral Ideas*, 2nd edn., vol. 2, London: Macmillan, 1924, pp. 745–6. See also Westermarck's *Christianity and Morals*, London: Kegan Paul, 1939.

4. E. Westermarck, *Ethical Relativity*, London: Kegan Paul, Trench, Trübner, 1932, p. 203; H. T. Buckle, *Introduction to the History of Civilization in England*, ed. J. M. Robertson, London: Routledge, 1904, p. 789.

5. W. James, *Principles of Psychology*, London: Macmillan, 1901, vol. 2, pp. 419–20.

6. P. B. Medawar, *The Art of the Soluble*, London: Methuen, 1967, p. 81.

7. The matter is fully treated by Englefield in the work mentioned in note 1 above.

8. Jens-Peter Green, *Krise und Hoffnung. Der Evolutionismus Julian Huxleys*, Heidelberg: Winter Verlag, 1981, pp. 331, 338. This work includes a full bibliography of both primary and secondary literature.

9. D. Cupitt, *The Sea of Faith*, London: B.B.C., 1984, pp. 112, 247, 258.

Chapter Eight: Miracles and the Nature of Truth

1. On the various meanings the word 'miracle' has been given see Antony Flew, 'Miracles', in Paul Edwards (ed.), *The Encyclopedia of Philosophy*, New

York: Macmillan, 1967, vol. 5, pp. 346–53. For a more recent discussion, see P. S. Wadia, 'Miracles and Common Understanding', *The Philosophical Quarterly*, 26 (1976), pp. 69–81.

2. C. F. D. Moule, *Miracles, Cambridge Studies in their Philosophy and History*, London: Mowbray, 1965, p. 17.

3. On unipeds and other medieval beliefs, see C. Lofmark, 'On Medieval Credulity', *Trivium* (special vol., for C. P. Magill, ed. H. Siefken), University of Wales Press, 1974, pp. 5–21.

4. H. R. Trevor-Roper, 'The European Witch-Craze of the Sixteenth and Seventeenth Centuries', in *Religion, the Reformation and Social Change*, London: Macmillan, 1967, pp. 127, 172. All my remarks on witchcraft are deeply indebted to this article; cf. Keith Thomas's more recent *Religion and the Decline of Magic*, London, 1971, which criticizes (p. 573) some details of Trevor-Roper's paper, but is in substantial agreement with it.

5. Trevor-Roper, *op. cit.*, p. 182; cf. Thomas, *op. cit.*, pp. 577, 579 and refs., and also R. S. Westfall, *Science and Religion in Seventeenth-Century England*, New Haven: Yale University Press, 1958.

6. This miracle (on which Pascal had based his defence of Jansenism) consisted of the sudden cure of his little niece (on 21 March 1656) of an ulcerated eye after touching a relic from the crown of thorns in the convent chapel at Port Royal des Champs, a Cistercian convent near Versailles.

7. John Wilkins (died 1672) said that miracles were limited to the days when Christianity was young and in need of supernatural testimony. Boyle too thought that miracles ceased "with the foundation of Christianity". And Newton wrote to Locke that "miracles of good credit continued in the Church for about two or three hundred years". See Westfall, *op. cit.* in note 5 above, pp. 89–90, 203.

8. J. M. Robertson, *Gibbon*, London: Watts, 1925, p. 66.

9. "The laws of nature ordain what each thing can do and what it cannot"; and superstitious fears can be dispelled "only by an understanding of the outward form and inner workings of nature". Lucretius, *On the Nature of the Universe*, English translation R. E. Latham, Harmondsworth: Penguin, pp. 44, 61–2.

10. 'Of Miracles', section 10 of Hume's *An Enquiry Concerning Human Understanding* (1748).

11. Cf. note 11 to chapter 9 below (p. 250). The uniformity of nature, as W. K. Clifford pointed out, is the basis of all our generalizations, indeed of all animal adaptation to environment. "The fish acquires his aquatic habits through the evolutionary process over countless generations on the understanding that the properties of water shall remain approximately constant". In the case of things which do change rapidly, we try to understand them by analyzing them into more durable constituents (*Lectures and Essays*, ed. L. Stephen and F. Pollack, London, 1879, vol. 1, pp. 293–4.)

12. Cf. A. Flew's criticism of Hume on this score: *Hume's Philosophy of Belief*, London: Routledge, 1966, pp. 197, 207; Flew's article 'Miracles' in *The Encyclopedia of Unbelief*, ed. G. Stein, Buffalo: Prometheus, 1985; and also Flew's introduction to his edition of Hume's essay: *Of Miracles*, La Salle, Illinois: Open Court, 1985.

13. D. Hume, *A Treatise of Human Nature* (1739), Book 2, part 2, section 6.

14. Mary Hesse, 'Miracles and the Laws of Nature', in *vol. cit.* in note 2 above, pp. 37–8.

15. G. F. Woods, 'The Evidential Value of the Biblical Miracles', in *vol. cit.* in note 2 above, p. 30.

16. R. Swinburne, *The Concept of Miracle*, London: Macmillan, 1970.

17. A. R. Vidler, *Christian Belief*, London: S.C.M., 1950, pp. 41, 52.

18. For a history of the discussion among theologians, see E. and M. L. Keller, *Miracles in Dispute*, English translation, London: S.C.M., 1969. For a well-argued rejection, by a theologian, of the historicity of Jesus's miracles, see G. Petzke, 'Die historische Frage nach den Wundertaten Jesu', *New Testament Studies*, 22 (1976), pp. 180–204.

19. W. Trilling, *Fragen zur Geschichtlichkeit Jesu*, 3rd edn., Düsseldorf: Patnos Verlag, 1969, p. 43.

20. *Ibid*, p. 102.

21. Howard C. Kee, *Miracle in the Early Christian World*, New Haven and London: Yale University Press, 1983, pp. 156–8, 292–3; and also Kee's *Medicine, Miracle and Magic in New Testament Times*, Cambridge: Cambridge University Press, 1986, pp. 73, 114–5.

Chapter Nine: German Metaphysics as a Refuge from Scepticism

N.B. Once full details of a book or article have been given in a note to this chapter, further references to that work, both in the chapter and in the notes, are sometimes given simply as page or paragraph numbers. On the meaning of 'A' and 'B' in references to Kant's *Kritik der reinen Vernunft*, see p. 143 above.

i. The Origin of our Ideas and the Quest for Certainty

1. Locke did admittedly observe that experience begins with complex situations and that these are only later analyzed into 'things' and 'qualities', as when awareness of a landscape precedes any awareness of its individual features (*Essay Concerning Human Understanding*, Book 2, chapter 1, paragraph 7). But he seems to forget this when he writes, in the next chapter, of "simple ideas", and when, in this one, he speaks of "simple" qualities such as yellow, cold, soft, bitter, etc. (paragraph 3), as if these were the earliest perceived.

2. D. Hume, *An Enquiry Concerning Human Understanding* (1748), section 4, part 1.

3. Leibniz, *Monadology* (1714), paragraph 28. In *The Philosophical Works of Leibnitz* (translated from the original Latin and French), with notes by G. M. Duncan, New Haven: Tuttle, Morehouse and Taylor, 1890, p. 222.

4. R. B. Braithwaite argues on similar lines when he maintains that some natural laws do have "a sort of necessity", but that this necessity derives from the deducibility of the law from some higher-level hypothesis supported by empirical evidence. See his *Scientific Explanation*, Cambridge: Cambridge University Press, 1953, chapter 9, especially pp. 301–2.

5. L. Wittgenstein, *Tractatus Logico-Philosophicus*, 5.1361 (Oxford: Blackwell, 1981, p. 108).

6. W. S. Jevons, *Pure Logic*, ed. R. Adamson, London, 1890, p. 263.

7. J. S. Mill, *A System of Logic* (1843), 9th edn., London: Longmans Green, 1875, vol. 1, p. 360 (Book 3, chapter 3, paragraph 2).

8. K. Popper, 'Philosophy of Science: A Personal Report', in *British Philosophy in the Mid-Century*, ed. C. A. Mace, London: Allen and Unwin, 1957, p. 173.

9. K. Lorenz, 'Gestaltwahrnehmung als Quelle wissenschaftlicher Erkenntnis' (1959), reprinted in his *Vom Weltbild des Verhaltensforschers*, Munich: Deutscher Taschenbuch Verlag, 1976, pp. 105, 108.

10. For detailed treatment of this matter, see F. R. H. (Ronald) Englefield, *The Mind at Work and Play*, Buffalo: Prometheus, 1985, chapter 2.

11. Hume wrote (*Enquiry*, section 4, part 2): "All inferences from experience suppose, as their foundation, that the future will resemble the past and that similar powers will be conjoined with similar sensible qualities. If there be any suspicion that the course of nature may change, and that the past may be no rule for the future, all experience becomes useless and can give rise to no inference or conclusion".

12. Mill makes this point when he says: "Though it is a condition of the validity of every induction that there be uniformity in the course of nature, it is not a necessary condition that the uniformity should pervade all nature. It is enough that it pervades the particular class of phenomena to which the induction relates" (*vol. cit.* in note 7 above, p. 358 n.; Book 3, chapter 3, paragraph 1).

13. Cf. above, p. 248, note 11 to chapter 8.

ii. Causal Connection—an Idea of Limited Usefulness and Empirical Origin

14. Compare B. Russell, *Principles of Mathematics*, Cambridge: Cambridge University Press, 1903, vol. 1, p. 486: "It is not worth while preserving the word *cause*; it is enough to say, what is far less misleading, that any two configurations allow us to infer any other". Cf. also Russell's paper 'The Notion of Cause' (1912, reprinted in his *Mysticism and Logic*, London: Longmans, 1918), and his *Human Knowledge*, London: Allen and Unwin, 1948, pp. 326 ff.

15. These complexes can only arbitrarily be regarded as individual events. When we speak of a 'condition' of an 'event' (such as the wind which moves the cloud and so allows the sun's rays to reach and warm an object on earth) we are making something indescribably complex, involving the concurrence of motion of millions of particles, into a distinct individual that can be enumerated. We invent such units by singling out ill-defined segments of the continuous space-time magma. Language and thought seem to be able to deal more easily with durable counters than with dissolving figures. And so, instead of assigning each morsel of experience to its enveloping matrix of continuous reality, we prefer to deal with events that have sharp outlines and are insulated by regions of empty space and time, and make them play the reciprocal parts of cause and effect. We may treat as an event any recurrent segment of the space-time world, or any recurrent selection of segments—for they need not be continuous. Recurrence is

essential, since otherwise our excerpt would be completely arbitrary, and nothing intelligible could be asserted of it. Absolute recurrence is not to be looked for, but by analyzing the larger events into components we can sometimes reach elementary events whose recurrence is more exact (cf. above, p. 98).

16. It is unfortunate that Mill in fact restricts his discussion to cases where the inference goes from what is earlier to what is later in time. However, in *vol. cit.* in note 7 above, p. 397 (end of paragraph 7), he seems to drop this 'antecedent-consequent' part of his definition of 'cause'.

17. A. Schopenhauer, *Über die vierfache Wurzel des Satzes vom zureichenden Grunde*, paragraph 23, in *Sämmtliche Werke*, ed. J. Frauenstädt, Leipzig, 1873, vol. 1, p. 88. English translation: *On the Fourfold Root of the Principle of Sufficient Reason*, La Salle, Illinois: Open Court, 1974, p. 127.

18. Mill put this point clearly. It is, he says (*vol. cit.* in note 7 above), "common to single out one only of the antecedents under the denomination of cause, calling the others merely conditions" (p. 378). Cf. Schopenhauer, as cited in previous note, p. 35 (paragraph 20); English translation cited, pp. 54–5.

19. Compare Max Verworn, *Allgemeine Physiologie*, 5th edn., Leipzig, 1909, pp. 36–7: "The idea of 'cause' has been applied to the totality of the factors determining an event. But the idea then dissolves into nothing, for it becomes identical with the idea of *conditions*. . . . This has long been recognized in mathematics, where in consequence the idea of cause has been completely abandoned. . . . In the same way natural science must strive more and more to eliminate this idea from its exact thinking".

20. E. Mach, *Erkenntnis und Irrtum*, 5th edn., Leipzig: J. A. Barth, 1926, p. 280. For a full account of the development of the notion of causation, see W. A. Wallace, *Causality and Scientific Explanation*, especially vol. 2, Ann Arbor: University of Michigan Press, 1974.

21. Hume wrote (*Enquiry*, section 7, part 1): "When we look about us toward external objects and consider the operation of causes, we are never able, in a single instance, to discover any power or necessary connection, any quality which binds the effect to the cause and renders the one an infallible consequence of the other. We only find that the one does actually in fact follow the other".

22. This point was made by Thomas Reid, in criticism of Hume in a letter written about 1788; see *Works*, ed. W. Hamilton, Edinburgh and London, 1863, vol. 1, p. 81. Dugald Stewart also explains the origin of the idea of causation by analogy with what he calls a "material vinculum"; some events and things seemed to be linked together in this way, and the idea of cause and effect is based naturally on this genuine experience. See his *Elements of the Philosophy of the Human Mind* (1792), chapter 1, section 2.

iii. Kant Versus Hume. Religious Implications

23. Hume, *A Treatise of Human Nature* (1739), Book 1, part 4, section 5 ('Of the Immateriality of the Soul').

24. This would not mean that the emotion *is* simply the molecular motion, or whatever physiological machinery is invoked. Any object presents different aspects; a bicycle or a cat looks quite different in front view and in side view.

Each of these aspects is just as real as any other. Likewise, an occurrence in a brain has both a psychological and a physiological aspect. When I say that I have a bit of a headache, or am very fond of a friend, it would be silly to hold that molecular motion in my brain—which admittedly forms one aspect of these phenomena—is the only aspect.

25. For a defence of the empirical origin of mathematical ideas, see Englefield, as cited in note 10 above, chapters 10 and 11.

26. Kant, *Prolegomena zu einer jeden künftigen Metaphysik* (1783), end of paragraph 60.

27. See my *Goethe and the Development of Science, 1750–1900*, Alphen Netherlands: Sijthoff and Noordhoff, 1978, pp. 107–110.

28. There are, Kant has said, *a priori* principles and empirical principles, the former being distinguished from the latter by their certainty. He now says that there must be *a priori* principles, for they are the only possible source of the certainty of the empirical principles, i.e. of those which are not certain.

iv. Kant's Fantastic View of Mind

29. For a statement of the biologist's view, and of its incompatibility with Kant's, see Lorenz, *op. cit.* in note 9 above, pp. 105–6.

30. Mill notes (*An Examination of Sir William Hamilton's Philosophy*, 5th edn., London: Longmans Green, 1878, p. 363) that although we may not be able to conceive an absolute commencement, or a time when nothing existed, yet we can conceive without difficulty a beginning and also an end to any portion of matter: "We see apparent annihilation whenever water dries up, or fuel is consumed without a visible residuum". To philosophers and scientists "the vapour which has succeeded to the water dried up by the sun, the gases which replace the fuel transformed by combustion have become irrevocably a part of their conception of the entire phenomena. But the ignorant . . . , if they were not told the contrary, would live and die without suspecting that the water, and the wood or coal, were not destroyed".

31. Lavoisier assumed in his quantitative investigations that the total weight of the products of a chemical reaction must be exactly equal to the total weight of the reacting substances; and finally he expressly stated what this implies, namely that matter cannot be created or destroyed. See his *Traité élementaire de chimie*, Paris, 1789, p. 140.

32. The contrary, Kantian, view was maintained by W. Whewell; see his *On the Philosophy of Discovery*, London, 1860, p. 349; "Such principles as have been mentioned [that material substances cannot be produced or destroyed; that the cause is equal to the effect; that reaction is equal and opposite to action] are not the results of experience, nor can be. No experience can prove them; they are necessarily assumed as the interpretation of experience. They were not proved in the course of scientific investigations, but brought to light as such investigations showed their necessity. They are not the results, but the conditions of experimental sciences. If the Axiom of Substances were not true, and were not assumed, we

could not have such a science as Chemistry, that is, we could have no knowledge at all respecting the changes of form of substances". It would be surely more correct to say that these generalizations are extremely broad, and that if they were not accepted as true, or were even proved false, a great many lesser generalizations would collapse with them.

33. Kant denies that we derive our idea of space by observing differences in the dimensions of objects, and claims that we need an *a priori* awareness of space before we can even perceive such differences (*Kritik*, A 23–4). But by the same argument the conception of colour would also have to be *a priori*; for if we have not this conception in advance, how can we appreciate differences in colour? Similarly with such ideas as intensity, heat, and weight. If the idea of space cannot be abstracted from observed spatial relations, neither can the idea of heat be abstracted from observed differences of temperature. In fact if discrimination between different qualities or sensations requires the pre-existence in the mind of an abstract conception which embraces the discriminated characters, then everything that goes to make up our experience must be supposed to be innate. To my mind there can no more be length or breadth without long and broad objects than there can be heat without hot or cold objects.

34. On this see F. R. H. Englefield, 'Kant as Defender of the Faith in Nineteenth-Century England', *Question*, 12 (1979), pp. 16–27; cf. also above, p. 170ff.

35. See, for instance, Kant, *Prolegomena*, note to paragraph 48; also paragraph 57: "Reason finds . . . no satisfaction in this view . . . which deprives it of all hope". And again (*Kritik*, A 2): "Reason, which is so desirous of this kind of knowledge, is provoked rather than satisfied by it".

36. The man, says E. Mach (*vol. cit.* in note 20 above, pp. 11–12) who investigates his psychological states and their mutual dependence does so in the hope of being able to explain them. But if at the end of his investigation he ascribes them to some "subject" which "has" them, then he is back at the position from which he started. He is like the farmer who got someone to explain to him how locomotives work, and then asked where the horses were which worked them.

37. Hume, *Treatise*, Book 1, part 4, section 6. On this whole matter see further W. James's remarks on the consciousness of self in *Principles of Psychology*, London: Macmillan, 1901, vol. 1, p. 304.

38. W. K. Clifford, 'The Philosophy of the Pure Sciences', in *Lectures and Essays*, ed. L. Stephen and F. Pollock, London, 1879, vol. 1, pp. 273–4.

v. What is Innate?

39. Kant, 'Über eine Entdeckung, nach der alle Kritik der reinen Vernunft durch eine ältere entbehrlich gemacht werden soll'. In *Gesammelte Schriften*, Prussian Academy edn., division 1, vol. 8, Berlin, 1912, pp. 221–2.

40. Schopenhauer, as cited in note 17 above, near end of paragraph 34; Frauenstädt's edn., p. 123; English translation cited, p. 181.

vi. The Problem of Free Will

41. F. von Schiller, *Über die aesthetische Erziehung des Menschen* (1795–6), edited by E. M. Wilkinson and L. A. Willoughby, Oxford: Clarendon, 1967, pp. 83, 135.

42. T. Carlyle, 'The State of German Literature' in *Critical and Miscellaneous Essays*, vol. 1, London: Chapman and Hall, 1894, p. 68.

43. Details in John Rogerson, *Old Testament Criticism in the Nineteenth Century*, London: S.P.C.K., 1984, pp. 36–7.

44. See my account of determinism in *J. M. Robertson. Liberal, Rationalist and Scholar*, London: Pemberton, 1987, chapter 8, section 2.

45. Nietzsche says, confusedly: "No one is responsible for his deeds, no one for his character. To judge is tantamount to being unjust" (*Menschliches Allzumenschliches*, vol. 1, aphorism no. 39). How is it still possible, if we are irresponsible, for us to be unjust? What else can 'irresponsible' mean except unable to respond to rational or moral considerations or persuasion? We say that someone is irresponsible when drunk or out of his senses because we know that the ordinary conditions of his behaviour have been changed. A responsible person acts with a view to the future, on general principles or in consideration of others. An irresponsible person shows an unnatural lack of concern for consequences. Both forms of behaviour are determined by mental and other conditions, but they are distinct and can in general be readily distinguished. There is no true psychological analysis in this denial of manifest differences. If a man's behaviour is determined by certain rational or ethical considerations, we call him responsible. This does not imply that his behaviour is not determined. In a later aphorism (no. 70) Nietzsche says that the guilt of a murderer, "if there is any", lies "in his educators, parents, environment, in us, not in him", and that this is why we are more revolted by an execution than by a murder. Nietzsche thus cannot help attributing blame, even if he does, as an afterthought, try and save the position by a change of words. Where he puts the blame is also questionable. And even if we are able to say why a man is a murderer, why he is cruel and ferocious, that does not make him less so.

46. R. Swinburne, quoted by Keith Ward, *The Turn of the Tide*, BBC Publications, 1986, p. 66.

47. Schopenhauer, as cited in note 17 above, paragraph 49; Frauenstädt's edition, p. 154; English translation cited, p. 226.

Chapter Ten: Morality, Religion and Reason

i. Egoistic Instincts and Social Instincts

1. Edward Westermarck, *The Origin and Development of the Moral Ideas*, chapter 5 (2nd edn., London: Macmillan, 1924, vol. 1, p. 117).

2. Westermarck, as cited in the previous note, chapter 34 (vol. 2, pp. 195ff).

3. C. Darwin, *The Descent of Man* (1871), Part 1, chapter 4 (new edn., London: John Murray, 1901, pp. 154–5).

4. Gilbert Murray, 'What is Permanent in Positivism', in *Stoic, Christian and Humanist*, 2nd. edn., London: Watts/Allen and Unwin, 1950, pp. 184–5.

5. F. R. H. (Ronald) Englefield, *Language, Its Origin and Its Relation to Thought*, London: Elek/Pemberton, and New York: Scribner, 1977.

ii. Religion and Social Behaviour

6. On this see D. P. Walker's fascinating study *The Decline of Hell. Seventeenth-Century Discussions of Eternal Torment*, London: Routledge, 1964.

7. Margaret Knight, *Morals Without Religion*, London: Dobson, 1955, p. 15; *Honest to Man. Christian Ethics Re-Examined*, London: Elek/Pemberton, 1974, pp. 189–92. This latter book includes a valuable sketch of the biological foundations of ethical behaviour.

8. 'Of Truth', in *The Philosophical Works of Francis Bacon*, ed. J. M. Robertson, London: Routledge, 1905, p. 736.

9. J. M. Robertson, *Letters on Reasoning*, 2nd edn., London: Watts, 1905, p. 18.

iii. The Relativity of Moral Principles

10. A. Schopenhauer, *Preisschrift über die Grundlage der Moral* (1840), paragraph 7.

11. An English translation of Kant's essay is included in Sissela Bok's *Lying. Moral Choice in Public and Private Life*, Hassocks, Sussex: Harvester Press, 1978, pp. 267–72.

12. For details, see J. M. Robertson, *A Short History of Morals*, London: Watts, 1920, pp. 409–10 and refs.

13. T. B. Macaulay, *History of England*, 5 vol. edn., vol. 2, London: Saint Martin's Library, 1905, pp. 209–10.

14. J. M. Robertson, *Letters on Reasoning*, 2nd edn., London: Watts, 1905, pp. 253–6.

iv. Innovation and Stability in Society

15. Quoted by R. P. Ericksen, *Theologians Under Hitler*, New Haven and London: Yale University Press, 1985, pp. 129, 151.

16. It is still not uncommon to hear that to credit animals with ideas is 'hypothetical'. Of course the ideas of animals are hypothetical, just as atoms, electrons, light waves and Julius Caesar are hypothetical. The only question of interest is whether they constitute a useful hypothesis. Animals do many things

which we can most easily explain by the hypothesis of ideas, adequate or inadequate. And W. Köhler has shown (in his book on the mentality of apes: *Intelligenzprüfungen an Menschenaffen*, 2nd edn., Berlin: Julius Springer, 1921) that it is sometimes the inadequate ideas which are the more fruitful hypothesis. So long as the animal behaves in the most appropriate way possible to the events of his environment we may be misled by the very perfection of the adaptation to the assumption of simpler mechanisms. It is when he makes mistakes that we are able to recognize the mistaken notions on which his action is based.

17. Noted by Ericksen, *op. cit.* in note 15 above, p. 183.

Chapter Eleven: Atheism and Empiricism

i. Is Atheism Reasonable?

1. The religious affairs correspondent of *The Guardian*, Walter Schwarz, recently suggested there (17 November 1986) that "in any parish the number of concepts of God is equal to the size of the congregation".

2. Keith Ward, *The Turn of the Tide*, BBC Publications, 1986, p. 45.

3. *Ibid.*

4. Walter Schwarz, writing in *The Guardian*, 27 October 1986.

5. Hugh Montefiore, *The Probability of God*, London: S.C.M., 1985, p. 107.

6. See my *The Origin of Language: Aspects of the Discussion from Condillac to Wundt*, La Salle, Illinois: Open Court, 1987.

ii. Absolutist Hankerings

7. My argument here is deeply indebted to F. R. H. (Ronald) Englefield's *The Mind at Work and Play*, Buffalo: Prometheus, particularly to chapters 17 and 18 of that work, where the relevant issues are discussed in detail and where, in particular, it is made perfectly clear that this standpoint does not entail solipsism.

8. The implications of this distinction between my observation of my own ideas and my observation of those of another person were clearly stated by W. K. Clifford in a paper of 1873, where he wrote: "If you and I . . . choose to contemplate another person, we shall say that the world which he directly perceives is really inside his brain, and not outside; but that corresponding to these changes that go on in his brain there are certain changes going on outside of him, and that in many cases there is such a correspondence of the relations of contiguity in one case to the relation of contiguity in the other that conclusions about the outer world may fairly be drawn from the world in his brain. But now, if instead of considering this other person, I consider myself, the case is rather altered. I shall conclude by analogy that this world which I directly perceive is

not really outside of me; that the things which are apparently made known to me by my perceptions are really themselves only groups of my perceptions; that the universe which I perceive . . . is really *me*. And—by analogy also—I shall conclude that there *is* something besides this, different from it; the changes in which correspond in a certain way to the changes in my universe" ('The Philosophy of the Pure Sciences', in *Lectures and Essays*, ed. L. Stephen and F. Pollock, London, 1879, vol. 1, p. 286.

iii. Empiricism and the Nature of Science

9. Keith Ward, *op. cit.* in note 2 above, pp. 62–3.

10. E. Mach, *Erkenntnis und Irrtum*, 5th edn., Leipzig: J. A. Barth, 1926, p. 232.

11. J. S. Mill, *A System of Logic*, 9th edn., London: Longmans Green, 1875, vol. 2, pp. 16–18.

12. W. S. Jevons, *The Principles of Science*, 2nd edn., London, 1877, p. 509.

13. Peter Medawar, *Pluto's Republic*, Oxford: Oxford University Press, 1984, p. 124.

14. Mill, *vol. cit.* in note 11 above, pp. 21, 23.

15. Mill, *op. cit.* in note 11 above, vol. 1, p. 333.

16. W. Whewell, *On the Philosophy of Discovery*, London, 1860, p. 253.

17. Mill, *vol. cit.* in note 15 above, p. 334.

18. *Ibid.*, pp. 349–50.

19. *Ibid.*, p. 266.

20. Jevons, *op. cit.* in note 12 above, pp. 512–3.

21. Mill, *vol. cit.* in note 15 above, p. 215.

Conclusion

i. The Framework of Our Beliefs

1. Boer's book was originally published as *Above the Battle? The Bible and Its Critics*, Grand Rapids: W. B. Eerdmans, 1975. My references are to the 1981 edition by the same publisher, entitled *The Bible and Higher Criticism*.

ii. Fundamentalism Past and Present

2. J. Barr, *Fundamentalism*, 2nd edn., London: S.C.M., 1981, p. xix.

3. *Ibid.*, p. 182.

4. J. W. Wenham, *Christ and the Bible*, London: Tyndale Press, 1972, p. 74.

5. Henry Preserved Smith, 'Biblical Scholarship and Inspiration', in *Inspiration and Inerrancy* (by several hands), London, 1891, p. 23.

6. A. Richardson, 'The Rise of Modern Biblical Scholarship', in *The Cambridge History of the Bible*, vol. 3, Cambridge University Press, 1963, p. 310.

7. J. Barr, *Escaping from Fundamentalism*, London: S.C.M., 1984, p. vii.

iii. Circumstances Favouring Religious Conformity

8. T. S. Eliot, 'Arnold and Pater', in *Selected Essays*, 3rd edn., London: Faber and Faber, 1951, p. 436.

9. Barr, *op. cit.* in note 2 above, p. 109.

10. A. Barnett, *The Human Species*, revised edn., Pelican Books, 1961, p. 162.

11. Hitler, *Mein Kampf*, vol. 1, near end of chapter 3; 97th edn., Munich: Franz Eher, 1934, p. 129.

12. M. J. Penton, *Apocalypse Delayed. The Story of Jehovah's Witnesses*, Toronto: University of Toronto Press, 1985, p. 260.

13. S. R. Gardiner, *The Thirty Years' War*, London: Longmans Green, 1874, pp. 183, 213.

14. On this, see W. Hollenweger, *The Pentecostals*, English translation London: S.C.M., 1972, p. 76.

iv. Thin Ideas and Strong Emotions

15. Alstair G. Hunter, *Christianity and Other Faiths in Britain*, London: S.C.M., 1985, pp. 40–41.

Index

NT = The New Testament
OT = The Old Testament

Page numbers in brackets following references to notes indicate pages where an author is quoted (or his views alluded to) but not named. Thus Haenchen 242 n37 (49) means that this author is alluded to on p. 49, where superscript 37 directs the reader to the note on p. 242, where Haenchen is named and details of his work are given.

*i.e. "a type of literature characterized by the expectation of a cosmic battle at the end of the present age between God and the hosts of evil, ending in a cataclysmic judgment on the wicked and the glorious vindication of the righteous" (Howard C. Kee, *Jesus in History*, 2nd edn., New York: Harcourt Brace, 1977, p. 24).